IN OUR HANDS

In Our Hands

The Struggle for U.S. Child Care Policy

Elizabeth Palley and
Corey S. Shdaimah

NEW YORK UNIVERSITY PRESS
New York and London

NEW YORK UNIVERSITY PRESS
New York and London
www.nyupress.org

References to Internet websites (URLs) were accurate at the time of writing.
Neither the author nor New York University Press is responsible for URLs that
may have expired or changed since the manuscript was prepared.

LIBRARY OF CONGRESS CATALOGING-IN-PUBLICATION DATA

Palley, Elizabeth.
  In our hands : the struggle for U.S. child care policy / Elizabeth Palley, Corey S. Shdaimah.
    pages cm
  ISBN 978-1-4798-6265-8 (hardback)
  1. Child care—United States. 2. Child care—Law and legislation—United States. 3. United
States—Social policy. I. Shdaimah, Corey S. II. Title.
  HQ778.63.P35 2014
  362.70973—dc23
2013049129

New York University Press books are printed on acid-free paper,
and their binding materials are chosen for strength and durability.
We strive to use environmentally responsible suppliers and materials
to the greatest extent possible in publishing our books.

Manufactured in the United States of America
10 9 8 7 6 5 4 3 2 1

Also available as an ebook

We dedicate this book to our parents and children:
Marian and Howard Palley and Amelia and Charlotte Vitale
Sue and Alan Silberstein and Cliel, Elad, and Sagi Shdaimah

CONTENTS

ACKNOWLEDGMENTS

This book is personally and professionally meaningful to us both. We would like to thank the people who helped us along the way.

Judie McCoyd, Marian Palley, and Doug Imig read pieces or entire drafts of the manuscript, providing helpful input as we were writing. David Super provided insights on the compromises that led to the CCDBG. Hannah Gardi, MSW, served as research assistant extraordinaire. She reviewed the manuscript and references, searched for literature, and was responsible for much of the information on QRIS. She also shared her boundless enthusiasm for the project. We cannot thank her enough. Debbie Gershenowitz, Clara Platter, Constance Grady, and Nancy Dowd also helped to shepherd this book through its several iterations.

We would like to thank the advocates, union representatives, and policy analysts whom we interviewed for this book. This book could not have been written without their help. Not only have they been unflagging champions for children and families in the United States, but they were also willing to take time out from their busy schedules to speak with us. Despite the sometimes overwhelming challenges they have faced, they have continued their work to make raising children in the United States a less stressful prospect. In addition to our thanks for their time in granting us interviews, we admire their hard work and perseverance in their continued efforts on behalf of all U.S. families. The same can be said for the academics and researchers who are cited in this book, upon whose shoulders we stand.

We would like to individually thank the friends and family who made it possible for us to write this book.

Elizabeth

First, I would like to thank the many women, child care providers and teachers, who have helped me to care for and educate my own children. If all children were able to receive the help that we have received from you, there would be no reason for this book. I would especially like to thank Sarah Voisine, Hilda Tellez, Ms. Candy, Griselda Calderon, Bernice, Patricia, and all of the wonderful teachers at the International School of Brooklyn. It is largely as a result of your hard work and dedication to my children that I had the time and ability to write this book.

Next, I would like to thank all of the people who supported me while we wrote this book. I would also like to thank my coauthor, Corey Shdaimah, who both challenged and supported me as we wrote this book. Without her coauthorship, I am sure this book would not be as good as it now is.

I would like to thank my parents for their support, in general, and their child care assistance. Whenever I had a schedule conflict in the past five years requiring me to teach or attend meetings and care for my children simultaneously, all I had to do was pick up the phone and I knew you would be here. In addition, when I was bleary-eyed from reading this manuscript and could no longer tell if there were typos or if the prose was clear, my mother was always willing to look at whatever section about which I had questions and give me helpful feedback. Thank you.

Last, I would like to thank my amazing husband Alex. I am lucky to be married to someone who not only coparents my children but also supports my career.

Corey

I am grateful to Elizabeth Palley for sharing the research, writing, and logistical aspects of what it takes to produce a book while juggling our own families and careers. I value our ongoing conversations as we grappled with the sometimes conflicting, often frustrating facets of U.S.

child care policy almost as much as the respect and friendship that we shared in the process.

Thanks to my parents, Sue and Alan Silberstein, who cared for me when I was a child and have encouraged me to pursue my dreams then as now. Their belief in me and their nurture of my interests, talents, and passions form the bedrock on which all else is built.

I feel extremely lucky to have found a career that I love and that allows me to balance work and family life. More important, my husband Amichai has supported me every step of the way. I am grateful to you, Amichai, for creating a shared vision for our family, and for fostering my dreams and making it possible for me realize them. I hope that our children, Cliel, Elad, Sagi, will be adults in a world where the roles of caregivers are appreciated so that they will be able to have a full range of options and opportunities in their lives, whatever family configurations they choose.

Finally, I thank all of those who helped care for my children over seventeen years of parenting. The first person who showed us what excellent child care looks like was Miriam, whose home day care my daughter Cliel (now a babysitter herself) attended in Tel Aviv. Thanks to the teachers and staff at the Terry Lynne Lokoff Federation Day Care Services, the Jewish Community Center's Robert J. Wilf Preschool and Kindergarten, and New Gulph Children's Center. We had two babysitters, Shawna Hinchey and Sam Dalke, and six au pairs from four countries: Jamnian Thinchuay, Anna Jakubas (who now has a beautiful daughter of her own), Carina Ozaki, Jaqueline Souza Edwards, and Ethiopia Sabahat. Two wonderful women provided child care for our children in the years that Elizabeth and I worked on this book. Alana (Nani) Nejaim De Holanda, our last au pair, captured our hearts and became part of our family. Sammy Flicker's calm presence, engaging conversation, and good care enriched our lives.

1

Introduction

Child care in the United States has long been seen as a personal concern rather than a societal responsibility. In a widely hailed analysis of work-life media coverage from 1980 to 2006, Joan Williams, Jessica Manvell, and Stephanie Bornstein (2007) critiqued media portrayals of women choosing to "opt out" of paid employment in order to "return" to their mothering role. Their telling title, "'Opt Out' or Pushed Out?," challenged the so-called opt-out revolution. They examined how the media dichotomy did not hold up when examined against the day-to-day realities that shape the choices of women and their families. Media coverage that focused largely on the choices of elite individuals did not discuss that for most women these "choices" are the product of systemic factors that are shaped by workplace and government policies. Though periodically the tragic death of a child in care is reported (Cohn, 2013; Newall, 2013) or an advocacy group issues a press release and is able to gain some media coverage, much recent media coverage of child care has focused on family choices.

In recent years, media coverage has focused on some of the dilemmas facing women and families regarding their need for child care (e.g., Chira, 2013; Graff, 2012; Quart, 2013; Slaughter, 2012). In a review of news articles from 2009 to 2011, surprisingly few focused on the so-called Mommy Wars, which became popular in the past decade and seemingly pit mothers who have opted to remain in careers while placing their children in child care against mothers who have opted out of the paid workforce to stay at home. Nearly all of the articles that referenced the

Mommy Wars did so to refute this stark bifurcation. Several pointed out that most U.S. families cannot afford to forgo paid employment, making the luxury of choosing to stay at home in lieu of paid employment an option for few (Clemetson, 2006). Such articles pointed out that most mothers of young children work outside the home (Tyre, Springen, & Juarez, 2006).

Whatever the Mommy Wars say about societal ambivalence regarding custodial care, the popular media have provided a number of examples of women who have been able to circumvent difficult choices. In one article describing "mompreneurs," Heath (2011) portrays superwomen who have managed to create their own careers while caring for children. Some have done this through economic necessity, like one twenty-eight-year-old single mother of three portrayed in the article; others desired fulfillment of their dual role of parent and professional. The article, which celebrates these extraordinarily successful women, also recognizes that they are "overachievers," and often pay a high price. In the words of one mompreneur, "The lack of sleep is the hardest part. The kids are up by 5:30. When I put my daughter down for a nap, I do as much work as I can. Sometimes I play hide-and-seek with my kids, and I hide in a good spot so I can write a business e-mail on my BlackBerry. You have to be creative as a mom. Any time a child is sleeping, I am doing work" (Heath, 2011). This is clearly not a template for all families, nor can it inform any kind of feasible broad-based policy solution.

Despite portrayals of women who have it all and some recognition that most mothers work, the popular media continue to focus on women's choices between work and family. This individualistic perspective obscures the role of government and workplace policies. In a recent example, Katie Couric hosted Michelle Cove, author of *I Love Mondays: And Other Confessions from Devoted Working Moms,* on her daytime show *Katie.* The 2012 book relies on anecdotes from women who love their jobs while simultaneously loving their children and caring for their families. The characterization of these stories as "confessions" reveals just how deeply conflicted U.S. women remain about work and family.

Cove does an important service in airing these conflicts and challenging the notion that one cannot be committed to *both* children and work. On her show, Couric (Peterson, 2012) invites feedback on three hypothetical scenarios, including one that involves a call from the school nurse's office five minutes before a work-related presentation. Couric invites audience members to show whether they would "choose work or your kids" by showing one side of a two-sided paddle: one side features a picture of two diaper-clad babies, the other a cartoon figure of a woman in front of a computer screen.

In response to Couric's hypothetical, Cove relates a situation that she faced and discusses a range of factors that might influence her decision, including the child's safety and level of discomfort. Cove, saying "it doesn't have to be one or the other," shows how adept mothers have become at minimizing conflict wherever and however possible. She also presumes relatively accommodating workplaces. However, her book and the Couric program discussion make it clear that the popular conversation remains focused on viewing these as individual conflicts that are essentially private matters. We can share and laugh about them for relief, and we can strategize about how to navigate the hurdles, but there is little in the way of critique for the broader systemic factors that produce or contribute to work-family challenges. They are simply not visible or intelligible as public concerns (Harrington, 1999).

The so-called Mommy Wars even fail to capture the experience of everyone who can financially afford to opt out of paid employment. Clemetson (2006) suggests that black middle- and upper-class professional women do not share all of the angst and concern regarding child care with their white counterparts. The choice of forgoing paid employment, even for those who can afford it in the short term, is further constrained by longer-term economic considerations. For professional black women, debates about self-fulfillment can seem incomprehensibly narrow against the need to build sustainable wealth and security for their families. The discussions also pale in comparison to worries about shielding sons and daughters from the perils that black children face growing up, and overlook the practical pull of extended families in need of financial support. Due to discrimination, black and other minority women may also have a harder time returning to work should they leave the workforce to care for young children, thus weighing a potentially higher career cost than white women. Black women may be aware and appreciative of the sacrifices made by earlier generations and the need to set an example for their own children and other black children (Parker, 2005).

These articles, as a group, suggest a potential turning away from the Mommy Wars. Yet, they remain focused on individual decision making. Despite our status as privileged professional women with advanced degrees and relatively flexible academic schedules, we too struggle to address our own child care needs, as do many of our friends, colleagues, and students (see Appendix 1). Like for many others, our caregiving is an ongoing rather than episodic life concern (Coiner & George, 1998; Wolf-Wendel, 2012). This book is our attempt to grapple with *why*, in the U.S., we have been unable to make any headway on a problem that touches so many families. Child care policy has been explored by many who came before us, and we add our own insights to this important debate.

Previous Literature

This book draws on some of the very important and extensive foundations that have been laid in the field of child care policy research but is unique in a number of ways. The most recent account that focuses on the trajectory of comprehensive federal child care legislation, by Zigler, Marsland, and Lord (2009), provides a rich insider analysis of the political process. Joan Lombardi (2003), also a political insider and analyst, lays out a blueprint for reframing child care in the United States as early childhood education. Other books, like the recent work of Joan Williams (2010), offer an academic legal analysis of U.S. child care policy (see also Alstott, 2004). Yet a third strain of writing in this area is exemplified by the work of Ann Crittenden (2002), who makes an excellent case with popular appeal describing the impact of the lack of affordable, quality child care on women and families. Mary Frances Berry's (1993) *The Politics of Parenthood* and Sonya Michel's (1999) *Children's Interests/Mothers' Rights* both provide comprehensive historical background on the development of American child care policy.

The many works of Sheila Kamerman and Albert Kahn inform the historical political background of American child care policy and provide a comparative perspective (e.g., Kahn & Kamerman, 1991; Kamerman & Kahn, 1976). Others also provide examples of comprehensive child care models in other countries and in the United States (Fagnani, 2012; Kunin, 2012; Waldfogel, 2010). In 2001, Sally Cohen investigated how U.S. politics and procedures for decision making have influenced the development of U.S. child care policy over time. Other related work, including *Protecting Soldiers and Mothers* (Skocpol, 1992), examines the history and development of child care policies in the United States in the context of U.S. social policy more generally. Still others (e.g., Spain & Bianchi, 1996) have focused on the impact of child care on women in the workplace.

Most of these excellent historical and legislative reviews were published more than ten years ago, and thus cannot address child care policy as it has evolved more recently. While there are no recent books that update this work, much of this information has been updated and expanded in important policy briefs by organizations such as the Institute for Women's Policy Research, the National Council of La Raza, and the National Association of Child Care Resource and Referral Agencies.

Despite the overwhelming need and apparent benefits of early child care and education programs, the limited role of government in assisting all families with the provision of care for children and the strategies that interest groups have adopted in an environment of limited political opportunities have hindered serious public debate about a universal child care policy in the United States. Public concern and financing of care for children in the United States have been framed and stigmatized as a poverty issue. Early education has been largely addressed as a separate matter, whereby family care needs are not considered. Paid family leave has been viewed by many as yet a third, and often separate, legislative and policy concern than either early education or child care. By some it is viewed as a threat to family autonomy or a threat to business interests. Others may view child care policy as a legitimate concern, but a lower priority than education or poverty. By addressing child care as a stigmatized poverty issue unconnected to the needs of a more universal working population, and by not considering it as an ongoing concern, public funding for child care is more likely to be subject to cuts in periods of economic downturn. This also means that there is less public attention to influencing or regulating the quality and type of care available.

Groups that might support a universal child care policy including paid parental leave do not see themselves as part of a broad social movement. This weakens all of the interest groups and players who support children and women's issues. The nature of race and class divisions can partially explain the lack of a unified social movement around this and other gender-related concerns (Weldon, 2006). In order for interest groups to work together, there must be a paradigm shift in how caring for children is characterized in the United States. Child care is not merely a problem for low-income families; parents from all income brackets struggle to find affordable, quality care that provides a solid early education foundation. These are connected themes, and integrating early education and universal care needs can be better addressed by a more comprehensive, unitary, nationwide policy. Problems that parents experience in trying to care for their own children are no longer simply individual problems but rather affect such a large percentage of the population that we, as a country, are experiencing a major social welfare crisis. Nonetheless, there has been limited social mobilization to propel any major social change.

The divides that exist between groups interested in supporting federal involvement in child care policy are historical (Cohen, 2001; Michel, 1999). Educational interest groups have focused on the need to monitor and better regulate preschools and prekindergartens. Child care and child welfare groups have focused on the need to expand the availability of quality care for low-income children and many women's groups have remained silent on these issues, sometimes advocating for paid parental leave (Palley & Shdaimah, 2011). Interest groups that might be concerned with child care are confronted by antitax groups as well as socially conservative coalitions that have formed a uniform agenda that includes the idea that government should not support child care or any policy that enables women to work more easily. Although some research has suggested that a majority of individual citizens in the United States might support a universal federal child care policy (Dobuzinskis, 2010), there is little in the way of social movement activity to support this type of legislation.

There are many factors that have contributed to the policy vacuum around care and education for young children in the United States. They include the larger political context, political trajectories and interests of the women's movement, the child care and early education movements, interest group politics, the declining role of labor unions in American politics, the separation of federal and state powers, antigovernment sentiment, and the influence of race on American public policy decision making. In the context of a political system of checks and balances that is designed to foster incremental change, more unity is necessary. Concern about insufficient government support, either federal or state, for child care is not new.

This book adds to the public and scholarly debates in several ways. First, we build on the important work that has come before us and pull the often separate strands together. Our analysis of their combined messages and conceptual frameworks leads to a more holistic picture. Our research also adds new empirical data and analysis to the debate. We review legislative debates, drawing on testimony before congressional subcommittees regarding four major pieces of proposed legislation. We first set up our analysis by examining the role of interest groups, which provides important backdrop that explains the interests and roles of different players in the child care debates, including groups representing the interests of women, unions, conservatives, racial minorities, and business. We carefully chose legislation to represent different eras (the 1970s, 1980s and 1990s, and 2000s) as well as different focuses (comprehensive child care, child care for low-income families, and emergency family leave). Interviews with policy advocates provide for long-term views of advocacy efforts as well as multiple perspectives from outside of government. The advocates with whom we spoke (and their organizations) have, over the years, had greater access to politicians at different times and have sometimes worked with competing agendas. The blending of their perspectives provides nuance and a rich understanding of the advocacy efforts around child care as it has evolved over the years, including a sober understanding on the part of advocates of what is lost and gained using different political strategies. We draw on social movement and framing literatures to analyze these interview data.

The Context

We wrote this book within the political context of a national budget deficit and calls for reducing spending rather than increasing services and tax revenues (Lowrey, 2013). Despite the introduction of new health insurance policies designed to address unmet health care needs during the first Obama administration, there is currently little public policy discussion about the development of new infrastructure or programs in the United States. States and local governments are faced with ballooning pension expenses and reduced budgets, limiting their ability to expand services. Policy debates in education have generally focused on improving rather than expanding services to include younger children. Recent pushes for pre-K education at the national level indicate some movement on this front (Allen, 2013). There is also currently some state and local advocacy to develop paid parental and sick leave (Taylor, 2013). These efforts indicate a renewed interest in child care policy and that the time is right to review the history of U.S. child care policy in order to better determine the path forward.

Most of the poor in this country are women and children. During the Clinton administration, the major public assistance law was changed to require almost all recipients to work in order to receive financial assistance. Most are mothers who receive benefits as heads of households with children. When these mothers work, they must find someone to help care for their children. Cross-national research has found a correlation between state-supported child care for children younger than three and both maternal ability to work and higher wages for mothers (Misra, Budig, & Boeckmann, 2011). Additional research suggests that cultural attitudes toward women and work affect the success of parental leave and public child care policies on women's earnings (Budig, Misra, & Böckmann, 2012). However, women's options are often limited by the availability of resources in their communities. Our culture simply does not place economic value on child (or other) care responsibilities. We have a patchwork of policies that provide temporary assistance to some people in certain circumstances and leave others to address child care as an individual concern. The existing laws frame child care as individual struggles that are largely faced by low-income families. However, this is far from accurate.

When we read testimony from the 1971 hearings on the Nixon-era bill to institute a federal child care program, we saw an emphasis on concerns about work-life balance and leveling the playing field for low-income children. The framing of the need and appropriate government response could have been written today. In fact, these concerns seem even more pressing today. Why, then, have we not progressed? This is especially curious when the problem of child care does not seem to affect any particular population but rather seems to be a universal concern of families.

Child care is not a women's issue but a family and societal issue, affecting everyone. Despite the entrance of many women who had traditionally served as caregivers into the U.S. labor market, there has been little or no national political discourse around parenting and child care as broad-based social needs (Palley, 2010). There are few national policies that support families as they care for their children in the United States. While multiple frames have been employed to advocate for child care, national funding for child care centers and programs primarily targets low-income children. More recent policies, such as state-based pre-K programs, are more universal, but do not address the extensive care needs of families. In this book, when we discuss child care, we consider early education to be one component of care, even though it is often separated from child care, especially custodial care, in public discourse.

We set out to understand why child care policy in the United States not only lags significantly behind that of our Western European counterparts but also is not on the forefront of any political campaigns or debates. Why, despite the apparent need for more universal legislation to address early child care and education needs in the United States, has there been such limited social mobilization?

The Design of This Book

In Chapter 2, we review the literature on framing and provide analytical lenses for the data that are presented in later chapters. We examine the particular policy context in which U.S. child care policy has been framed. This includes a background on federalism, devolution, campaign finance, and the use of symbolic politics in framing as well as the influence of the structure of government and government procedures on policy development.

Chapter 3 explores the history of child care debates in the United States. In it, we examine the four major pieces of federal legislation that have addressed child care in the past forty years. These bills are the Nixon-era Child Care Development Act, the Act for Better Child Care Services, the Child Care Development Block Grant, and the Family and Medical Leave Act. In this chapter, we examine the language and arguments that were used in the legislative hearings and debates as well as the resulting legislation. We also examine the arguments put forward by the major proponents and opponents who testified on these policies as well as other concerns that were raised during the hearings.

Chapter 4 focuses on the role of advocacy organizations that would appear to be the most likely proponents of a comprehensive child care policy. We use a historical lens to examine why the current women's movement has not fully aligned itself with the interests of caring for children. More specifically, we examine the role of unions in pioneering child care programs and advocating for child care policy. In addition, we look at the role of child advocacy organizations, including those focused on child welfare and child development broadly and those focused on education for young children. Last, we review the role of the conservative movement and the shift in strategies to counter the expansion of government involvement in child care and in the policy arena more generally during and following the Nixon administration.

Chapter 5 examines the current benefits that are available to parents in the United States to help them care for their children. It includes a review of U.S. tax law benefits for child care, the Child Care Development Block Grant, a piece of the Personal Responsibility and Work Opportunity Reconciliation Act (1996), the Family and Medical Leave Act, and Head Start. The chapter also includes a discussion of the predominately state-based pre-K movement.

Chapter 6 analyzes the limitations of these existing policies and the unmet needs for child care that result from the piecemeal child care landscape in the United States. We contrast these with model programs. The chapter begins by drawing on the literature that documents the increasing number of women in the workforce since the 1970s as well as changing employment patterns for women. This chapter examines data on the impact of balancing work and family on women and families as well as alternatives to our current system of addressing the societal need to care for children. It also includes a review of literature on models of child care, including the U.S. military policy and European policies that were often suggested as alternatives by advocates and that have proven financially and politically viable in other countries.

In Chapters 7 and 8, we present data collected from advocates, researchers, and funders to provide an insider perspective on why women's rights and children's care needs have been considered as separate issues during the late twentieth and early twenty-first centuries. We draw on interviews with key players in the national policy formation around early childhood education and child care subsidies for poor women, many of whom share a unified vision despite the schism in their advocacy efforts. In these chapters, we present the challenges that our respondents identified as well as their assessment of future prospects. We also analyze these data in light of framing and social movement theories.

Chapter 9 concludes this book with the observation that developing adequate child care policy in the United States has been and will remain complicated. A paradigm shift that characterizes caring for children as a universal social problem is needed. This is predicated on the recognition that families with working parents (both married and single) must provide care for their children and our interest in ensuring that all children receive quality care. Last, this chapter provides suggestions for how to frame child care policy to make it more politically salient across social class and political affiliation in our current political climate. This may be needed to increase social mobilization, which may, in turn, help effect broader social change and the development of more expansive child care policies designed to help families care for their children.

2

Framing

Caring for very young children in the United States has not been framed as part of larger universal policies to support families. As a result, it has been left on the sidelines of major political discourse. Framing, or the identification of a problem, affects the success of policy debates and is a major factor in the way that issues are constructed and debated in the public policy arena (Bosso, 1994). The targeted population of a policy and the perceived worthiness of that population also affect public policy support for programs (Rochefort & Cobb, 1994; Schneider & Ingram, 1993). Framing may be influenced by the nature of our legislative system, the historical context, and key stakeholders and interest groups.

Historically, there have been multiple ways that the child care needs of American children have been framed. During the Johnson administration, Head Start was created to help low-income children start school without being "left behind" their peers and as a means to address intergenerational poverty. Later, during the Nixon administration, child care was framed as a universal need and government involvement was seen as either necessary, in part because of the breakdown of the traditional American family, or overly intrusive ("Soviet-like"). Through the 1970s and 1980s, the shift was toward a need to provide support for poor families, and in the 1990s and 2000s the debate centered on balancing the needs of women in the workplace and employers' rights.

A crucial component of framing is the successful transformation of a private trouble into a public problem (Mills, 2000). The first stage of the policy process involves problem identification or recognition (Blumer, 1971), which is critical in determining which problems will become part of the formal public policy agenda. Problem definition and framing are dynamic and, often, actively contested processes that continue throughout the debates over the trajectory of public problem formation at all stages of the process. Frames help to define not only how a social problem is understood but also the extent to which troubles are included or excluded from public policy solutions.

According to Bosso (1994), policy analysts have shown interest in problem identification because it is "critical to success or failure in policy formulation" (p. 182). In 1974, Goffman defined the term "frame" as something that helps individuals "to locate, perceive, identify, and label" a concept (p. 21). Frame analysis has been used in social movement research to help researchers identify the processes by which "individual interests, values, and beliefs" become aligned with the goals and ideologies of social movements (Snow, Rochford, Worden, & Benford, 1986, p. 464). Political scientists have sought to understand the impact of legislative policy framing policy on public perception. Druckman (2001) notes that a framing effect occurs when "in the course of describing an issue or event, a speaker's emphasis on a subset of potentially relevant considerations causes individuals to focus on these considerations when constructing their opinions" (p. 1042). Other research has looked at how elites use framing to influence public opinion (Chong, 1996; Druckman & Nelson, 2003; Schneider & Jacoby, 2005). Using opinion polling data, Schneider and Jacoby (2005) suggest that changes in "elite political discourse" affected the way that people perceived government spending for public assistance. Looking at data from 1992, 1996, and 2000, they found a dip in the percentage of people who favored public spending for child care for welfare recipients in 1996 when the Personal Responsibility and Work Opportunity Reconciliation Act (PRWORA) legislation, which created Temporary Assistance for Needy Families (TANF), was passed.

Issue framing focuses on how we define a problem. Rochefort and Cobb (1994) identify several aspects of problem definition including causality, severity, incidence, novelty, proximity, and crisis. Problem definition, including the perceived worthiness of the affected population, influences public policy solutions (Rochefort & Cobb, 1994; Schneider & Ingram, 1993). Policymakers may also be hesitant to recognize a problem if there is no obvious solution (Rochefort & Cobb, 1994; Wildavsky, 1979). For example, it has been easy for politicians to ignore the growing gap between the wealthy and the poor in the United States because there is no clear or simple strategy to address it.

Problem definition, in turn, shapes policies. If a problem is identified as a relating to women, then the policy to address it will also address women and what are perceived as women's concerns. If an issue is framed as a problem of poverty, then the policy solutions that are proposed will relate to poverty. U.S. child care needs are currently framed in several different ways. Frames include understanding children's need for care as a result of the need for women to work, the need for children to receive quality care, the need for poor children to start school without being "behind" their peers, and the need to address intergenerational poverty. Frames may, at times, overlap, leading to the omission of public policy or the drafting of policies that circumscribe public discussion or have led to what has been described by both Pierson (1993) and Palley (2012) as policy feedback.

Similar policies can be framed to address the needs of different populations. For example, there was a change in the major public assistance benefit (often referred to as "welfare") for families with young children from Aid to Families with Dependent Children (AFDC) (Title IV of the Social Security Act, 1962) to Temporary Assistance for Needy Families (TANF) (PRWORA, 1996).[1] AFDC was an unlimited benefit that existed to provide assistance to single mothers caring for children. Because the children were considered to be a major beneficiary of the law, the benefits did not end until the children reached the age of majority. TANF, on the other hand, provides time limited assistance to families (mostly to mothers). Families are considered to be the major beneficiary of these benefits. As a result, children are not explicitly named, and benefits can end long before the child reaches majority.

Caring for young children in the United States has not been framed in major policy debates as a part of larger universal policies to support families. As Linda White (2009) notes in an article examining the differences in development of U.S. and French child care policies, "all programmatic ideas rest on some normative justification and frames are in part deployed to take advantage of extant norms to make one's position seem not just reasonable but also appropriate" (p. 319). Whereas in France child care is regarded as a right of citizenship, in the United States it is seen as a private obligation. Since the 1700s, the French have provided early education through publicly funded centers. The U.S. child care system, on the other hand, was developed as a private nonprofit and for-profit system. This history has shaped the norms that influence how care for children is seen in the respective countries (White, 2009).

In most industrialized societies people assume that women both care for families and children and work outside the home. As a result, these nations have developed universal policies to address the need to care for children (Heymann, Earle, & Hayes, 2007). Despite the significant number of women with young children in the U.S. workforce, public policies regarding care for children, including support for nonparental child care and parental leave policies to enable working parents to care for their children, have, until recently, been on the sidelines of any meaningful public discourse. Much American social welfare policy views certain types of family matters as "off-limits" to government intervention, and equates support with illegitimate interference (Katz, 1996; Morgan, 2006). Intervention in the realm of child care has, at times, been caricatured by conservatives (Zigler et al., 2009) as extremely intrusive into family, precluding serious consideration of whether support must always come with such interference and, if so, how competing concerns may be balanced. This narrow and, often, extremist perspective limits the equality of women with children; it also limits the societal obligation to care for children. Outside of the narrow context of addressing child care for the poor, child care has largely been seen in the United States as an individual problem that each family must resolve on its own.

Advocates are aware of this challenge. In the 1990s, many, including the National Association for the Education of Young Children, the Children's Defense Fund, and the National Women's Law Center, made a systematic effort to reframe child care as part of early childhood education (Media Strategies Group, 1999, cited in Imig, 2001). This effort was made to garner greater public support for child care and was based on research that suggested that the U.S. public considered child care as a personal problem but considered education to be a more public concern. By reframing child care as both caring for children and educating them or by changing the name of nursery to pre-K, they believed that they would increase their chances of obtaining public funding to support early child education and care programs (Rose, 2010). One challenge of this reframing was that "[w]hile people prioritize education and see it as a public responsibility, when they consider all of the reforms that schools need, early education is frequently at the bottom of the list" (Bostrom, 2002, Introduction). This framing also excludes the care needs of families and children.

In addition to framing, the political strategies used by organizations to further their agendas have played a key role in the development, or lack thereof, of an adequate policy solution to address U.S. child care needs. One of the strategies has been to seek incremental change in part by seeking additional funding for existing programs. Pierson (1993) refers to the process by which existing policies affect the development of future policies as policy feedback. Michel (1999) found that existing early education and care policies were shaped by the identification of interests, which created incentives for the development of separate early education and care programs. At present, an additional factor that seems to be affecting the development of a movement to address child care problems in the United States is public perception of child care as a private struggle. Advocates have therefore focused on narrower solutions such as universal pre-K, quality rating systems, and child care needs for the poor. This has led to public policy framing that limits discussions and debates as either work support or equalizing programs for the poor or education- and quality-focused policies. In the next section of this chapter, we review factors that influence the framing of child care and its absence from the national agenda. These include the U.S. federal system, devolution, the structure and procedures of government, American exceptionalism, campaign finance, and the use of symbolic politics in framing.

General Political Context

In her 2001 book in which she reviewed three major pieces of child care legislation between 1970 and 2000, Cohen investigated how the structure of government and the procedures for decision making shaped laws that address child care in the United States. She found that in the 1970s, only one committee had jurisdiction over child care bills, leading to some unity. The House Select Committee on Children, Youth and Families, which operated from 1983 through 1991, was also instrumental in agenda setting during that time. This committee helped draft and push the Act for Better Child Care Services (ABC). However, in the 1990s jurisdictional "turf battles" among the House committees over child care legislation influenced what became the Child Care Development Block Grant (CCDBG) (Cohen, 2001). During the legislative debate, there were four committees under which child care fell. During the 1990s, ideological partisanship also thwarted several efforts to pass child care legislation. In addition, Cohen notes that presidential interest played a role in the extent to which this issue was even addressed. For example, Jimmy Carter, president from 1976 to 1980, was not interested in child care, and therefore no legislation was considered during his tenure. Cohen (2001) also ascribes a role for interest groups, which provided key information that influenced legislators such as the Heritage Foundation in the 1990s and the Children's Defense Fund in the 1970s.

The U.S. Federal System and Devolution

The U.S. federal system and recent moves toward devolution affect nearly every aspect of social welfare policy in the United States, including child care. "For child care, the question is not whether devolution is inherently good or bad. Rather, it must focus on how devolution affects children and families relying on publically subsidized care" (Cohen, 2001, p. 251). Cohen notes that in 1994–1995 federal funding for child care exceeded state funding in nearly every state, a trend that has continued. In fiscal year 2011, federal CCDBG funding was $7.8 billion whereas state funding was only $2.1 billion, much of which was required in order to be eligible for federal matching money (Office of Child Care, 2011).

The roots of federalism in the United States are in the U.S. Constitution and the Federalist Papers, articles that were drafted to broaden support for the U.S. Constitution. In Federalist 39, James Madison introduced the idea of a federal government as a substitute for the loose confederation of states that had existed prior to the Constitution (Madison, reprinted in Nivola & Rosenbloom, 1999). He advocated a federated system that retained strong state power largely because he believed that the states would be "unlikely to look kindly at their abolition and replacement with a national government" (Nathan, 2008, p. 13). In Federalist 28, Alexander Hamilton suggested that the existence of both state and federal governments would protect individuals from government interference, as each could limit and control the other. "If their rights are invaded by either, they [e.g., citizens] can make use of the other as the instrument of redress" (Hamilton, reprinted in Nivola & Rosenbloom, 1999, p. 78). He saw the role of the federal government as largely providing military protection for the states.

The ideas and compromises that emerged from these principles and the debate regarding the proper role of government and desire to limit government authority are embedded in the U.S. Constitution. The U.S. Constitution delineates the relationship between the federal and state governments, in addition to checks and balances among the different branches of government. This section examines the role of the separation of federal and state governments as well as federal and state funding that exists to support child care.

Article IV, section 1 of the U.S. Constitution sets out the obligation that states honor and enforce laws, records, and judicial decisions of other states, with the federal government responsible for setting out procedures for fulfilling this obligation. "Full Faith and Credit shall be given in each State to the public Acts, Records, and judicial Proceedings of every other State. And the Congress may by general Laws prescribe the Manner in which such Acts, Records and Proceedings shall be proved, and the Effect thereof." The Tenth Amendment of the U.S. Constitution declares that all rights not explicitly given to the federal government are reserved to the states. "The powers not delegated to the United States by the Constitution, nor prohibited by it to the States, are reserved to the States respectively, or to the people." The combination of Article 4 and the Tenth Amendment demonstrate that the founders of the United States intended to provide states with power of their own and authority over their citizens. Family policies have largely been considered state matters. Nonetheless, through poverty-based programs, the Pregnancy Discrimination Act (1978) and the Family and Medical Leave Act (1993), the federal government has taken a role in shaping child care policies in the U.S.

General limits to the state governments specifically vis-à-vis citizens arise from the first section of the Fourteenth Amendment: "No State shall make or enforce any law which shall abridge the privileges or immunities of citizens of the United States; nor shall any State deprive any person of life, liberty, or property, without due process of law; nor deny to any person within its jurisdiction the equal protection of the laws." The Fourteenth Amendment grants power to the federal government to oversee these limitations on the state in the fifth section, stating, "The Congress shall have power to enforce, by appropriate legislation, the provisions of this article." The fifth section of the Fourteenth amendment further provides the federal government with the power to enforce individual rights against incursion from the states: "The Congress shall have power to enforce, by appropriate legislation, the provisions of this article."

Though its role was originally limited to national defense, the U.S. federal government has expanded over time in part as a result of Supreme Court decisions interpreting the meaning of both the Tenth and the

Fourteenth Amendments to enable either greater or lesser federal power. Morton Grodzins, however, claims that the idea that the federal, state, and local governments ever had discrete functions is fictitious. Citing legislation as early as the late eighteenth century, he notes "the Northwest Ordinance of 1787 [which] gave grants-in-aid to states for public schools" as a key example of their interwoven historical functions (Grodzins, 1999, p. 55).[2]

In the early 1990s, the Rehnquist Court began relying more heavily on concepts associated with federalism, enabling them to, among other things, overturn the Guns Free School Zone Act (*U.S. v. Lopez*, 514 U.S. 549, 1995) and pieces of the Violence Against Women Act (*U.S. v. Morrison*, 529 U.S. 528, 2000) as well as the background check requirements for the purchase of firearms in the Brady Act (*Printz v. U.S.*, 521 U.S. 898, 1997). This is notable because only two congressional statutes had been overturned on federalism grounds in the fifty years preceding the Rehnquist Court decisions. This trend has continued. States' rights are more often invoked and more likely to be upheld in courts. As we will see in Chapter 3, federal versus state responsibility for child care oversight and provision has often been a central component of legislative debates.

There is a pendulum shift between eras when the federal or state governments have more power. Richard Nathan, a noted political scientist with the Brookings Institute, notes that "[i]n liberal periods, liberal activists are likely to view the center as their best bet for getting things done—as do conservative groups in conservative times. It is not federalism that these groups care about. It is advancing their interests" (Nathan, 2008, p. 21). Federalism is often used as an argument to advance particular interests, but both conservative and liberal groups use it in a manner that would appear inconsistent. Federalism, when invoked, is generally invoked not as a value in itself, but as a means to achieve issue-related goals, like same-sex marriage or antiabortion legislation. For example, during the New Deal era, there were broad-scale national efforts to address poverty in the United States. These efforts included the development of national social security (which was upheld by the Supreme Court in 1937; see DeWitt, 1999) and Aid to Dependent Children. In later years, school lunch programs, nationally funded work and education programs, as well as Medicare and Medicaid were enacted (Jansson, 2009).

One result of our multifaceted government that fractures powers is the difficulty of enacting comprehensive policy. However, fractured powers may also provide multiple avenues through which advocates can seek change. In the child care legislation hearings held during the Nixon administration, many public-sector workers and child care experts noted that the cost of creating a child care system to address the needs of the population was simply too great to be shouldered by state and local authorities. While the resources and scope of a broad-based child care system make the federal government the preferred site of policy change, in the absence of large-scale national efforts to address this need, states have begun trying to address the child care needs of their populations. One might conclude that the federalism-based approach has been successful in some states that have made efforts to address child care policy needs on their own in the absence of a comprehensive federal response. For example, in the absence of paid family leave, New Jersey and California both offer paid family and medical leave for employees, and Washington State has approved such leave but has not yet allocated funding for it.[3] In July 2013, Rhode Island approved paid family leave in a law that will begin to be implemented in January 2014 (WPRO Newsroom and the Associated Press, 2013). At approximately the same time, the Senate Committee on Appropriations included $5 million in the budget to support states to plan and implement state paid leave (U.S. Department of Labor, n.d.-a; U.S. Senate Committee on Appropriations, 2013). Other states require family leave benefits in companies with as few as ten workers, whereas the federal legislation applies only to employers of over fifty employees. Efforts to address quality child care provide another example of the interplay between state and national governments in the area of child care policy. For example, a quality star rating system has been started in states, but its extension has been encouraged by federal dollars. Though some states and localities have made efforts to address child care needs, these policies affect relatively few U.S. residents, and none provide universal access to care for children younger than four (Palley, 2010).

American Exceptionalism

As a result of America's history as a British colony that had been oppressed by an imperial government that abused its powers to deprive citizens of rights and properties without benefit or consideration, the U.S. constitutional framers distrusted government and sought to limit the role and power of the federal government, as noted above. The distrust of government was complemented by the relatively open opportunities for U.S. immigrants; the United States was perceived as largely unpopulated and rich in natural resources, and many of the European settlers who founded the nation believed that if people worked hard, they could buy land and succeed.[4] There was a limited role for the state in helping people. Assistance centered on little other than protecting possessions and facilitating property transfer (Jansson, 2009).

In Louis Hartz's (1955) seminal work, *The Liberal Tradition in America*, he suggested that in striving for modern reforms, the United States differed from its European counterparts. Because European nation-states had histories of community-centered feudalism, they were more likely to adopt Marxist ideals that relied on collective action to challenge feudalism. The United States was less drawn to Marxism, which was not compatible with its much more individualized historical cultural and ideological base. The United States was founded on Lockean ideas of liberalism, which included the notion that all people are created equal and have basic natural rights such as the right to social contracts, which should not be infringed upon by government. Lockean values stress individualism as well as limited government and equality (Hartz, 1999; Nivola & Rosenbloom, 1999). Lockean ideas of liberalism suggest that individuals should be able to care for their own families and that the role of the government should be limited so as not to interfere with individual or business contracting. Thus, the ideological opposition to child care in the United States is likely based, at least in part, on the belief that people should be able to find and provide care for their own children and that such family and work matters are not an appropriate role for government. As Hartz (1955) noted, "a society which begins with Locke . . . stays with Locke, by virtue of an absolute and irrational attachment it develops for him, is indifferent to the challenge of socialism in the later era as it was unfamiliar with the heritage of feudalism in the earlier one" (pp. 5–6). In other words, as a nation, we are set in our ways.

It was not until the late nineteenth and early twentieth century, during the Progressive Era, when the United States began to deal with the effects of industrialization, that the country began to regulate working conditions, public health, and housing. As a result of the Great Depression during the 1930s, we created our first national social welfare programs (Jansson, 2009). In general, however, social welfare programs have been created in the United States only as a response to crisis rather than a consistent political ideology because they are viewed by many as anathema to conceptions of individual responsibility and success on individual merits (White, 2009). It follows that the United States has developed child care policies that are primarily responsive to low-income families.

Agenda Setting against a Backdrop of Limited (Federal) Government

According to E. E. Schattschneider (1960), "The flaw in the pluralist heaven is that the heavenly chorus sings with a strong upper-class accent" (p. 35). Because of its history as a democratic federalist system rooted in Lockean liberal ideals, in the United States it is difficult for those not in power to raise new issues and for these issues to gain political attention. Because of their concerns about government power generally, the founders of the United States set up a government in which participants, both those within and outside of government, could easily obstruct government initiatives. For this, political scientists Charles Lindbloom and Edward Woodhouse (1993) note, we have paid "a high price, a price that appears to be rising in an era where collective problems have risen high on humanity's agenda" (p. 88).

The conservative movement has been largely successful in creating antigovernment discourse in which social benefits are generally provided only on a less eligibility basis and the development of *any* new social benefits is heavily challenged. This leads to a process called "non-decision making," in which "the range and type of issues and alternatives considered will represent the interests and most salient concerns of previously legitimized political forces" (Cobb & Elder, 1971, p. 902) and other potential concerns never gain access to the decision making arena (Cobb & Elder, 1971). When seen in this light, it makes sense that child care policies have been left off the national agenda.

The twentieth- century conservative movement, a movement largely opposed to any government intervention to support social welfare, arose in reaction to the New Deal in an effort to limit government involvement in worker's rights. Two of the leading conservative groups that emerged during that era were the Liberty League and the National Association of Manufacturers. Both groups were founded by small numbers of wealthy industrialists. Both groups sought to limit the power of labor unions to protect or enhance worker rights, and both opposed New Deal policies designed to help workers (Phillips-Fein, 2009).

During the mid-twentieth century, conservative economists Frederick Hayek and Ludwig von Mises conceded that the market was irrational but argued that giving government power to regulate it simply led to corruption. They believed that the market promoted freedom and did not trust the will of the majority (Phillips-Fein, 2009). They suggested that unlike mainstream economics, which relies on modeling, it was impossible to understand all of the variables that affect the economy. For these reasons, they claimed that the market would better regulate itself. They also opposed progressive taxation as well as the existence of a central bank (e.g., the Federal Reserve) (Zernike, 2010). Their opinions were persuasive to conservatives and, "[t]he ideals that they outlined would inspire resistance to the federal government, labor unions, and the regulatory state throughout the rest of the 20th century" (Phillips-Fein, 2009, p. 41).

The rise of the current conservative movement is largely attributed to William Buckley, who founded the *National Review* in 1955, and to Barry Goldwater, a five-term senator from Arizona who opposed the New Deal. The *National Review* provided a venue for conservative thought and, in the 1970s, provided free ads to organizations such as Young Americans for Freedom, which both supported Ronald Reagan's vision of conservatism and founded a conference in 1974 to train young conservative leaders (Bjerre-Poulsen, 2002). Barry Goldwater's supporters also championed Ronald Reagan's rise to power. The key principles of Reagan and post-Reagan conservatism were "trickle-down economics" and, because he viewed government as hostile toward business, promotion of smaller government and laissez-faire ideals (Phillips-Fein, 2009).

Two large conservative think tanks, the Heritage Foundation and the American Enterprise Institute (AEI), both of which have been supported by wealthy business owners, spend their resources furthering a conservative agenda, seeking to reduce the role of government in the provision of social welfare. The Heritage Foundation promotes tax cuts, welfare reform, privatization, and school choice. In 1984, it had a $10 million budget and over one hundred employees. By 2007, the Heritage Foundation's annual budget was $40 million and it had $150 million in assets (Hoplin & Robinson, 2008).

One of the founders of AEI, conservative economist Murray Weidenbaum, who worked for AEI, along with George Gilder, "helped to shape the developing popular critique of the ineffectiveness of liberal regulatory initiatives, by arguing that they hampered the economy and warped the moral sense of the nation" (Phillips-Fein, 2009, pp. 178–179). In the mid-1970s, the Business Roundtable, a group of five hundred CEOs from the nation's largest companies, formed with the idea that political leaders would be more likely to listen to them than to paid lobbyists or middle managers. Like the AEI, they favored less government regulation and lower taxes (Phillips-Fein, 2009).

In the early 1970s, the New Right was born (Gottfried & Fleming, 1988). Though both the Old Right and the New Right believed in free enterprise and limited government, as well as what they define as traditional values, the New Right was a more populist movement focusing attention on social issues such as control over schools and family morals (e.g., abortion, the Equal Rights Amendment, and gay rights). Jay Van Andel, founder of Amway, took a leadership role in the Chamber of Commerce in 1979, bringing with him a strong antiregulation sentiment. Working with Richard Lesher, who became president of the U.S. Chamber of Commerce in 1975, they developed Citizens Choice. This grassroots arm of the Chamber of Commerce allowed nonbusinessmen to support the chamber's efforts to defend capitalism and promote free enterprise (Phillips-Fein, 2009).

During the early 1980s, Christian Evangelists such as Jerry Falwell and Pat Robertson played a key role in spreading the word of the New Right and inspiring political participation of Evangelical Christians in elections. Traditional conservatives remained more focused on economic issues as well as affirmative action, forced busing, and the Civil Rights Act and were less focused on the Equal Rights Amendment, gay rights, and abortion (Gottfried & Fleming, 1988). Ronald Reagan ran for president in 1980, largely on a platform of fighting government regulation, with a focus on opposition to issues such as school busing and abortion. He appealed to Christian Evangelicals and corporate and working-class America. During his campaign against President Carter, with his message of tax cuts and deregulation, he received strong support from corporate America (Phillips-Fein, 2009).

In 1984, Freedom Works, otherwise known as Citizens for a Sound Economy, a group largely supported by the Koch Foundation, a well-known supporter of libertarian causes, was founded. Its goal was largely to oppose the regulatory state. It was not until 2009 that this group gained momentum by connecting itself with the Tea Party movement. The Tea

Party movement began largely as a grassroots effort, in part out of fear of the bailout and mounting government debt at the end of the George W. Bush administration. At the beginning of the Obama administration, Tea Party activists adopted the ideology of Freedom Works (Zernike, 2010), with the underlying belief that government cannot be trusted.

An April 2010 *New York Times*/CBS random-digit-dialing poll of approximately 1,580 people, 881 of whom identified as Tea Party supporters, reported that Tea Partiers were mostly white, older than the general public, and more affluent than other voters in the survey. Though the movement was created and organized by young people, only 17 percent were younger than forty-five years old. While they were reportedly conservative on social issues, their primary concerns were economic. Interestingly, though the majority of those polled were recipients of, or lived with recipients of, government programs such as social security and Medicare and did not wish that these government programs be altered, a common sentiment they held was that government size should be reduced. Many were inspired to action or membership because of fears that their place in the middle class was at risk and by distrust of government activity (Zernike, 2010). This distrust of government often translates into positions that oppose government involvement in the regulation or expansion of any government services. This environment helps to ensure that child care policy is not at the forefront of government agenda setting, as it would require expansion of both the federal role and federal funding.

Campaign Finance

Campaign finance has been a major tactic used by conservative antitax advocates. Campaign finance has a significant effect on the extent to which advocates succeed in having legislation proposed or kept off the national political agenda. Campaign finance shapes the legislative process in a number of ways, including direct media communication, push polling, and other soft money spending. The campaign funds provided by businesses afford them a disproportionate impact. Although they represent fewer "voices" than some other organizations, their monetary contributions provide powerful sway; this means that the concerns of large business donors might unfairly outweigh the concerns of other constituents. Because politicians have become so reliant on larger and larger amounts of money to run and to win, conservative viewpoints that are promoted by the wealthy are amplified, giving them a disproportionate voice in the political arena. Child care advocates do not have the same resources as those who have set the national agenda, which has often led to child care being left out of the national discourse.

Direct contributions to campaigns and regulations surrounding public communication by political action committees (PACs) and limitations on individual donations to political campaigns (currently set at $2,500) (Federal Election Commission, 2011) impact the policymaking process. Children are at a disadvantage in our political system since they tend not to have money and cannot vote. Parents who can afford to participate in financing campaigns generally do not need assistance finding affordable high-quality care. Given the nature of the campaign finance system, those who can afford to get their issues placed on the political agenda are less likely to be concerned about children and parental care. Women and children's rights organizations operate with much lower funding than business, corporate, or union interests and have less of a unified focus. Therefore, these groups have had difficulty getting concerns related to child care including paid parental leave on the national agenda. Unions may be most likely to lobby for child care and family leave rights. However, their collective bargaining rights continue to be threatened across the nation. As a result, they have not been able to focus on the extension of benefits for their members but rather are more focused on ensuring their very existence (Greenhouse, 2011).

In a recent review of 20,000 organizations that made political contributions either directly to candidates or to PACs or spent money on direct advertisement, we found that little was spent by organizations supporting early childhood care and education (Center for Responsive Politics, n.d.-a). In 2012, all of the top twenty spending lobbying organizations represented business interests. The biggest spender, the U.S. Chamber of Commerce, spent $136 million lobbying in 2012, more than three times the amount of the second highest spending group, the National Association of Realtors (Center for Responsive Politics, n.d.-b). Of the top ten spending organizations in 2011–2012, the only one that even considers child care to be an issue (albeit a minor one) was the organization that placed tenth, the Service Employees International Union (SEIU). SEIU made $18 million worth of contributions to federal candidates and to PACs and used $31 million on outside spending, spending on advertisements not directly connected to the campaigns of candidates but either supporting or directly challenging legislative candidacy. Two of the "heavy hitters," organizations that have made large political contributions since 1989, are the American Federation of Teachers (AFT) and the National Education Association (NEA). Among other concerns relating to working conditions, health care, and public education, the AFT notes that one of their key issues is the importance of high-quality early childhood education to prepare children for school-aged learning (American Federation of Teachers, n.d.). Early education is not one of the key issues supported by the NEA. None of the top twenty single issue contributors during the 2011–2012 election cycle focused on early education or care. Furthermore, of groups listed as women's groups, those that seek to "enhance women's rights and influence legislation regarding issues that primarily affect women," none of the top contributors identify child care as a primary issue. The largest contributor was EMILY's List, which contributed $3.1 million to elect prochoice women to Congress. The top lobbyists include the National Women's Law Center, which spent $190,000 lobbying during the 2011–2012 election cycle. This was the only group listed by the National Center for Responsive Politics that considers child care among other issues affecting women (National Center for Responsive Politics, n.d.).

Though there is no hard evidence that campaign finance affects efforts to garner support in Congress for more expansive child care policies, it seems likely that it would. After all, such policies cost money—tax dollars—and many businesses spend tremendous amounts of money to ensure that they will not be taxed heavily—or forced to contribute to social spending, particularly new social programs. By examining the impact of campaign spending during the 1996, 1998, and 2000 elections, including the amount of airtime afforded candidates, Stratmann (2009) found that both incumbent and challenger funding influences election outcomes. Several researchers have demonstrated that campaign finance influences voting behavior and corrupts the political process (Glantz, Abramowitz, & Burkart, 1976; Goldstein & Freedman, 2000; Wilson, 2010). The voting process is easily subject to manipulation through advertisements. Much funding is used to influence voting practices by priming voters through framing issues in the media in order to affect voting patterns (Wilson, 2010). Priming involves exploiting and activating existing knowledge structures and beliefs to shape perceptions in policy debates and influence voting practices (Druckman, 2004; Wilson, 2010). For example, during the 1988 George H. W. Bush campaign, advertisements featuring William Horton were aired. Horton (referred to in the campaign as Willie Horton), an incarcerated African American man, kidnapped, raped, and stabbed someone while released on a weekend pass. His image was used in campaign advertisements to portray Bush's political rival, Michael Dukakis, as weak on crime. This advertising tactic was criticized as intentionally playing into racialized stereotypes and latent racism, which has been documented by scholars (Mendelberg, 2001). If people are primed or given images that associate blacks with violence, such as the Horton advertisement, they are less likely to agree to support programs or candidates that they believe will promote programs that they think will benefit "inner-city" residents, whom they may perceive as poor black criminals. These racially coded words have become more subtle as overt racism has been challenged; one study found that the term "inner city" was also used to prime support for more punitive crime policy (Hurwitz & Peffley, 2005). There is significant social psychology research indicating that people do not accurately retain and weigh information and are likely to be influenced by advertising. "Individuals have limited memories, an inability to gather all relevant information and correctly weigh factors and the tendency to be influenced by biased or irrelevant information" (Wilson, 2010, p. 688; more generally Simon, 1982, identified this concept as "bounded rationality" in the 1950s).

Business plays a huge role in shaping the interests of legislators through campaign contributions. A recent *New York Times* article indicates that Americans for Prosperity, a conservative nonprofit group largely financed by billionaires David and Charles Koch, was one of the main contributors to the campaign of Wisconsin governor Scott Walker (Lipton, 2011). Josh Israel and Aaron Mehta of the Center for Public Integrity reviewed campaign financing for the top Democratic and Republican candidates in the 2010 election cycle. They found that corporations or business interests represented nine out of the top ten contributors to Congressman Boehner (R-OH), and all of the top ten to Congressman McConnell (R-KY), five of the top ten to Senator Reid (D-NV), and two of the top ten to former speaker of the House Nancy Pelosi (D-CA). Eight of Pelosi's top ten and five of Senator Reid's biggest contributors represented either labor unions or trial lawyers (Israel & Mehta, 2010).

All PACS, including those representing liberal, conservative, and nonpartisan groups, spent approximately $297 million on all types of communication (independent communications, electioneering communications, and other communication costs) that require FEC reporting during the 2010 election cycle, and the top four PAC contributors to candidates all represented private companies, including the National Association of Realtors, Honeywell, the National Beer Wholesalers Association, and AT&T. Six unions were among the top twenty PAC contributors to candidates. None of the top twenty PAC contributors during the 2008, 2010, and 2012 election cycles were organizations whose primary focus was either women or children, with the arguable exception of the American Federation of Teachers, which focuses on the K–12 education sector (Center for Responsive Politics, 2013b).

The four largest spending conservative groups together spent $97.6 million in preparation for the 2010 elections. These organizations are 501(c)(4) nonprofits and therefore need not report information about their donors, who are able to remain anonymous. All unions combined spent $46.7 million during this election cycle.). The largest identifiable organization spending money to further women's interests was Women Vote, which spent $1.1 million, nothing near the levels of contributions from conservative groups or unions. While unions have often represented interests of the broader working public and have been allies in advocating for the ABC and the Comprehensive Child Development Act, no large groups were identified as having spent money on communication to further children's issues (Farnam & Keslo, 2010). EMILY's List, one of the more prominent organizations that is considered to be a leading women's issues PAC (www.opensecrets.org, n.d.) and has a mission to elect "pro-choice, Democratic" women to office (www.emilyslist.org, n.d.), does not take a policy stand on child care or any of its related policies such as family sick leave, maternity leave, or early education. Essentially no one is spending money to encourage an expansion of family policy in the United States, and a lot of money is being spent to reduce government oversight and spending. This helps to keep issues such as child care, for which there is limited spending, off of the national agenda. It also seems to suggest that if child care advocates could convince Conservatives that child care is an issue worth supporting, they may be more likely to get this issue on the national political agenda.

Given the Supreme Court decisions regarding campaign spending, it seems unlikely that the role of campaign financing in elections will diminish anytime soon. The first Supreme Court case to rule on campaign finance law was *Buckley v. Valeo*. In *Buckley v. Valeo* (1976), the Court upheld legislation allowing Congress to limit individual campaign contributions, require disclosure of contribution information, and develop public financing for elections, but not to regulate expenditures. In its decision, the Supreme Court equated campaign finance with free speech. The ruling in *Valeo* allowed for unlimited soft money spending and "issue advocacy." It held that regulations could limit First Amendment rights to free speech only to combat the appearance of corruption. However, when considering campaign expenditures, the Supreme Court held that candidates must have "unfettered opportunity to make their views known so that the electorate may intelligently evaluate the candidates' personal qualities and positions on vital political issues" (424 U.S. 1, 52–53). Several scholars have suggested that the Court did not give sufficient weight to the role of political strategists in creating messages. It is not simply information that is being transmitted by candidates, but candidates use advertising to manipulate voters much in the way that corporations do to convince people to buy their products (Thurber & Nelson, 2000; Walker Wilson, 2010).

The 2002 McCain-Feingold Act (formally referred to as the Bipartisan Campaign Reform Act) barred corporations and unions from electioneering communications in an effort to address the impact of "soft money." This act limited spending on ads that named federal candidates within thirty days of a primary and sixty days of a general election. However, much of this law was overturned in *Federal Election Commission v. Wisconsin Right to Life, Inc.* (551 U.S. 449, 2007), which excluded both corporations and labor unions from the limitations on soft money spending on advertising that relates to issues ("issue ads") as opposed to advertising spent in support of specific candidates.

In the most recent Supreme Court ruling to address campaign finance, *Citizens United v. Federal Election Commission* (130 S.Ct. 876, 2010), the Court held that individuals and organizations have a First Amendment right to spend money on political campaigns. In other words, the Court ruled that corporations share First Amendment rights. This bill allows individuals to spend unlimited amounts of money on supporting political candidates as long as they are not clearly "electioneering communications." The Court interpreted "electioneering communications" to include basically anything other than directly soliciting votes for a particular candidate. According to this ruling, wealthy individuals can spend as much money as they want and neither their identity nor the amount of money that they spend is reportable to the Federal Election Commission unless the money is spent in support of a specific candidate. In response to *Citizens United and Speechnow.org v. FEC*, a D.C. Circuit Court of Appeals decision following the *Citizens United* case, a new type of organization known as a super PAC was formed. Super PACs are "[t]echnically known as independent expenditure-only committees[.] Super PACs may raise unlimited sums of money from corporations, unions, associations and individuals, then spend unlimited sums to overtly advocate for or against political candidates. Super PACs must, however, report their donors to the Federal Election Commission on a monthly or quarterly basis—the super PAC's choice—as a traditional PAC would. Unlike traditional PACs, super PACs are prohibited from donating money directly to political candidates" (Center for Responsive Politics, 2013a). Recent data from the Center for Public Integrity indicate that Super PACs or candidate-specific PACs have been created by former aides following the *Citizens United* decision and now "rival the candidates' own money and operations in size and scope" (Confessore, 2011). "Though many of these groups are required to disclose their donors, several, such as Karl Rove's American Crossroads, have nonprofit sections that need not disclose donors" (Confessore, 2011).

Symbolic Politics and Framing Campaign Issues

Language is used symbolically in politics to define need. "A symbol is anything that stands for something else. Its meaning depends on how people interpret it, use it or respond to it" (Stone, 1997, p. 138). Deborah Stone suggests that there are four important aspects of symbolism that shape policy debates: (1) narrative stories, (2) synecdoche, (3) metaphors, and (4) ambiguity. The language and symbols that are used in public discourse also shape how issues are perceived (Edelman, 1988). Causal stories (Stone, 1989) affect the urgency and significance of policy debates. Narrative or causal stories provide an explanation for how a problem arose. With respect to child care policy, there are several narrative stories:

(1) that government is trying to impose on family decision making, (2) that child care centers are dangerous places for children, and so parents should be responsible for caring for their children, (3) that parents have the responsibility to find and pay for their child's care unless they are very poor, and (4) that many families with working parents need help. We argue that the first three narrative stories seem to have gained more attention than the final one, making federal support for child care weak.

Ruth Rosen (2007) found two causal stories for the child care crisis. Both of these stories, lack of efficient organizing or balancing and women's choices, imply solutions that are individual rather than societal. In her critique, Rosen (2007) offers a counter-causal story, claiming, "Such contentious stories conveniently mask the reality that most women have to work, regardless of their preference. They also obscure the fact that an absence of quality, affordable child care and flexible working hours, among other family-friendly policies, greatly contributes to women's so-called 'choice' to stay at home" (p. 14).

Rosen's causal stories explain that the reason most families with children whose parents work struggle is a dearth of accessible and affordable child care. All of these causal stories offer different explanations for why parents struggle with child care. They are informed by values about the respective roles and responsibilities of parents and government, and conceptions of choice, agency, and fundamental rights (Alstott, 2004). According to Stone (1989), the importance of causal stories begins when identifying whether an issue will reach the formal agenda, but causal stories are equally important in the "formation and selection of alternative policy responses" (p. 283). Stone notes that people with the power to remedy a problem often benefit from its existence and so have no incentive to make changes (Durkheim & Sidel, 1998; see also Goffman, 1974). Regarding child care, she notes that the reference to maternal deprivation of children with working mothers is consistent with the idea that men should be the breadwinners. Though as a society we have largely accepted working motherhood (e.g., Sarah Palin was a working mother who was largely supported by conservatives), it has been framed as a *choice*. The view that women are entitled to work if they so desire and that families must manage child care if they choose to do so has affected the framing of child and family policy in the United States.

Synecdoche is a figure of speech in which an example is used as a typical case of a larger dynamic or problem. In other words, "the whole is represented by one of its parts" (Stone, 1997, p. 145). For example, the mythical welfare queen driving a Cadillac was used as a symbol to indicate that women on public assistance were taking advantage of the benefits system and getting rich, and the idea of "dependency" to represent a complex web of pathological behaviors associated with poverty helped to fuel punitive welfare reform (Schram, forthcoming). With regard to child care, often the media provide horrific examples of children who are harmed or sexually abused in child care centers or by home care providers, conjuring up a specter of danger that discredits the entire concept of child care and reinforces preferences for maternal care (Cohn, 2013).

Metaphors imply some sort of comparison. For example, if advocates indicate that a system or policy is fragmented, that is usually a metaphor for a need to integrate the system. Another example of a metaphor is a slippery slope; for example, although the suggested policy is not a problem in and of itself, it might lead to other problems or to other types of government intervention that would be problems. These arguments were made by many who opposed the unpaid Family and Medical Leave Act (see the discussion in Chapter 5), suggesting that if unpaid leave were passed, ultimately advocates would seek paid leave, and that would be expensive for businesses.

Similar to the research on priming that we discussed earlier, research in the mid-1990s and early 2000s found that white attitudes toward African Americans influenced the likelihood and the extent to which they supported welfare (Gilens, 1999; Hurwitz & Peffley, 2005). Though public opinion polling has suggested, and continues to suggest, that most voters do not explicitly support or oppose policies as a result of explicit racial implications, many are affected by racial coding (Gilens, 1996; Sears & Henry, 2003). Racial coding is the use of words or other language as code for people of a particular race, often African American. In one experimentally designed study, those who thought that a majority of blacks were poor and who associated being black with being lazy were less likely to support welfare spending (Gilens, 1999). Using the 1991 random-digit-dialing National Race and Politics Survey, Gilens (1999) found that white beliefs about blacks, particularly regarding their work ethic, strongly influenced the extent to which they supported welfare, defined as AFDC, Food Stamps, and General Assistance, that is, cash benefits for low-income families and other government-supported poverty-based programs.

Stone also notes the multiple meanings of symbols and posits that their potential ambiguity can make collective action possible (Stone, 1997). The group Zero to Three conducts and translates research for policymakers on the developmental needs of children ages zero to three and is funded by government and philanthropic grants. It works to "promote the health and development of infants and toddlers" and has used the slogan "Early Experiences Matter" to galvanize a political constituency for early care and education (www.zerotothree.org). This may mean different things to different people, such as a push for quality standards in infant care or a push for leveling the playing field by providing opportunities to low-income children. Zero to Three's somewhat ambiguous rallying cry may be a useful frame to draw together constituents from groups that have previously worked on separate aspects of child care.

As noted throughout the book, most child care policy in the United States indeed targets low-income families, despite the fact that child care concerns apply more broadly. This limited framing of the issue has led to policies that do not accurately reflect the broad-based needs of U.S. families. However, the source of poverty-based policies has its roots in the very real differential impact that inadequate child care has on low-income families and the perceived need to prioritize. In the United States, poverty disproportionately affects blacks and Hispanics. Using the Luxembourg study as a mechanism for cross national analysis, Misra, Moller, Strader, and Wemlinger (2012) demonstrate that child care and parental leave policies operate as a mechanism to keep both single and partnered mothers out of poverty. According to the American Community Survey, between 2007 and 2011, 25.8 percent of blacks and 23.2 percent of Hispanics were living below the U.S. poverty line (approximately $22,000 a year for a family of two adults and two children), while only 11.6 percent of whites were (9.9 percent for whites with no Hispanic origin) (Macartney, Bishaw, & Fontenot, 2013). In addition, in 2011, one in five children (22 percent) in the United States was living in poverty, and 38 percent of black children, 32.3 percent of Hispanic children, and 23.3 percent of biracial children were living in poverty (Macartney, 2011). In 2011, 45 percent of children came from low-income families, in which yearly earnings were less than $45,622 (e.g., 200 percent of the federal poverty line), and 26 percent of children younger than three were living in poverty (Annie E. Casey Foundation, 2013). In 2009, 24 percent of families with children younger than six lived in poverty. Moreover 44 percent of single-mother-headed households with children younger than six were living in poverty (DeNavas-Walt, Proctor, & Smith, 2010).

Conclusion

There are multiple factors that affect the way child care policy has been framed in the United States. The theories that we have covered all point to the importance of how child care debates are shaped by ideological, structural, and financial forces. The framing of child care policy has been influenced by U.S. political traditions such as Lockean liberalism; the separation of powers in our political system, not only between states and the federal government but also within the legislature; the influence of campaign finance; and the movement toward devolution. As a result of conservative advocacy efforts, social programs have often been framed as expansive government spending that interferes with the family. The narrative story that seems to have held most sway over politicians since the 1970s is that if one chooses to have children, then one must shoulder the responsibility and financial burden to care for them without any assistance. This, of course, is consistent with Lockean liberalism. Child care also seems to have been influenced by a politics that is divided by race and class, pitting potential child care constituencies against one another, with one group focused primarily on education and the other primarily on custodial care as a work support. The ubiquitous need for child care assistance and regulation has been unable to bridge these gaps. In the chapters that follow, we explore how groups developed bifurcated interests as a result of existing policy and framing, thus creating adversaries out of potential allies.

3

History

Much of the debate around policies is decided prior to the introduction of the problem into the political process (Cobb & Elder, 1983). This chapter explores the history of U.S. debates around child care, as well as the history of the interest groups that have been involved in the debate (outlined in Chapter 4), to provide a partial explanation for the way in which child care and other family care policy has been framed in the United States. Some of this legislation has been reviewed most recently by Cohen (2001), who focused on the impact of government structure and other institutional factors on the debate. In this chapter, we look at how child care developed as a public policy and how the public and legislative debate has been framed differently at different times.

Early History of Nonrelative Child Care

Nursery schools, preschools, and day care centers have different histories. Though early child care centers can be identified as early as the 1820s, there was a large increase in their number in the late 1800s. This increase was primarily due to the poverty and social dislocation experienced by new immigrants, which drove many mothers into the paid labor market. Most of the original child care centers were established to help keep children out of orphanages and were run by charitable organizations. Child care was primarily custodial. At this time, many perceived that because women's natural role was to care for children at home, there was something wrong with needing child care. As a result, many child care centers were linked with social welfare services, and in order to get services, families were required to meet with social workers (Michel, 1999; Steinfels, 1973). The focus on child care as a pathological need was exacerbated by the dual function that social workers and child care centers were to serve, which was not only to keep children safe but also to inculcate their families with middle-class American values. The trend continued through the 1970s in the debates around child care legislation during the Nixon era. At that time, proponents focused on the integrating and socializing effects of child care and the education that children could receive while in care, particularly targeting immigrant families (Comprehensive Child Development Act, 1971). Zylan (2000) notes the creation of distinct agencies designed to serve different interests related to the care and education of children. The Children's Bureau (1912), the Women's Bureau (1920), and the Federal Office of Education (1867) often had competing interests that ultimately undermined the development of a comprehensive child care policy in the United States. The Women's Bureau was concerned with protecting women's labor-related interests (equal rights with men in the labor force) and tended to align itself with labor unions, whereas the Children's Bureau was primarily concerned with child labor and the needs of abused and neglected children (Skocpol, 1992; Zylan, 2000). The Women's Bureau perpetuated the idea that a woman's role as mother "needed to be protected at all costs" (Zylan, 2000, p. 613). The use of women's role as caregiver and nurturer indeed helped leverage support for women, but was a double-edged sword that reified this role for women and led to a separation of interests between women's roles as parents and their role as workers in the paid labor force. Child care was often viewed more as a working women's issue than a child welfare concern. The Office of Education's mandate was to encourage local education policies. It, therefore, did not address how child care providers functioned as educational institutions while their parents worked, even though this was often a reality. The Children's Bureau supported national and state preschool and kindergarten programs to help families and improve mothers' ability to care for their children, but the Office of Education wanted to give local districts more deference as a result of southern segregation, which was a prime concern when the Children's Bureau was developing its education mission and policy. As a result, these two federal agencies and their constituencies split, with the Children's Bureau focusing on welfare based programs and the Office of Education developing the educationally focused Head Start programs that gave high levels of discretion to local authorities. In the mid-twentieth century, the Children's Bureau strongly supported mothers' pensions based on the belief that mothers should not be working outside of the home and that maternal care was superior to the care that children could receive in day nurseries (Rose, 1999). Ultimately the Children's Bureau aligned itself with the changes in public assistance and the view that it was essential to help poor mothers develop their ability to care for their children (Zylan, 2000). This view became policy, and since then public child care spending has been linked to public assistance in the United States.

In the early twentieth century, though relative care was still the most common form of care, there was an expansion of day care centers to serve low-income families. Many centers had rigid entrance criteria including the requirement that women be either widowed or deserted. During the Progressive Era, there was a rise in single motherhood, often as a result of desertion. Single mothers represented social breakdown and an affront to the widely held middle-class belief that men should pay for the costs of families and women should raise children. This led many potential advocates of child care to focus their energies on seeking mothers' pensions rather than child care assistance. Day nurseries ultimately enabled women to work, even as many charity workers and advocates believed that this was antithetical to their natural role (Rose, 1999).

Day care as education, including kindergarten and nursery school, has a slightly different trajectory than that of day nurseries or day care for poor children. Kindergartens were initially established in the United States in the early twentieth century; they primarily served poor children in public schools and were seen as providing a potential benefit for all and, thus, received broad-based support. In the 1920s, partial-day nursery schools sprang up to address the educational needs of the privileged. At the same time, private pay institutions with trained teachers, often associated with institutions of higher education, were created and generally served well-educated professional parents and were used to promote independence among children (Rose, 1999).

During the Great Depression, day care centers were set up to provide jobs for women through the Works Progress Administration. Of the federal funding for these centers, 95 percent was allocated toward wages. However, these programs provided only eighteen months of relief and employed only untrained teachers (Rose, 1999). In 1941, as a response to the need to have women work while men were away at war, Congress passed the Lanham Act, which provided funds for child care. At the same time, many states allocated public funds for child care. At the end of the war, women were expected to stop working and return home to care for their children. In 1946, Lanham funds were withdrawn from child care. Between the years 1945 and 1960, child care became a marginal service that could not meet the needs of working mothers largely because middle-class women were expected to be home raising their children and not working in the paid labor market (Michel, 1999).

Head Start was established in 1965 as part of Lyndon Johnson's war on poverty. It was placed under the administration of the Office of Education. In the mid-1960s, Sargent Shriver, the director of the Office of Economic Opportunity, was faced with a surplus of Community Action Program money. When he consulted personnel in the Office of Economic Opportunity to determine where to focus the funds, he realized that over half of the poor in the United States were children (Vinovskis, 2005; Zigler & Muenchow, 1992). Ed Zigler quotes Shriver as saying, "It is clear that it is foolish to talk about a total war on poverty if you were doing nothing about children" (Zigler & Muenchow, 1992, p. 2). Head Start was begun as an idealistic way to combat U.S. poverty. It was originally envisioned as a pilot program with the intention of serving twenty-five hundred children in the summer of 1965. While still on the drafting board, the program was highlighted by the Johnson administration. Given the perceived increase in tax revenues foreseen by the administration, Johnson budgeted $18 million for the summer program and millions more for the program to begin on a year-round basis starting even before the summer pilot began (Zigler & Muenchow, 1992). At the same time, the Republican minority was trying to place early childhood education under the auspices of the Department of Education rather than the Office of Economic Opportunity (where Head Start was located) (Vinovskis, 2005).

Head Start's planning committee comprised both researchers and politicians, with few early childhood educators, and it was designed to address the education needs of youth who were at risk for future school failure and poverty. Though several of the researchers believed that a comprehensive early childhood program could change a child's IQ, others felt that helping children to develop better social and school readiness skills would, in and of itself, provide the children with a valuable benefit (Zigler & Muenchow, 1992). The broad goals were to develop self-esteem and self-discovery promoting activities as well as provide basic medical services to participants (Vinovskis, 2005). The original program did not emphasize cognitive development and, as a result, there were quality concerns that, according to Zigler, remained into the 1990s. As a result of political considerations and the goal of using Head Start to employ poor women as the program developed, there were no national requirements about teacher training. Another reason that no particular model of education was promoted by Head Start was that early childhood educators themselves could not agree on any one model. In addition, several local communities objected to outsiders telling them which curriculum was best for their communities (Zigler & Muenchow, 1992). A key aspect of the Head Start program was parent participation (Karch, 2010; Vinovskis, 2005; Zigler & Muenchow, 1992). Parental participation has been credited by some as increasing the political involvement of parents of Head Start children and helping them develop capacity-building skills (Karch, 2010; Schneider & Sidney, 2009).

When the original Head Start national evaluation study (Westinghouse/Ohio) was released, Richard Nixon was the president. Though there were some positive findings regarding the achievements of students who participated in the yearlong program, the data demonstrated that the summer program accomplished little. Many of the positive findings were also considered to be weak, and the IQ advantages seemed to fade after a year. Another study, the Coleman Report, found that school quality had little impact on student performance. Though Zigler and Muenchow (1992) note that the findings of this report have since been largely discredited, the report set the stage for political debates about the legitimacy of government funding for early childhood education. According to Zigler, the idea of evaluating Head Start as one national program was, in and of itself, flawed, since there was considerable variation among sites (Zigler & Muenchow, 1992). In a reanalysis of Head Start data, Marshall Smith and Joan Bissell of Harvard found that children who had participated in yearlong Head Start programs demonstrated educationally significant improvements when compared to the control group participants (Zigler & Muenchow, 1992).

Another reason it can be hard to gauge the success of Head Start is because it has never been funded well enough to meet needs (Currie, 2001; Improving Head Start for School Readiness Act, 2008). In 1969, President Nixon established the Office of Child Development, which was to include Head Start, but at the same time Nixon did not increase Head Start spending. "The Nixon administration was clearly on record wanting to do something to help young children, but its support for Head Start was lukewarm" (Zigler & Muenchow, 1992, p. 75). The original per-child expenditure for Head Start was essentially created out of thin air and was, according to Zigler and Muenchow (1992), probably far too low to ensure a quality program. Several respected early educators opposed the summer pilot on the grounds that it was too short in duration to make a difference and that the budget was insufficient to provide a quality program. The budget for Head Start shrank from $349 million in 1967 to $325 million in 1970 (Zigler & Muenchow, 1992). In

1972, the Office of Management and Budget (OMB) recommended a three-year phase out of Head Start.

Robert Finch, the Secretary of the U.S. Department of Health, Education, and Welfare, helped Zigler, the director of the Office of Child Development, challenge the OMB proposal by noting that they should not, as the Westinghouse/Ohio report had, be focusing on IQ because Head Start was "not only about school performance but also health, nutrition, and attitudes toward self and society" (Zigler & Muenchow, 1992, p. 83). They noted the success of Head Start in both identifying physical disabilities and providing medical services to poor children. Apart from the political challenges facing Head Start, Zigler was concerned about the quality of the programs (Zigler & Muenchow, 1992).

In 1967, the Social Security Act was amended to provide money for day care, primarily for women receiving (or formerly receiving) public welfare (Steinfels, 1973). In the mid-twentieth century the distinction between care and education became somewhat blurred as more middle-class women went to work and began enrolling their children in private care nurseries. This led to significant class differences in the type and nature of the care that young children received, a phenomenon that still exists (Rose, 1999).

Legislative debates of the past fifty years around child care reveal a continued ambivalence about the appropriate role and purpose of government in child care and early education of young children. In the following section, we draw on the legislative debates surrounding the Comprehensive Child Development Act (1972), the Family and Medical Leave Act (1990), and the Act for Better Child Care Services (1988) to illustrate this ambivalence and to provide a window on how proponents and, in rarer cases, opponents have framed child care for the legislative record. Legislative testimony does not provide a full story, as much happens beyond the public eye. However, testimony provides a view of the discourse and legitimating arguments put forth in the public arena by advocates, legislators, and interest groups and is thus an important component of understanding public policy (Burstein & Hirsch, 2007).

Comprehensive Child Development Act (CCDA)

Evidence of the historical framing of child care can be seen during the Nixon administration (Michel, 1999). In 1971, President Nixon vetoed the Comprehensive Child Development Act (CCDA) (92nd Cong., S2007; Klein, 1992), which would have provided federal funding for universal preschool including Head Start. This act stressed not only that services should be available to the poor, working, and middle classes but also that programs should be educationally based as opposed to purely custodial. This was termed "quality care."

The child care debates of the Nixon era can be characterized by a number of features: the comprehensive nature of the need, the high cost of care, the high level of moral appeal, the need for flexibility and local influence—including parental involvement—in the programs, the importance of research to ensure quality programs, and the need for extensive federal funding to support this program. Perhaps the most striking component of the early 1970s debate was just how *comprehensive* a program was contemplated. Using model programs that had been pioneered by unions as pilot projects in Baltimore and other locations, the early preschool programs were seen as centers that could use the child care setting to help families with medical and dental services, parenting skills, and nutrition and to ensure school readiness. Such services were viewed as enabling parents to work and as a means to equalize opportunity. They contained a socialization component reminiscent of the early child care movement that would now be viewed as paternalistic and xenophobic. Some testimony sought to overcome the reticence of parents to entrust their children to the care of strangers and was also designed to inculcate values and language skills to immigrant children. A major tension in the debate about this legislation was the extent to which it was realistic to develop a universal program, for example, whether the funding would actually be available to make it successful—a problem that had plagued Head Start. Another key feature of the testimony was what many suggested was the obviousness of the problem and the remedy (92nd Cong.,

S2007, 1971). Kenneth Young of the AFL-CIO cited figures compiled by the Women's Bureau of the Labor Department regarding the growing number of children of working mothers, then estimated at 12.3 million children younger than fourteen (May 25, 1971, p. 434).

In 1966, the Office of Economic Opportunity reported that 2.2 million children between the ages of three and five should be involved in Head Start and that few such programs existed for any children younger than three (May 25, 1971, p. 252). Dr. Lourie, the medical director of the Hillcrest Center and the president of the Joint Commission on the Mental Health of Children, presented a Joint Commission Report. He noted, "Studies indicate that most children, regardless of class or race, whether in the ghetto or suburbia, do not receive the needed support and assistance from our society." Furthermore, "Although maternal employment apparently does not affect the child's physical or mental health if good substitute care is available, there is presently a severe and critical shortage of high quality care available for children of working mothers." Another report, titled "Urban Education: Problems and Priorities," published by the Republican Coordinating Committee, which comprised Republican members of the House and Senate, noted that "[e]arly childhood education programs should, as a matter of priority and urgency, be expanded to include all five and four year olds and perhaps three year olds, from impoverished neighborhoods who could benefit from this experience" (92nd Cong., S2007, 1971). This Republican group recognized the need for expanding early childhood education programs but believed they should focus on benefits for low-income children.

The programs were debated with a high level of moral appeal. Senator Walter Mondale (D-MN) testified that providing holistic child care programs to aid working parents, while providing services such as medical screenings and education components, was an imperative of a fair society. "I think the other thing is that the American people must realize that there is no answer to the unfairness of American life that does not include a massive preschool comprehensive child development program. Anything less than that is an official admission by this country that we don't care." Mondale's language evokes the "equal playing field" language that came later in American politics and is sometimes conveyed today in discussions around school readiness and Head Start programs.

As noted above, some witnesses were concerned about whether the expansive nature of this program was financially feasible. Many of those who were concerned about the cost of the program suggested that over-reaching would lead to failure and that it might make more sense to either start with more money, as suggested by the Children's Development Fund founder Marian Wright Edelman, or develop the program more slowly, with a priority focus on the poor, as suggested by Joe Niemeyer, the president of Bank Street College of Education (92nd Cong., S2007, 1971).

Some, such as the director of the Black Child Development Institute Maureen McKinley, questioned the validity of "color blind programs which attempted to meet the needs of individuals without coming to terms with the reality of racism and its impact." She was further concerned that white researchers would "continue to describe, define, and program for black children, because we are finding that their interpretations are leading us down a dead end street. . . . Even though we believe research is essential, we cannot be supportive of efforts which are lodged in and perpetuate racism in the belief that black children are inferior" (p. 372). McKinley wanted to ensure the role of the black communities and leaders in determining program goal setting and implementation, how success would be measured, and how the outcomes would be used.

Congress debated whether the federal government should provide the money and whether or not a state-led agency was necessary. There was also debate over the extent to which child care should include educational components. The final bill did not stress education, though it was proposed in earlier legislation (HR 13520), nor did it require that large units of government be the federal grantees (Klein, 1992). Despite the fact that the Child Development Act of 1971 was passed in both the House and the Senate with bipartisan support, it was vetoed by President Nixon. Concerns were raised during the testimony that ranged from the need to support and educate low-income children to providing support to their families to the economic needs of businesses to have fully committed workers. However, none of these arguments was sufficient to win over Nixon. Playing to the right, in his veto comments President Nixon suggested the potential "family weakening" role of the law and compared public child care to practices in the Soviet Union (Klein, 1992, p. 34; Michel, 1999; Nixon, 1971). After Nixon's veto of the CCDA, child care policy became and has since remained a political issue that is divided along class lines (Dinner, 2010). No similarly comprehensive bill has been attempted since 1971.

Act for Better Child Care Services (ABC)

Several unsuccessful efforts were made between 1971 and the present to reintroduce the child care debate. In 1975, the Child and Family Act of 1975 (S 626, HR 2966) passed both houses of Congress but was vetoed by President Ford. In 1977 and 1978 Senator Cranston (D-CA) held hearings on child care and child development and then introduced the Child Care Act of 1979. However, when he could not form a consensus among child care advocates, experts, and policymakers, he ultimately withdrew the bill. In 1983 Senators Dodd (D-CT) and Specter (R-PA) developed the Children's Caucus, with the intention of developing support for child care legislation (Zigler et al., 2009).

A comprehensive child care policy was again proposed in 1988. Senate Bill 1885, the Act for Better Child Care Services (ABC), sought to "Provide for a Federal Program for the Improvement of Child Care, and for other Purposes." The Alliance for Better Child Care (the Alliance), a coalition of "more than one hundred education groups, including child advocates, labor unions, child care scholars, and other interest groups led by the Children's Defense Fund supported and lobbied for this legislation" (Zigler et al., 2009, p. 53). At this time, the Alliance agreed that a universal program was too costly and believed that advocating for such a program was "politically impractical" (Cohen, 2001, p. 93). When reviewing the proposed bill, the National PTA made their support contingent upon changes to severely limit the ability of religious organizations to gain access to funds. Though perceived by some in the Alliance as merely a technical change, it was problematic for the U.S. Catholic Conference and several other religious groups. Ultimately, all but the secularists agreed to a bill that would allow religious organizations to receive vouchers for child care that could not be used for religious instruction (Cohen, 2001).

The ABC was introduced by Senators Dodd (D-CT) and Chaffee (D-RI), with thirty-seven cosponsors. It carried a $2.5 billion price tag. Hearings were held before the Senate Committee on Labor and Human Resources, Subcommittee on Children, Family, Drugs and Alcoholism on March 15 and June 28, 1988. During the June 28 hearing, Senator Dodd summarized the purpose of the proposed legislation:

> ABC is designed to provide the seed for this national partnership [of the Federal and local governments, child care providers and parents] through a three-pronged approach. First, ABC would make child care more affordable by targeting three out of four dollars directly to low-income and working families for child care services. Second, ABC would make child care more available through a system of grants and loans, recruitment and training, and resource and referral networks designed to help States broaden the number and variety of child care services. Finally, the ABC bill would increase the quality of care by establishing minimum Federal health and safety standards and by providing funds to the States for training, technical assistance, consumer education, and salaries for child care workers. (S1885, p. 210)

Researchers, policy analysts and interest groups, working parents, child care providers, the business sector, and representatives of local governments provided oral and written testimony. Noticeably absent, in contrast to the Nixon-era CCDA debates around child care, were union voices as well as those of interest groups representing racial and ethnic minorities. The CCDA debate was also different in that it was very much about socialization of children into American values and the moral value of providing comprehensive care, including health care, through day care centers that would serve outreach purposes to children and their families. ABC debates, with some exceptions, were much less *explicitly* value based or ethically grounded, and focused much more on economic cost-benefit assessments. Indeed, a number of supporters in their testimony distanced themselves from altruistic or social motivations.

In 1988, across party lines, liberal and conservative voices recognized child care as a problem. Most recognized the increasing number of working mothers and the dearth of child care slots. Senator Hatch's (R-Utah) testimony was representative of this position:

> Now this is a serious problem, and I think that conservatives as well as liberals ought to join together to solve this problem. I don't think this is a Democrat problem or a Republican problem; this is a bipartisan problem of families that we really have to solve.
>
> In my home State of Utah, we have a need for 100,000 licensed child care slots. We have only 18,000. We know that many of the other 82,000 children are being cared for one way or the other, but the fact is some of them are not. . . . We know that about 55 percent of all women in this country work. In Utah, it is 59 percent . . . [and if it rises as predicted] this is going to put a lot more pressure on the need for child care than we have right now. (S1885, p. 4)

There was also fairly widespread agreement that women receiving welfare benefits, or low-income mothers, would require child care assistance if they were to enter or return to the paid labor market.

A small number of witnesses pointed to more deep-rooted societal or cultural attitudes that lay at the base of inaction, which were not easily rebutted through rational cost-benefit analysis or appeals to the changing workplace. This was largely because they were normative and value-based assumptions that found little place in the subcommittee testimony. Dana Friedman, for example, noted the suppressive impact of the societal belief that child care difficulties are to be borne within the family, rather than be a legitimate topic of public concern and support: "Millions of men and women are going to work each day carrying in their lunch pails and briefcases the right amount of private guilt, the proper level of subdued expectation, and the perfect amount of stress which serves as the fulcrum in what we call 'balancing work and family life'" (S1885, p. 96). She asked policymakers, who may have been unaware of the day-to-day struggles facing most Americans, to think carefully about the characterization of child care problems, noting, "The question of when a personal problem becomes a public responsibility is at the heart of society's ambivalence to child care support" (S1885, p. 98).

Fran Haynes, a parent witness, also spoke to deeper attitudes that underlay responses to child care needs when she opened with "the statement that I am tired of being punished for being a mother. . . . [W]e were all children at one time, and if we did not have quality child care in some form or another, would we have turned out to be the quality adults we are today?" (S1885, p. 17). Despite some consensus on the type and scope of the problem that gave rise to the need for some government involvement on child care, conservatives largely spoke out against ABC. They did so on several grounds, including concerns over the exclusion of religiously based child care in any government scheme, the specter of intrusion into parental decisions regarding care for their children, and the impact of regulation on the market and on family care providers.

Although conservative voices were overwhelmingly outnumbered in the hearings, they too raised more basic concerns that ABC would supplant "grandmothers" caring for their children and would also privilege mothers' work outside of the home. They opposed ABC on the grounds that it would provide either economic incentives or an expression of societal preference for out-of-home child care and, in the words of Robert Rector of the Heritage Foundation, "discriminate against or exclude 'traditional' families" (S1885, p. 341). They expressed concern over what they deemed a heavy-handed federal intrusion into local government and into the family. Most of the conservatives who testified agreed that some relief for families raising children was warranted, but they favored other bills. William Mattox of the Family Research Council was opposed to ABC or other bills that "invariably limit parental choices by favoring certain child care arrangements over others" (S1885, p. 360) and offered two alternatives: "The Federal Government can: (1) decrease family expenses by offering free or subsidized child care services, or (2) increase the disposable income of families by reducing taxes or offering cash benefits to help parents bear the cost of raising children" (S1885, p. 360). William Bentley Ball, testifying on behalf of the Association of Christian Schools International, opined what he saw as excessive government intrusion.

> The ACSI has a lot of concern about a simple blank check being given to government in this terribly sensitive area . . . the blank check, it seems to us, is accentuated by the fact that you will have a 15-member commission, which is going to create minimum standards to which all State regulation must conform, and it seems that the bill therefore—and I think many of the people who have argued for the bill today believe that it does set the stage for total government control of all child care and religious education in child care. That being so, we are concerned therefore as religious institutions that the bill will be potentially extremely intrusive in religious child care. (S1885, p. 161)

These explicitly value-based assessments of ABC however, were rarer than data-driven testimony. This does not mean that value-based assessments were not present implicitly. Indeed, it could be argued that values or concerns that were not explicit held more sway than what was conveyed in the public record, as despite little disagreement on the data regarding women's work, childhood development, and the situation of child care in the United States, the bill was not signed into law.

Many of the witnesses cited studies that showed the importance of a variety of factors that influence healthy childhood development. According to Professor Deborah Phillips of the University of Virginia, research on the impact of the early childhood environment consistently points to the same factors: "group size, the caregiver training, and especially important for infants and toddlers are the ratios of staff to children. Also important, you will get a consensus among experts and practitioners alike, is the issue of parental access to child care, and that as well is addressed in the ABC bill. Parents should be able to walk into their child care programs at any time, unannounced" (S1885, p. 272). As noted, there was very little disagreement on the data regarding factors that influence quality care and concerns about access. Other witnesses reiterated similar factors and none refuted their importance to children and families.

One of the problems regarding provision of quality care, on these measures, was the status and pay of low-wage child care workers. Diana Pierce, of the Institute for Women's Policy Research, reported on the abysmal working conditions, poor salaries, paucity of benefits, and lack of training. In order to illustrate how low child care wages were, she drew the following comparison: "To put these salaries in context, California's welfare reform legislation the GAIN legislation mandates that no welfare recipient be required to take a job for less than $5.14 per hour. Below that level, with even one child, and the costs of child care and medical benefits, the State has determined that a family would be more impoverished by entering employment than be remaining on welfare. Yet almost half of child care workers' earnings are at this level, often with families to support" (S1885, p. 121). Despite the dire state of child care employment, few mentioned this, and child care workers voices' were largely absent from the debate.

Parents who testified brought a variety of concerns to the table, all of which provided anecdotal support for the research data on accessibility, affordability, and quality of care. Parents struggled to find appropriate care for their children, whether they had children who had disabilities or were parents whose children had no specialized needs. Affordability was a factor, but even parents who could afford child care struggled, as testimony bore out. The litany of parental struggles included those with pre-school-age children, older school-age children with no after-school care, a child with a disability, and children who were improperly cared for, were injured, or died in child care settings. Michael Brooks, whose infant son died in child care, noted that this was an area where he had expectations from his government: "As a citizen, I look to my government, whether State or Federal to act on my behalf, to monitor and regulate industries and services that I as an individual cannot, to serve and protect myself and my children from unwarranted dangers" (S1885, p. 17). Parents, and those who work with parents in job training and welfare programs, also testified on the high numbers of parents who wanted to work but could not due to the paucity of safe and affordable child care options.

Local government witnesses included state governors, mayors, and agency heads in their individual capacity and as representatives of broader constituencies. These witnesses were largely supportive of ABC. They saw the legislation as a tool to help develop infrastructure, uniform standards, and supplemental funding for existing state efforts. Mayor Carrie Saxon Perry of Hartford, Connecticut, testified in her role as mayor as well as on behalf of the U.S. Conference of Mayors:

[O]ur State government has done much to increase the supply of afford-able day care. The State has raised the reimbursement to $75 per week for both family day care, previously $30 per week, and center care, previously $45 per week. The corporate tax credit cap has been extended to $1 million for employers who subsidize child care costs for their employees. Zoning laws have been changed so that family day care may not be barred from a residential neighborhood. . . . Despite all the best efforts of State govern-ment and local governments and the private sector, however, too many parents are unable to find safe and affordable day care for their children, and the lives of too many children are in jeopardy. Our children need more help from the Federal Government, and they need it now. (S1885, p. 59)

Together with their general support, local government witnesses raised several concerns. Elliot Ginsberg, commissioner for Connecticut's Health and Human Services Department and secretary of the National Council

of State Human Service Administrators, voiced a concern about the possibility of mandates without money. "I would say that the issue is one
that is tied to the question of whether there will be dollars to provide for
those standards. That is to say, I don't believe it is one where people do
not believe that the standards that we have provided for in Connecticut
or elsewhere are standards that are necessarily things that they would
object to. It is a question that it does cost dollars to provide for those"
(S1885, p. 332). Subcommittee members invited advocates to respond
to concerns raised by conservatives. The state witnesses confirmed that
states that had implemented standards had not seen a drop in available
child care slots. They also confirmed that business incentives, which were
suggested by some of the conservative witnesses as a preferable solution,
had not proven a viable or sufficiently comprehensive solution to the
problem. Most employers were so small that even with incentives they
could not create workplace child care programs. These programs were
lauded, but witnesses also made clear, both in prepared testimony and in
response to questions from the members of the subcommittee, that they
were extremely limited and did not reach the overwhelming majority of
employers or their workers. For this reason, witnesses did not see these
programs as a substitute for a more comprehensive and diverse solution
backed by the federal government.

Local government witnesses also informed the subcommittee of the
need for flexibility, and questioned the structure for setting out standards
in the bill. Then governor of Arkansas Bill Clinton illustrated the difficulties of setting up uniform standards in his depiction of a private-sector
experiment that had to be restructured when employees who lived in
a rural area did not bring their children the long distances they had to
travel in order to enroll them in on-site child care. Witnesses suggested a
number of alternatives, such as voluntary standards, the need for broad-
based representation on the legislatively created body that would set the
standards, and the need for great flexibility at the state level.

While child care monies were provided in a number of other proposed
legislative attempts that year, both sponsors and witnesses saw these as

supplemental; they did not preclude the need for more comprehensive policy. These were viewed as largely replicating piecemeal solutions that were already in place. Witnesses alternatively referred to the state of child care as a "non-system," "patchwork," and "full of potholes." Each of these suggested solutions not only was inadequate for the needs addressed, but also did not reach all of those who could potentially benefit from a more comprehensive child care. For example, Commissioner Ginsberg of Connecticut explained why the subsidies proposed as part of welfare reform did not supplant the needs addressed by ABC. He pointed out that the subsidy did not speak to the inadequacy of the supply, which ABC would address, for example, in developing "a comprehensive child care system. It transcends the issue of affordability provided in welfare reform legislation, while also providing a blueprint for improving the quality, the supply, and the coordination of child care services. It addresses the fact that families of every income bracket are desperate for solutions to the lack of quality care settings" (S1885, p. 318). Cost-benefit analyses relating to individual business as well as national productivity played a prominent role in testimony on behalf of the ABC. Some emphasized long-term cost of not having a policy to help children stay safe and reach their social and educational potential. Others pointed to the loss in productivity when workers worried about children, or had to scramble for patchwork care that resulted in higher rates of absenteeism and lateness. A number were careful to distance the business rationale from perceived liberal agendas, such as Senator Tom Harkin (D-IA), referring to a report submitted by Philip Johnston, secretary of the Massachusetts Executive Office of Human Services: "You talked about the Committee for Economic Development that was set up by President Reagan . . . the chairman of the committee was the former chairman of Proctor and Gamble. This committee is comprised, as you know, Mr. Chairman, of top corporate officers in America. . . . [T]hey recommend that we spend per year on early intervention programs, including childcare—$11 billion a year. That is about five times what we are proposing. And these were not leftist liberals that were asking that. These were corporate managers of America" (S1885, p.

270). Business representatives such as Roger Hall from Corporate Realty International pointed out that while they may be interested in child care for altruistic reasons, this was not the main thrust of their support. He noted that the provision of child care by corporate leaders, who could afford to do so, was evidence that it was economically prudent. Support of ABC by business leaders was used to indicate that comprehensive child care policy was not merely the right thing to do, but was also good for business.

In July 1988 ABC was unanimously voted out of the Labor and Human Resources Committee, and a new bill, with bipartisan support, was reintroduced in 1989. However, the bill had a harder time getting through the Senate. President Bush also opposed a block grant approach to child care. In the end, the bill was negotiated into a compromise that led to funding for child-care-related programs such as the Child Care Development Block Grant, Head Start, and Early Childhood Education Fund (Klein, 1992). Since the demise of ABC, the United States has never come close to legislating comprehensive federal child care policy that would address the needs of a broad-based constituency. Though ABC was less comprehensive than CCDA, which had been proposed seventeen years earlier, it still contained some universal components. Unlike CCDA, which was framed to address a universal need, however, ABC framed child care needs as primarily a poverty-based concern.

In the section that follows, we trace the more recent history of attempts to fashion piecemeal responses to the child care crisis that continues to plague U.S. families in an economy in which parents' work out of the home is increasingly necessary for survival.

The Child Care Development Fund (CCDF)

The Child Care Development Fund was initially created with money from the Child Care and Development Block Grant Act of 1990 (CCDBG), the next major child care legislation to be seriously considered by the federal government. The CCDBG was part of the deal designed to avert "automatic across-the-board, cuts in most federal programs" stemming from the Gramm-Rudman-Hollings Act. David Super, general counsel for the Center on Budget and Policy Priorities from 1993 to 2004, explained, "The Democrats agreed to significant cuts in many domestic programs and the new budget rules (which stifled new spending initiatives successfully for future years) in exchange for getting several spending initiatives that they had been pushing for the previous year or two. The biggest were Medicaid and Earned Income Tax Credit expansions, but the package also included . . . CCDBG" (personal communication, January 27, 2012). Because it was the result of political compromise in the time of crisis, there is virtually no contemporaneous discussion in the legislative record.

Following the logic of poverty-based federal child support, these funds were intended primarily to support low-income children and families, although some money was directed toward child care quality. In its first year, the CCDF provided $750 million to states, of which 75 percent was allocated to vouchers for families with incomes up to 75 percent of the median state income and 25 percent was allocated for quality improvement as well as for before- and after-school programs. Its initial goal was to address the needs of those with limited financial resources and to address the quality of its programs. Nonetheless, it included no licensing or regulatory requirements for child care agencies or providers (Zigler et al., 2009).

By 2000, according to Zigler et al. (2009), "more than half of federal CCDF funding came from TANF" (p. 58). He noted that child development was not part of the goal of the 1996 Personal Responsibility and Work Opportunity Reconciliation Act (PRWORA) that amended the Social Security Act and created Temporary Assistance for Needy Families (TANF). These changes came as part of a reconceptualization of welfare from serving families with dependent children to serving families needing temporary assistance. Welfare changed from an entitlement program to one providing time-limited support to low-income families to enable women to move from welfare to work; the new program was also designed to curb their childbearing.

During the PRWORA legislative debates around changing the conceptualization of welfare, surprisingly little attention was paid to the development of the CCDF. Several legislators noted the importance of child care and the additional funds that would be needed to support it. However, others pointed out that the additional need for child care resulting from the increased workforce participation of women with young children would render CCDBG insufficient.

President Clinton and several others including Senator D'Amato (R-NY) suggested that one of the strengths of 1996 welfare reform bill over previous bills was its increased funding for child care. President Clinton noted that the bill provides "child care so that mothers can move from welfare to work, and protects their children by maintaining health and safety standards for day care" (National Archives and Records Administration, Office of the Federal Register, 1998, p. 1234). Senator Hutchinson (R-TX) noted that the bill provided $4.5 billion more than the previous law for child care. Although its child care emphasis was noted in passing by a few senators, such as Senator Bingaman (D-NM), Senator Murray (D-WA), Senator Kennedy (D-MA), and Senator Moseley-Braun (D-IL), only three senators heavily stressed the importance of child care: Senator Feinstein (D-CA), Senator Hatch (R-UT), and Senator Simon (D-IL).

Senator Murray expressed concern that these additional funds would still be insufficient: "It is vital that parents return to work. But we have to help ensure that our children receive adequate health care, nutrition, and are not left home alone, or, worse, to wander our streets." Senator Bingaman (D-NM) noted that "[a] good bill would encourage adults to work without threatening the well-being of children or unduly burdening the States that need welfare assistance the most. It would enable flexibility in planning at the State and local levels, without dismantling the social safety net." Among his other complaints about the PRWORA, Senator Bingaman noted that "The nonpartisan Congressional Budget Office has said that, over six years, this bill falls . . . $2.4 billion dollars short in child care resources."

Senator Moseley-Braun noted, "The fact is, with regard to able-bodied, anybody who can work, should work, and anybody who can work ought to take care of their children. But this bill makes no provision for that, and that is a fundamental problem." She asked, "What do these people do with their children? . . . So, if you are able-bodied and can find a job, you must, under this legislation, come off welfare, you have reached the time limit, you have to go to work. What if you have a 3 year old child? Where does that child go? There is inadequate money, as the Presiding Officer, I know, is well aware, inadequate money to pay for child care." Senator Hatch, a strong believer in "family values," criticized a compromise that would allow states to sanction families with young children if the mother could not afford child care for children between the ages of five and ten. He explained, "We put those parents in a catch 22 situation, either they lose benefits or leave their child—a 6, 7, 8 year-old at home alone. I do not understand, again, the logic of that kind of thinking." Last, Senator Feinstein noted,

> In order to move people into work, there must be affordable child care for parents. This bill does not provide anywhere near enough funds. The child care block grant is awarded to states based on their current utilization of Federal child care funds. In California, there are approximately 1.8 million children on AFDC. California currently provides child care subsidies and/ or slots for approximately 200,000. The Child Care Law Center estimates that under the welfare reform bill, as more parents are required to work, as many as 418,00 preschool children and 650,000 children ages 5 to 13 may need child care. This would be a 600 percent increase in the need for child care slots.

The concerns raised on both sides of the aisle underscore that child care is problematic not just for women receiving welfare benefits, but for all women, especially low-income women. Senator Simon noted that the limitations on benefits would not come with sufficient supports: "[Y]ou can stay on welfare 5 years, maybe only 2, but we are not going to provide any job for you, we are not going to have any day care for your children."

At the same time that welfare reform was poised to send low-income women into the workforce with insufficient child care supports, the establishment of the Child Care Bureau in 1995 led to optimism for those involved in child care advocacy. However, in 2006, it was subsumed under the Office of Family Assistance in the Department of Health and Human Services. Currently, its primary role relates to families on TANF (Zigler et al., 2009). Advocates were very upset by this change because they felt it reflected the Bush administration's view that child care was a concern of only extremely low-income families, and a group of child care advocates submitted an open letter of protest (H. Blank, personal communication, February 1, 2013; Zigler et al., 2009). In 2010, the Office of Child Care was established to oversee both Head Start and Child Care. This new office linked Head Start and federal funding for child care, thereby giving it more prominence (Blank, 2013). However, this office is also housed within the Department of Health and Human Services and thereby relegates all American child care policy to a poverty-based concern.

The framing of child care in the CCDBG and the placement of child care oversight into the Department of Health and Human Services suggest that child care was, and remains, an issue primarily seen as one that affects low-income families, particularly those eligible for other public benefits.

Family and Medical Leave Act (FMLA)

The next federal bill that attempted to address the needs of parents to care for young children was the Family and Medical Leave Act (FMLA), which was signed into law in 1993. Though this act provides only twelve weeks of leave, it is, in fact, the only U.S. law that is designed to address the universal need for child care, albeit only in temporary or emergency situations. However, the FMLA is unpaid and is available to only approximately 59 percent of the working population (Klerman, Daley, & Pozniak, 2013). Therefore, though it recognizes the universal need to care for young children, it does not actually provide for that need.

The current version of the FMLA was introduced in Congress annually between 1986 and 1993, when it was ultimately passed. Testimony around the FMLA provides a window on the very limited understanding of the purpose and goal of child care as temporary relief for working parents. On two separate occasions, this bill had sufficient support to pass in both the House and the Senate; however, largely because of the opposition of the Chamber of Commerce, the National Federation of Independent Businesses, and the Society for Human Resource Management, it was vetoed by both President Reagan and the first President Bush (Lenhoff, 2004). The resulting legislation represented a compromise between business needs and the needs of individuals caring for family members.

Two features of the debate, occurring just a few years prior to welfare reform, are striking. One is that workers who cared for their family were described in language that noted their obligation and responsibility to young, elderly, and sick family members. This was balanced against the need to protect the jobs of such workers who were fulfilling their responsibility. Although some of the lawmakers stressed the greater burdens on poor families, many referred to the growing number of women in the workforce and how common (if not universal) the problem of reconciling work and family obligations had become recently. The rhetoric of responsibility pervading this debate is an interesting contrast to the testimony provided on the CDA proposed during the Nixon administration. The new rhetoric situates the debate in an era when responsibility was a common political mantra. Also striking is the recognition of mothers as breadwinners in both single- and dual-parent families as a nearly universal necessity rather than just a requirement for low-income families. There was very little to suggest that mothers should or could stay home. Also of interest is the focus on business, which is likely a result of the direct impact of the proposed legislation on employers generally, in contrast to the strict child care bills that put obligations primarily on government but not on the private sector (with the exception of child care providers).

The Senate subcommittee for Children, Family, Drugs, and Alcoholism heard testimony on January 22, 1993, and the House Subcommittee on Labor-Management Relations of the Committee on Education and Labor heard testimony the following day. Both chambers heard similar views on the bill, with the overwhelming majority in favor of the legislation. The FMLA was one of the first orders of congressional business to be passed in anticipation of the newly inaugurated President Clinton signing it into law. There was less outside testimony before subcommittees on the FMLA than was the case with the other bills we reviewed. One reason may be that prior versions of the proposed legislation had been discussed over the course of eight years, and much testimony had already been collected. Representative Marge Roukema (R-NJ), quoting Yogi Berra, called the hearing "déjà vu all over again," claiming that while Congress was "dithering," countless Americans had lost their jobs to care for sick loved ones (HB1, p. 2). Advocates for the bipartisan legislation were confident of its passage and likely saw no need for much in the way of new arguments. Like those debating the other bills we have reviewed in this chapter, the FMLA hearings included far less testimony from witnesses who opposed the bill.

Robert Reich, secretary of the U.S. Department of Labor, testified in both houses.[1] He described the dilemmas faced by American families in a changing workforce. He and others, like Senator Wellstone (D-MN), testified on the growing number of dual-earner families, often due to necessity, as well as single parents. "If you don't have family and medical leave, if they don't know that they can take time out and go back afterward to their jobs, there is a great deal of insecurity. There is a great deal of insecurity in the economy and families. Given that new work force, this becomes more urgent than ever" (SB5, p. 6). Support for the FMLA on the basis of work-family struggles was bipartisan. Senator Bond (R-MO) described the FMLA as consonant with a conservative, family-focused agenda.

There is a great conservative case to be made for passage of family leave. As a society, we need to make family obligations something we encourage rather than discourage. As a society, we should never force a parent to choose between a sick child and his or her job. We should never force a parent to choose between caring for an aged parent and a job. We should never force a mother to leave her newborn days after its birth just in order to stay employed. Those are devastating effects of the lack of a family leave policy, and they invite family hardship and breakup.

The need to keep our families stable and intact is the greatest challenge facing our country today, and I believe our ability to do so will affect our long-term prosperity and well-being. (SB5, p. 16)

Representative William Ford (D-MI), who called the FMLA "pro-family," cited the support of the Conference of Catholic Bishops. "To one degree or another, almost everyone agrees with the core principle of this legislation: to protect family values and America's children" (HB1, p. 5).

Like others, Bond also noted that the FMLA's 1993 iteration heeded calls for shared employer-employee responsibility in the workplace. Describing the bill as a "unique opportunity to forge a bipartisan consensus on children and family issues in this Congress," he asked for Republican support (SB5, p. 17). Senator Coats (R-IN) noted that eighteen changes were made since the prior congressional session to address concerns of business, making it a "better bill" (SB5, p. 17). While Republicans and some Democratic supporters described the compromises as positive, more liberal supporters, such as Senator Metzenbaum (D-OH), viewed the bill as watered down and too narrowly tailored and were frustrated with opponents who called for further compromise.

As we sit here and talk about this legislation, we should remember that 95 percent of the businesses in this country would not even be covered, and 60 percent of the workforce would be unprotected. I understand that's necessary from the standpoint of compromise in order to pass the legislation. But I am old enough to remember that when we tried to pass Social Security legislation, minimum wage legislation, unemployment compensation legislation, employment discrimination legislation, and then even before my time, workers' compensation, there was always a hue and cry that it can't work, that it will destroy the American free enterprise system, and that it is an unnecessary burden. (SB5, pp. 11–12)

Metzenbaum portrayed opponents' concerns as scare tactics. Other supporters of the bill in both chambers, including Judith Lichtman of the Women's Legal Defense Fund, Diane Duval representing Businesses for Social Responsibility, and California Assembly Majority Whip Gwen Moore, used the experiences of other countries, individual states, and businesses that had implemented family leave policies to belie concerns over productivity, loss of jobs, and competitiveness. Citing the positive experiences of member companies from a variety of industries and states with voluntary family leave policy, Duval testified that family leave policies reduce turnover and its attendant costs and enhance morale and productivity. Her written House testimony was supplemented by articles from the popular press highlighting the benefits of family leave policies.

As with the other bills, the testimony of personal experiences, provided only in the Senate, was powerful. Rudy Fernandez, the father of triplets, was denied three weeks of vacation that he had accrued and been promised by his employer. He was unable to help his wife shuttle his three premature babies from hospital to hospital or help care for them at home. "Right before [his] pension vested" he was laid off, with the three weeks of earned vacation time serving as his only severance pay (SB5, p. 23). The reason for termination that the sleep-deprived father was given was that he appeared tired at customer sites. The contrast between his employer and his wife's was stark; his wife had benefits that allowed her to stay home with her medically needy children for some months, although she, too, ended up choosing not to continue to work when offered only a full-time option for her return. Ms. Fernandez opened her testimony with the observation that, as a social worker, she had seen cases of abuse and neglect that were a result of parents' inability to properly care for their children when unable to take time off, particularly in the area of medical need. Michael Skubel, whose daughter Jacinta suffered from a rare, unpredictable, and life-threatening chronic illness, had always received stellar employee reviews. During a family medical crisis when his wife was pregnant and his daughter was hospitalized in the intensive care unit, Michael asked for five weeks of leave, at which time he was fired. Dr. Howard Pearson, president of the American Academy of Pediatrics and director of a camp for children with serious illnesses, was the only expert witness to provide oral testimony in either chamber. He supported parents' testimony with expert medical opinion regarding the importance of parental presence for children's ability to cope with and heal from serious illness.

Personal testimony depicted hardworking, loyal employees facing real family needs, a point that was highlighted when Senator Kennedy elicited long, dedicated work histories. These personal testimonies showed how callous employers can (and do) retain employees by manipulative tactics that exact high prices from families and are also bad for business as a result of their impact of employee performance. Parents wanted to prevent what happened to them from happening to others, and viewed the FMLA as a family support safety net. Lucy Skubel explained, "I came here today to tell my personal story, not because it is a particularly favorite story of mine to relate to anyone, but because I wanted you all to understand the urgency that families feel in seeing that family and medical leave is signed into law. . . . We know that denying family and medical leave is denying families, plain and simple" (SB5, pp. 25–25).

In order to balance the sense that these stories might be outliers, Senator Chris Dodd (D-CT) warned anyone who thought that something like this could not happen to her or him: "Well, you're kidding yourself. It will. It may not be as dramatic. But it may be your parent, it may be a spouse—but at some point you will be put in the situation of having to choose between being with your family and being a good employee. All we are trying to do with this bill is to minimize that conflict so that you can be the good employee, and you can be the good parent, spouse, or child in the case of an elderly parent you are caring for. But I promise you—I promise you—for those of you who have never been afflicted

with this, I promise you it will happen to you" (SB5, p. 34). Senator Ted
Kennedy similarly countered the belief that family emergencies can be
avoided. Poignantly describing his own ability to stay by the side of a son
who was battling cancer, Kennedy hoped that the FMLA would afford
this to all employed parents.

Senator Lichtman, like Senator Dodd, underscored the broad appli-
cability of the FMLA beyond parents care for children.

> Indeed, because the Family and Medical Leave Act addresses such a wide
> range of family needs, our coalition of advocates has been broad as well,
> representing the concerns of women, children, labor, persons with dis-
> abilities, seniors, the civil rights and religious communities, and health
> care providers. And as you noted, we are putting a list of all the organi-
> zations who have endorsed this legislation and that have worked on its
> behalf as members of this coalition into the record formally. (SB5, p. 37)

The four-page list of sponsors included women's groups, unions, religious
groups, and medical experts, as well as early education and child care
providers and advocates. The Service Employees International Union
and AFL-CIO pointed to the health needs of a growing proportion of
the over-fifty-five workforce as an impetus for the FMLA.

Oppositional responses were offered in both chambers and came
solely from the business sector. Written testimony in the House from the
National Federation of Independent Businesses was typical in that it supported the "concept" of the FMLA, but preferred to permit employers and
their employees to work out flexible policies that accounted for their needs
and the contingencies of specific workplaces without government intervention. Representative Harris Fawell (R-IL) testified that he was opposed
not to the idea of leave but to the mandated uniformity: "[W]hat I oppose
is the notion that a national personnel leave plan can be mass produced in
Congress for all of America's diversified employers and employees, public and private, in a way which is actually beneficial to them and to the
country. A 'one-size-fits-all' requirement such as the one in this legislation

ignores the diversity of America's workforce and infringes on the ability of employers and employees to negotiate the types of benefit packages that are best suited to their particular needs" (HB1, p. 9). Similar concerns were echoed by Republican legislators in both houses. John Boehner (R-OH) testified that polls showing voter priorities did not indicate popular support for the FMLA, despite supporters' claims.

Michael Losey, president of the Society for Human Resource Management, focused in his House and Senate testimony on what he called "practical and administrative issues": "The vast majority of our membership, practicing practitioners, believe that leaves are an enlightened and appropriate thing in today's workforce and workplace. They are overwhelmingly in favor of this. The problem is the issue of mandate, the cookie cutter, as others have referenced here today . . . it will be our members who will be charged with implementing what we will decide here" (HB1, p. 68).

Among the modifications sought were changes to labor regulations to allow employers more freedom in granting partial days without incurring costs and a counterbalance to potential employee abuse of health benefits provided under the Consolidated Omnibus Budget Reconciliation Act (COBRA), which requires employers to retain former employees on their health benefits for a period of eighteen months, subject to any required employee contribution. The FMLA debate as it related to COBRA revolved around when COBRA eligibility would begin; opponents worried that employees who did not intend to return to work would take advantage of the FMLA so as to delay the start of COBRA benefits, effectively adding an additional twelve weeks to their health care coverage, which would incur employer expenses. Proponents of the law pointed to the unlikelihood of this type of fraud largely due to the high expenses borne by employees under COBRA coupled with no proof that fraudulent claims or practices had been reported in states where family leave policies were in effect or with companies that had adopted voluntary leave policies.

In a Congress that was largely supportive of the FMLA, business concerns such as these were greeted with skepticism. In both chambers, legislators doubted whether *any* amendments would assuage concerns raised by opponents, despite their conceptual support. Senator Dodd doubted the detrimental business impact:

> [T]he idea that somehow this is going to be a tremendous burden, I've got to believe that companies that have looked at this with their sharp pencils at Aetna and AT&T, two we've talked about here this morning, have concluded that from a business standpoint, it makes a lot more sense for them to have this kind of a policy in terms of their own fiscal bottom-line needs—given the costs associated with not having someone on the job and accommodating health care needs—than it does to terminate people, go out and rehire, and go through the tragic costs, putting aside the needs of their own employees and people who have to try to make ends meet. (SB5, p. 57)

Secretary Reich was more conciliatory, although equally unyielding. Reich likened the FMLA to child labor laws, noting that "occasionally the government" has got to step in and provide a floor" (HB1, p. 34). Some also worried about "cafeteria plans" forcing workers to make untenable choices, and testified that family leave should not be subject to being weighed against other benefits such as health care.

Reich, like other proponents, gave two types of justifications for mandated family leave. The first was a business justification, indicating that the FMLA was necessary because not all American employers "understood that it was in their interest" to treat workers as "key assets," noting it was no longer an economy where untrained workers could be treated "as fungible, as cogs in a wheel" (HB1, p. 31). His other arguments were less about good business than about fairness in a broader sense and the impact of individual business practices on other businesses and on society more generally: "Some companies, in fact, can spoil it for other companies. Even enlightened companies have to suffer when there are irresponsible companies that are not offering family and medical leave because it changes the climate of labor and management relations. A worker who can't get the job back because he or she had to go and attend to a sick child or rela- tive, well, that worker tells another worker, who tells another worker, and before you know it, in the entire workplace a lot of companies are faced with a less trustful, less trusting workforce" (HB1, p. 19).

Another societal concern that Reich hoped the FMLA would address echoed Senator Kennedy's description of his desire that all U.S. employ- ees have the freedom to care for family members that he, as a privileged member of society, had enjoyed. This is the development of a two-tiered workforce where high-level executives and managers have flexibility while the vast majority of other employees do not.

There was much debate around whether the FMLA was a proverbial "camel's nose under the tent" or a slippery slope to broad government intervention into labor practices. Opponents worried that this was the case; some supporters denied the existence of a broader agenda. Still oth- ers hoped that the FMLA was the start of a more universally applicable leave policy. Representative Gwendolyn Mink (D-HI) noted provisions in the law calling for studies of the FMLA's impact following implemen- tation; indeed the FMLA has been studied and reported on by the gov- ernment since its inception. It has shown some success and limited but growing uptake (see Chapter 5).

Conclusion

Our review of the trajectory of key federal child care proposals provides further support for Phillips and Zigler's (1987) claim that child care has long been a contentious U.S. policy that is driven neither by research nor by the day-to-day realities of America's working families, but by ide- ology. The legislative debates about policies that affect child care also highlight differences in how federal involvement in child care policy has been perceived and portrayed over time. We have moved from a society in which the idea of national child care was a real possibility to one in which the discussion of child care has become one of supporting poor women to work and allowing new parents a few weeks of unpaid leave.

We see a broad vision of the CCDA giving way to a "more realistic" but severely limited conception of child care as an emergency work support in the case of illness, childbirth, or adoption or a temporary safety net for extremely low-income families. In the chapters that follow, we will examine why despite a rich history of advocacy and apparent need, no broad-based social movement has coalesced around a national role for child care in the United States.

4

The Role of Interest Groups

The term "interest group" "refers to any group that, on the basis of one or more shared attitudes, makes claims upon other groups for the establishment, maintenance, or enhancement of forms of behavior that are implied by the shared attitudes" (Truman, 1964, p. 33). In contrast to political parties, interest groups exist to further a relatively narrow agenda.

> On a simplest level, when we speak of an interest group we are referring to an organization that tries to influence government. . . . Interest groups are organizations that are not part of the government they are trying to influence. . . . Interest groups are distinct from political parties because political parties run candidates for office under their banner, whereas interest groups do not. On the other hand, it is difficult to distinguish between interest groups and social movements because social movements are composed of interest groups. (Berry, 1997, p. 5)

In a recent meta-analysis of literature on interest groups, Hojnacki, Kimball, Baumgartner, Berry, and Leech (2012) found that the majority of groups studied between 1996 and 2001 had some influence on the policy process. As has become clear in our review of the history so far, different interest groups have played different roles and have advocated for their interests during the history of the debates around the expansion of public child care in the United States.

In this section, we explore how interest groups sought to influence the development of child care policy in the United States. We examine the roles of the women's movement, unions, and early childhood and education coalitions as well as the history and role of the conservative movement in the framing of child care debates, drawing on the legislative review of the previous chapter. We note that at different points in time, different groups have sought to define or frame this debate in different ways.

The Women's Movement

In the late 1960s, liberal, radical, and African American feminists viewed child care as a right. There was tremendous grassroots support for universal child care (Dinner, 2010). In the early 1970s, however, there was no consensus among feminist organizations regarding the need to advocate for greater access to child care for women. Many felt that advocating for child care would put them in a position where they were de facto accepting that women were biologically more prone to care for children, a position that many organizations rejected. Zigler et al. (2009) note that "feminists' silence and divisiveness on the issue made a more powerful statement than any advocacy they took" (p. 20).

When it was originally founded, the National Organization for Women (NOW) identified child care as a fundamental right and a means to further women's equality (Dinner, 2010). During NOW's first annual conference in 1966, the organization adopted a position that indicated the need for "child-care facilities [to] be established by law on the same basis as parks, libraries, and public schools, adequate to the needs of children . . . as a community resource to be used by all citizens from all income levels" as an integral part of advancing women's equality (NOW, 1966).

In the early 1970s, the Women's Strike for Equality, led by Betty Friedan, sought to ensure equal access to employment for women, universal child care, and unrestricted access to abortion (Carmody, 1970).

Radical and socialist feminists saw the nuclear family and, as a result, motherhood, as the root of women's oppression. They viewed raising children as a community responsibility and universal child care as a mechanism to release women from the confines of patriarchal families (Dinner, 2010; Firestone, 1970; Umansky, 1996).

In contrast to politicians and child development experts who sought to use early childhood education to overcome the disadvantages that children from low-income communities purportedly experienced, feminists viewed child care as a boon for their own children. Feminists believed that child care would offer children the opportunity to form relationships with other children and adults, broadening their experience beyond their isolation in the nuclear family (Dinner, 2010, p. 577). In its support for child care, the feminist movement merged with the earlier maternalist reformers. They became key supporters of the only piece of comprehensive child care legislation ever proposed in the United States, the Comprehensive Child Development Act (CCDA) of 1971.

Following Nixon's veto of CCDA, radical and socialist feminists turned away from seeking a state policy to address child care and several powerful sections of NOW began to focus on tax policy rather than universal child care programs (Dinner, 2010). "Feminists mobilized for universal child care as critical to women's liberation, but Nixon used the very challenges that universal child care posed to normative gender roles and to the organization of the family to legitimate his veto of the CCDA" (Dinner, 2010, p. 625). Divisions in the women's movement over sexuality and the potential role of men in providing child care affected the women's movement's ability to unify on issues of child caring (Dinner, 2010).

Though black women involved in the National Welfare Rights Organization supported publicly funded child care, they were skeptical of a national program, fearing it would put low-income children in poor-quality care while their mothers were forced to work low-wage jobs (Dinner, 2010). Furthermore, they wanted to be able to choose the care for their children (Kornbluh, 2007). The child care policy goals of black and white feminists often clashed:

The notion that women had a right to child care created a shared policy concern, although not an identity of interests, among African American and white, middle-class and working-class feminists. . . . The political implementation of feminists' vision for universal child care highlighted divisions within the coalition: Bella Abzug and Shirley Chisholm, women's liberationists and welfare rights activists, disagreed about the extent to which the needs of poor women should be prioritized over those of middle-class women. The universalism of rights language never erased the differences in women's economic, social, and political positions, but it did give feminists across these differences a broadly shared goal, a starting point from which the divergence in their visions might be debated and negotiated. (Dinner, 2010, pp. 626–627)

The defeat of the CCDA revealed and exacerbated partisan splits around the role of government in child care, particularly at the federal level. This led to something of a vacuum in advocacy for federal child care involvement. This coincided with the economic recession of the 1970s, which set the stage for the retreat of the federal government from social welfare programs.

Later, in the 1980s and 1990s, many women's groups focused on fair wages and ending employment discrimination while simultaneously seeking to distance themselves from child care advocacy. The poor working conditions and low wages of child care workers raise class conflict, which may have further led feminists away from child care advocacy (Zigler et al., 2009). As noted earlier, the next major federal legislation that showed any real possibility for enactment was the Family and Medical Leave Act (FMLA). The support of the women's movement for this bill was indicative of the shift away from comprehensive child care as its own issue and a move toward a greater focus on equality in the workplace.

When FMLA was originally proposed in 1987, several organizations, most notably NOW and the Women's Legal Defense Fund (now the National Partnership for Women and Families), wanted the bill to focus on antidiscrimination policy and ensuring equal treatment and therefore sought a bill to protect parents. Organizations such as 9 to 5, the National Association of Working Women, and the Coalition for

Reproductive Equality wanted a bill that would provide women with special protection. In the 1970s, these groups had advocated for the gender-neutral construction of disability (Conway, Ahern, & Steuernagel, 1995). Other groups, such as the Children's Defense Fund, the Junior League, the AARP, and the U.S. Catholic Congress, sought a bill that would focus on the family rather than on parents (Wisendale, 2003). Though they compromised to support the FMLA, as noted in Chapter 3, their compromises left the United States with a very narrowly applicable law.

Leading women's rights organizations, many of which supported paid family and medical leave in the early 1990s and which theoretically would support federal child care policies, do not currently see these as core issues. In 2007, the Multistate Working Families Consortium published "Family Values at Work: It's About Time." This report documented the difficulties that families experienced while trying to balance paid work and family care responsibilities. It identified a policy agenda including mandatory workplace flexibility with extended leave for new parents and paid leave, paid sick leave, broadening the FMLA to include all employers with twenty-five or more employees, and laws to require employers to attend school activities. It was published with the assistance and support of ACORN, the AFL-CIO, the Center for Law and Social Policy, the National Partnership for Women and Families, 9 to 5, the National Employment Law Project, and Take Care Net; noticeably absent were the largest women's advocacy groups. Furthermore, in a 2009 review of the websites of three of the largest women's advocacy organizations, NOW, the Feminist Majority, and the National Partnership for Women and Families, only the National Partnership identified universal paid family leave as a core issue.[1] None referenced quality child care (Palley, 2010). Based on a review of these websites in 2013, this continues to be true. Though NOW lists paid family leave and women-friendly workplaces as topics of interest, their key goals are to address economic justice for women, sex discrimination, lesbian rights, violence against women, and racism (now.org).

While economic justice arguably includes creating the space to allow women to care for children, it has not always been identified that way. The

Feminist Majority focuses its energy largely on antidiscrimination policies and equal rights for women in the workplace in addition to women's health care (feminstmajority.org). They do not focus their attention and energies on women who require access to child care. These organizations now prioritize individual rights policies rather than family support policies. In recent years, the women's movement has been seen as more representative of privileged white women; this is nothing new (Goldberg, 2009). According to Jaffe (2013) feminists do not champion causes of the working poor, including home care workers, nurses, and female contingent workers. She suggests that the issues of rich women who are juggling children in high-paid careers are not where feminist discussions should lie. Rather, they should focus on what Dana Pearce (1978) called "feminization of poverty," which is the disproportionate number of women among the world's poor. Women are overrepresented in the growing service sector, and much of that work is paid for at poverty wages. "[M]ost women still work in female-dominated industries that have long been underpaid, precarious, and without benefits" (Leonard, 2013). For many of these women, child care is a paramount concern. They cannot afford private care centers, and many must place their children with neighbors or friends where they are not certain that their children will be safe, let alone provided with the opportunity to learn socialization or other skills (National Association of Child Care Resource and Referral Agencies, 2011). Michel (1999) too recognizes the competing views on policy regarding child care coming from different social classes. Many rich and upper-middle-class women who lead women's organizations may be able to afford high-quality care in the private sector. This may account for their lack of emphasis on child care policy. However, child care is a potential rallying point for all women that may be used to help bridge long-standing class divides among women.

Unions

Union interest in child care can be traced to the 1920s, when trade unionists sought protective legislation for women. This protective legislation excluded domestic workers and agricultural workers, who were primarily nonwhite. In 1954, when the child care deductions were introduced, they were reluctantly supported by the Congress of Industrial Unions (CIO) and opposed by the American Federation of Labor (AFL). Both groups saw the entry of women into the workforce as competition for men's jobs (Berry, 1993).

Where it existed, initial union involvement stemmed from the provision of and advocacy for child care for the children of union members. These activities were at their height in the 1960s when unions were able to provide more extensive benefits to members and unions were key stakeholders in developing programs. Using templates that were pioneered in union pilot projects in Baltimore and other locations, the early preschool programs were part of comprehensive union-based centers that could help families with medical and dental services, parenting skills, and nutrition and ensuring later school readiness. These programs became the model for Nixon's comprehensive child care plan. The CCDA was designed to provide child care for already-working parents and had heavy backing by unions, particularly the AFL-CIO, the International Ladies' Garment Workers' Union, and the Amalgamated Clothing Workers of America (a division of the AFL-CIO).

The decline in popularity and political importance experienced by unions in the past quarter century has provided an impetus for unions to become more involved with workforce populations that were previously excluded, such as immigrants, women, and other low-wage workers (Dowell, 2003). Over a nearly thirty-year period beginning in the early 1970s, child care workers began to organize locally and nationally. The movement gained traction and successfully unionized some sectors of the child care workforce (Whitebook, 2002). What eventually became the Center for the Child Care Workforce began in 1977 as a grassroots organization in San Francisco and was later absorbed into the American Federation of Teachers Educational Foundation. It has been a key resource in providing information and advocacy for the education, training, wages, and working conditions of child care workers (Center for the Child Care Workforce, n.d.).

Unions have acted locally more than nationally, such as in the efforts to unionize child care workers in Philadelphia (Dowell, 2003) and increase benefits for working parents in New York (Eidelson, 2012). This is perhaps a function of the lack of uniform support by unions for child care, despite support in certain geographic areas or employment sectors. Union leaders currently tend to see paid family leave as one of a number of issues related to working conditions. They vary in their support for paid family leave depending on the makeup of the union and the union's leadership (Gerstel & Clawson, 2001).

In contrast to their heavy involvement in support of the Nixon-era child care bill, unions were noticeably absent from the ABC debates of 1988, as they have largely (with some important exceptions) remained today. Unions did participate in the FMLA debates. The only union making a statement at the subcommittee hearings in either the Senate or the House of Representatives for the FMLA was the Service Employees International Union (SEIU). In their testimony before the House's Subcommittee on Labor-Management Relations of the Committee on Education and Labor, the SEIU noted,

SEIU members work in the rapidly growing service industries where low wages and few benefits are increasingly the norm. We view parental leave as part of a package of decent minimum standards which will bring greater security and stability to America's working families.

Since the mid-eighties, SEIU has led the way in championing the work and family agenda at the bargaining table as well as in State houses and on Capitol Hill. We have negotiated new benefits to help our members cope with the work and family balancing act. But as a 1987 survey of our members revealed, family policies are sorely lacking in low-wage service industries. Consequently, we came to the conclusion that a bargaining solution—employer-by-employer—is not sufficient to guarantee minimum family benefits for all workers.

It is telling that the SEIU, which testified in the House, represents a member base that has a relatively high percentage of low-wage women workers compared to many other employment sectors. Although they did not provide written and oral testimony during the hearings, many unions and local affiliates were included in the list of "endorsing organizations" of the legislation in written testimony by Judith Lichtman of the Women's Legal Defense Fund. These included the AFL-CIO, the Amalgamated Clothing and Textile Workers, and the American Postal Workers Union, among many others.

Between the hearings on the Nixon bill and the passage of the FMLA in 1993, union membership decreased from 28.8 percent of the workforce in 1972 to 15.85 in 1993 and has since decreased even more, to 11.9 percent in 2010. Unions have more recently been put on the defensive in several states regarding collective bargaining rights (see Krugman, 2011, on Wisconsin). Another shift in union activity is from the focus on benefits to workers as parents to greater involvement in improving child care through work with on-site child care providers and improving conditions that affect the workplace environment, pay, and quality of care. Unions have also been working to protect the rights of child care workers, who have been described as one of the most undercompensated labor sectors. This is the case despite the fact that childcare workers are better educated than the general population (Dowell, 2003).

Madeleine Kunin (2012), three-time governor of Vermont and political activist, sees an important role for labor. According to the U.S. Bureau of Labor Statistics, 10.5 percent of working women are union members. The percentage of women union members has increased, with women representing 44 percent of all union members in 2007. In some unions, women make up more than half of the membership (Ciazza, 2007). The growing number of women in labor unions raises the likelihood that family issues will be front and center on union policy agendas. Kunin (2012) quotes from her interview with Netsy Firestein, a founder of the Labor Project for Working families, who sees the primary obstacle as one of competing priorities rather than a lack of interest: "Women make up the majority of workers in the growing sectors of service workers, nursing home workers, and hotel workers," she explains. "Having women in leadership in the unions makes a big difference for work-family issues. Nobody in labor ever says, 'No, we don't agree with these issues.' It's just that they say we have fifty other things that are ahead of you. At the moment it's all about losing jobs and health reform. Our struggle is how we get these issues on the plate so they're not the last to be taken care of" (pp. 198–199). Despite the increase in women union membership and perhaps the growing number of women in leadership roles to which Firestein alludes, women are still not proportionally represented in union leadership positions. In 2005, Bronfrenner (cited by Ciazza, 2007) estimated that women represented only about 21 percent of union leadership. As proof of the promise of labor as a central advocate for child care policy, Kunin (2012) points to the pivotal roles of unions in the passage of progressive New York and California family leave policies. Past leadership and advocacy roles for unions underscore the important nexus of employment and custodial care, and may also bridge lower- and middle-income constituencies that are often at odds over the focus of child care policy. They also provide a bridge between those who need child care and those who provide it; unifying those voices in mutual self-interest might help further a more comprehensive child care agenda.

A Child Care/Early Education Movement

Proponents of early education trace their roots back to nineteenth-century custodial care approaches, but the two movements have often interacted in ways that scholars and activists see as working at cross-purposes (as noted in Chapter 3). In 1898, the first national organization to address child care was formed. The main goals of this organization, the National Federation of Day Nurseries (NFDN), were to "Americanize the poor" and to provide emergency assistance for poor women and families (Koven & Michel, 1993; Michel, 1999). The NFDN, Catholic Charities, and the National Association of Colored Women (blacks were excluded from NFDN) were responsible for setting up seven hundred nurseries by 1912 (Michel, 1999). NFDN did not seek government funding but did try to use municipal and state governments to regulate facilities (Michel, 1999). Both the NFDN and the Children's Bureau were strongly opposed to child care and early education for children ages zero to two, believing that it was better for children to be in parental care at that time (Michel, 1999).

Early childhood education advocates relied heavily on social science research to try to expand the provision of child care. Much of this research focuses on improving the outcomes for low-income or at-risk youth and, as such, has been used to support funding for low-income children in early education programs. This research began with the Perry Preschool Program in the 1960s, which was studied using an experimental design. Its effects have been longitudinally studied for at least forty years. Three- and four-year-old children were given two and a half hours of educational services a week. The average class size was about twenty to twenty-five students, and each class had four teachers. In addition, each student and a parent received an hour and a half home visit per week. Approximately 125 students took part in the study over five years. Socioeconomically matched pairs from the same community were assigned to a control group that did not receive services. The study demonstrated that children who had participated in the intervention group were more likely to be of average intelligence (rather than have an IQ of less than ninety) at age five, to score higher on achievement tests at fourteen, and to be employed at nineteen. As adults, at age twenty-seven, they were significantly less likely to have had multiple arrests, significantly more likely not to live in poverty, and significantly more likely to have graduated from high school. A cost-benefit analysis of this program that considered reduced government expenses for elementary and secondary education services, social services, and criminal justice services as well as the higher taxes the participants could pay based on their higher mean earnings calculated that the return for every dollar spent on preschool was just over $7. The cost of the program was approximately $7,500 per child while in the program in the 1960s, and the benefit per participant in reduced government expenditures over the decades that they were tracked was approximately $44,700 (Barnett, 1996). Though some research has suggested that the IQ advantages were short-lived, this program essentially established that IQ could be altered by one's education (Kirp, 2007).

Similar to the Perry Preschool Program, the Abecedian Program provided full-day early intervention services for 111 high-risk children for the entire year from 1972 to 1977. The mean age of the children in the study at the outset was 4.4 months. They were provided intensive yearlong services until age eight. Like the Perry Preschool Program, the and Abecedian program included home-visitation components. At age twenty-one, these children had higher IQs, were less likely to have spent time in special education, spent less time in special education when they were placed in it, scored higher on achievement tests, were more likely to be in higher education, were more likely to earn more, and were less likely to be on public assistance or incarcerated than were their peers. The results of the Abecedian Program were superior to the results of the Perry Preschool Program (Heckman, 2008).

Head Start was established 1964 as a part of President Lyndon Johnson's war on poverty, and in 1965 the Federal Office of Education was tasked with administering it. As noted earlier, this program grew out of the civil rights movement and was designed to address the needs of youth who were at risk for school failure and poverty. Its goals were to address the needs of the whole child including the child's social, emotional, health care, and psychological needs. Head Start programs include everything from teaching children how to brush their teeth to parental instruction on how to care for and parent a preschool-age child (Currie, 2001; Improving Head Start for School Readiness Act, 2008). Though some research demonstrated that though children not in Head Start tend to catch up to their Head Start peers by third grade, other research demonstrated that children in Head Start are less likely to be held back or assigned to special education classes (Kirp, 2007). In the late 1970s, despite research that initially demonstrated limited success of Head Start, the media confused the Perry Preschool Program with Head Start and began attributing the successes of the Perry Preschool Program, a program with smaller class sizes and college-educated teachers, to Head Start.

Within a decade of the beginning of Head Start, the CCDA was proposed. In their recent book, *The Tragedy of Child Care in America*, Zigler et al. (2009) argue that the cause of CCDA's failure was the inability of the Senate and child care advocates such as Marian Wright Edelman to compromise on who would control CCDA. Advocates and the Senate sought more federal control and the Nixon administration wanted more local control. According to Zigler et al., Edelman simply did not believe that Nixon would veto CCDA during an election year. He notes that her "unwillingness to compromise made the bill unpalatable even to politicians who were originally among the supporters" (Zigler et al., 2009, p. 35).

Following Nixon's veto of CCDA, during the fiscal recession that followed, child care activists "shifted their political energies from rights articulation to heightened battles over funding, eligibility criteria, and community control" (Dinner, 2010, p. 621). This may in part have been a response to concerns that government involvement in early education or care programs might lead to paternalistic interventions or programs that do not meet the needs of minority populations, as was raised in the subcommittee testimony. Educational advocates, notably the American Federation of Teachers, did not enter the child care debate until 1975, at which time they supported a more limited bill, the Child and Family Services Act of 1975, which died in committee (Klein, 1992).

As a result of the lack of progress during the 1980s and 1990s toward improving and expanding child care, "advocates deliberately sought to reframe the issue away from care and toward education" (Rose, 2010, p. 216). Rose (2010) suggests that the framing of preschool away from child care may have had unintended consequences of diminishing the value of child care and separating the issue from the care for children younger than preschool age, despite its equal importance. Rose (2010, p. 217) quotes Lois Salisbury of the Packard Foundation: "To improve kids' opportunities you need to start with four year olds and work down, rather than diluting the effort and being unsuccessful, as we've always been." She suggests that universal pre-K programs have to keep this clearly in mind when working with what they believe is a more winnable campaign.

In the 1980s, advocates also shifted their focus away from federal programs toward the state level. One battleground for early childhood advocates was Illinois. In 1985, because of the lobbying of pro–early childhood education groups, Illinois enacted legislation that provided funds for at-risk children to receive preschool education. The coalition of early education groups that was active in furthering this legislation was supported and heavily influenced by Irving Harris, a Chicago philanthropist who focused on child welfare. In the 1990s, Harris convinced the McCormick Tribune Foundation to further finance preschool initiatives. In 2006, Governor Blagojevich signed legislation to provide preschool for all. The opposition questioned whether the funding would ever really be available to reach this goal (Kirp, 2007). In 2007, Governor Blagojevich noted, "It's a civil rights issue. Low income kids have a right to a level playing field" (Kirp, 2007, p. 19). Although early education might have been viewed this way in Illinois, it has not been viewed this way at the national level.

At the same time, An Ounce of Prevention, a group initially funded by Irving Harris, and the Buffett Early Childhood Fund worked together to develop Educare. Educare is a model public-private partnership that provides education for at-risk children in Chicago from birth to age five. This group received public funds from Head Start, Early Head Start, and the Child Care Development Block Grant as well as some funding from Chicago Public Schools to develop schools for at-risk children ages zero to five (Educare, n.d.). Other foundations that have supported it and have begun working to further the goals of An Ounce of Prevention include the Bill & Melinda Gates Foundation, the Irving Harris Foundation, the J. B. and M. K. Pritzker Foundation, the W. K. Kellogg Foundation, and the George Kaiser Family Foundation. The goal of this group is to develop "an integrated strategy of practice, policy and research that is changing the way America thinks about early childhood education" (Educare, n.d.) and to "attack the achievement gap that takes root early in life and puts children in poverty at great disadvantage." Though they identify a need to change the way that people in the United States view early childhood education, the primary goal of Educare is to address the needs of those at risk or disadvantaged. This is a different perspective from that taken by groups seeking to further the rights of women in the workplace. This focus reinforces the existence of programs primarily designed to address the needs of the poor.

Conservative Influences

Though conservative groups have always played a role in the development of U.S. social welfare policy, they began to heavily influence the framing of child care policy during the Nixon administration. The Heritage Foundation and other powerful conservative groups came into existence shortly after the Nixon veto of the CCDA (Cohen, 2001). At present, neither social nor economic conservatives seem to be actively engaged in opposing child care policies. In *Grand New Party*, Ross Douthat and Reihan Salam (2008) suggest that there is a political vacuum around child care. Neither the left nor the right addresses the needs of working parents. Economic conservatives are relatively quiet about child care. Douthat and Salam suggest that if the right can come up with solutions to address the needs of families, such as tax relief policies for parents with children at home, they could win over working-class parents. Though child care is clearly not a major issue for the American Enterprise Institute (AEI), they have posted a study on their website by Douglas Besharov decrying the high public cost of child care and Head Start (American Enterprise Institute, 2007; Besharov, Myers, & Morrow, 2007). The AEI website also cites his work, noting that Census Bureau surveys underestimate participants in publicly funded programs (Besharov, Morrow, & Fengyan Shi, 2006). Besharov notes that much government documentation does not consider infrastructure and other costs thereby underestimating the full cost of these programs (American Enterprise Institute, 2007; Besharov et al., 2007). In another, more dated article published in 1994 that was posted on the AEI website, Besharov criticizes the patchwork system of child care that has been developed in the United States and calls for block grant funding to eliminate overlapping services.

Business groups, which tend to be economically conservative, have been remarkably silent on issues of national or state involvement in child care policy. However, the concerns of business were often present in the legislative debates around the FMLA and used to justify some of the extremely limiting provisions of the legislation that was ultimately signed into law. Their involvement in this legislation is clearly the result of the FMLA intervening directly in the employer-employee relationship, whereas measures to address child care such as the CCDA and ABC did not (except in the case of worker rights for child care providers). While some businesses have noted that family support policies can be economically beneficial, most businesses are resistant to being regulated.

One of the U.S. Chamber of Commerce's 2010 priorities under education and workforce development was "to build the case for states and localities to provide access to quality pre-K programs for all children," providing some evidence that reframing child care as early education was sufficient to garner some business support, though, notably, they indicate no role for the federal government (U.S. Chamber of Commerce, 2010). By 2013, early childhood programs were no longer on the list of priorities (U.S. Chamber of Commerce, 2013). Other groups such as the National Small Business Association, though taking no position on child care and early education, strongly oppose paid sick leave requirements, which is one way that parents can care for their children without experiencing workplace penalties.

Americans for Tax Reform (ATR, n.d.) "oppose all tax increases as a matter of principle. [They] believe in a system in which taxes are simpler, flatter, more visible, and lower than they are today. The government's power to control one's life derives from its power to tax." As a result of their ideological opposition to taxes, this group would likely oppose the expansion of any public services that may cost money, such as tax benefits to parents, more public child care, and/or early education programs that are funded by tax dollars. In the past few years, the Tea Party movement has been outspoken about their opposition to any increases in taxes or increases in the provision of public services. The Tea Party, a populist movement heavily supported by rich businessmen, does not support government funding for public, particularly social, programming, identifying this as the overreaching of government power (Zernike, 2010).

The socially conservative Christian Coalition seems to take no position on child care or early education in its 2010 legislative agenda. Perhaps this is because child care and family leave legislation is not a major part of any national policy debates. However, documents retrieved from the Christian Coalition's website in 2010 state their position: "Feminists demand that child care arrangements be federally funded so that the rearing of children can be turned over to child care providers and thus not be burdensome or interfere with a woman's career aspirations" (Crouse, 2004). The organization also opposes the regulation of quality care, noting that parents should be able to make choices regarding what type of care their child receives and from whom without government intervention (Flakoll, 2009). However, in a question-answer forum on the Focus on the Family (2010) website, one responder, though citing a preference for at-home maternal care, notes, "Safe, clean, loving childcare facilities are a necessity in today's culture. They are especially needed by the millions of mothers who are forced to work for financial reasons. They are particularly vital to the many single parents who are the sole breadwinners in their families. Thus, we need not question the wisdom of providing well-supervised centers for children whose mothers and fathers require assistance in raising them." This shows that there is some recognition among conservatives that some mothers must work and will need child care assistance, although this is only when it is viewed against the alternative of state support for women who cannot otherwise afford to take care of their own children.

The Independent Women's Forum focuses on the poor quality of U.S. public education in its policy statement paper, "Keep Uncle Sam Away from Toddlers: The Case Against Government Funding for Preschool."

This study notes that increased federal funding for preschool (e.g., pre-K) may crowd out private care providers. They question the fairness of subsidizing specific services rather than subsidizing children, ultimately noting that tax benefits would better allow parents to choose what they believe are the best services for their children (Lukas, 2009).

Child care is not on the list of issues identified by the Family Research Council, a leading conservative research/advocacy organization. The closest they come to mentioning child care is identification of a strong need for parental authority in all areas of a child's life absent abuse or neglect, particularly in regard to education. "Government should empower parents to control the upbringing of their children and minimize its interference with the exercise of parental authority, except in cases of demonstrable abuse or neglect. Specifically, public policy should protect the right and maximize the power of parents to choose the form of education they wish for their children, be it public schools, secular or religious private schools, or home schooling" (Family Research Council, n.d.). Child care itself is not explicitly mentioned anywhere on their website.

Though not primarily concerned with child care or child welfare, organizations promoting conservative ideals tend to include child care funding with other public welfare programs and the fear of government overintrusion into the family or businesses. For example, in the 1970s, the right wing mobilized in order to defeat CCDA using a "profamily" stance. Organizations such as the Olin Foundation spent $370 million on research and think tanks between 1953 and 2005 to further their public policy ideas (Smith, 1991; Zigler et al., 2009). Other conservative think tanks such as the Heritage Foundation, the Eagle Forum, Concerned Women for America, and the Family Research Council all have sought to promote conservative public policies and have strongly opposed government intervention in child care. As noted earlier, many of these groups began following the Nixon veto of CCDA. "By trumping economic concerns with its double aces of family values and religious rhetoric, the New Right manages to win over Middle America, once the hotbed of the populist movement" (Zigler et al., 2009, p. 46). This includes many fundamentalist Christians who tend to oppose policies that might support what they view as nontraditional family structures and working mothers (Imig, 2001).

Conclusion

Child care policy has a complex history in the United States that has been influenced by multiple forces: the need for women to work, the large scale reentry of men to the labor force following the world wars, the desire to help equalize opportunities for poor children and ameliorate problems caused by segregation, educational policy, conservative antitax politics, and the role of campaign finance in our political system. Groups representing a variety of often competing interests have stymied progress on child care policy. Even when groups such as labor unions, feminists, progressive businesses, ethnic groups, and religious groups have united to pass or nearly pass more comprehensive legislation, these efforts have been thwarted or severely circumscribed by powerful socially and economically conservative groups, which have played on racial and class divides as well as American biases against government intervention. U.S. political culture and the political history surrounding child care policy in the United States have influenced how policies have been framed. In the following chapters, we examine the perspective of elite advocates on current policy debates. Much of the framing used by these advocates can be understood as a result of the influences of U.S. political culture and history.

5

Current U.S. Child Care Policies

The United States has no comprehensive child care policy, but rather a patchwork of programs that do not have universal child care as their prime focus. The FMLA remains the only major national legislation enacted in the past twenty years that specifically addresses child care needs, albeit on a short-term basis. There have also been some recent local movements to pass paid sick leave, another short-term care solution, particularly in San Francisco and New York City. One exception to a trend of defunding in the wake of a struggling economy is the recent funding of programs to supply care and education for young children through state-based universal pre-K programs for children ages three and four (Pew Center on the States, 2009) and the recent attention that President Obama has given this campaign (Obama, 2013). Funding for these initiatives, overall, expanded annually from 2005 to 2011. The ten-year Pew initiative that helped to fund these initiatives ended in 2011 (Pew Center on the States, 2011; Watson, 2010). Research has shown an increase in the supply and quality of programs for children where states have experimented with universal pre-K programs. Georgia's pre-K program was designed as a universal program to obtain broad-based support for addressing the needs of poor children. The program's universal application may have protected the program from funding cuts (Rose, 2010). In many places, the vagaries of funding, changes in eligibility and other requirements, and changing regulations can adversely affect programs and the families that rely on them (Schilder, Kimura, Elliott, & Curenton, 2011). During the 2011–2012 academic year, state per student pre-K spending reached a ten-year low. Though four-year-old enrollment in state-funded programs has doubled in the past ten years and approximately 28 percent of four-year-old children were enrolled in state-funded pre-K programs during the 2011–2012 school year, adjusted for inflation per capita state spending has declined by $1,100 (Barnett & Carolan, 2013).

In most places, pre-K programs are limited to partial-day programs that do not address the family care needs of working parents and are designed more to meet educational and school-preparedness goals (Barnett, Carolan, Fitzgerald, & Squires, 2012). They typically provide only a couple of hours of daily "education," although in some locations mixed-delivery systems with options for center-based care can be combined with full-day care (Schilder et al., 2011). Individual families grapple with limited child care choices and support, but discussion of these struggles rarely makes it on to national or even statewide public policy agendas. In this section, we review the major U.S. public policies affecting parents' ability to provide care for their children. They include U.S. tax policy, the Child Care Development Block Grant, Head Start, and the Family and Medical Leave Act.

The U.S. Tax Code

In 1954, the income tax code was revised to provide child care deductions for widowed, divorced, and low-income working women, thereby encouraging poor women to work and dividing low-income and middle-class women's interests regarding child care (Dinner, 2010). The child care tax deductions were expanded to a broader population including the middle-class families whose children received in-home child care, but these expansions benefited only those who make enough money to pay taxes. They also provided better benefits for in-home services, thus discouraging institutional child care (Dinner, 2010; Simkin, 1972).

The U.S. tax code currently includes some child care benefits for families who pay others to care for their children in order to work or to seek employment in the paid labor market. Families with dependent children up to age thirteen are eligible for up to up to $3,000 in child care expenses and up to $6,000 in expenses for two or more children (IRS, 2013). Although the amount of this tax credit has been increased slightly in the past thirty years, it has not kept pace with inflation. This credit cannot exceed $2,100 for families making less than $15,000 and $1,200 for families making more than $43,000 (IRS, 2013; National Women's Law Center, 2012).

In order to receive this benefit taxpayers must provide the social security number of the person who has cared for the child(ren). Many care providers are not legal United States residents or are paid nominal amounts and do not wish to pay taxes on their earnings. Arguably, requiring tax payments may elevate the status of caregivers so that they are less likely to be exploited and can benefit from Social Security. However, given the cost of care and the difficulty many families have obtaining it, this additional requirement may disadvantage those at the lower end of the economic scale. Because this tax benefit is nonrefundable, it primarily benefits the middle and upper classes who have higher tax liabilities.

In addition to the child and dependent care benefit, married couples making up to $110,000 ($55,000 filing separately) and single parents making up to $75,000 are eligible for up to a $1,000 child tax credit for each child younger than eighteen. In order to be eligible for this credit one must earn over $3,000 a year and will be eligible for either 15 percent of one's tax liability or $3,000, whichever is less. At incomes greater than $110,000, the tax credit is gradually phased out. A portion of this tax credit is refundable (IRS, 2011b). Employers that provide dependent care savings accounts allow employees to use pretax income of up to $5,000 annually for child care costs paid to licensed provider agencies or others who provide their social security numbers. Families can use dependent care savings accounts (if available) and/or tax exemptions for child care of no more than $5,000 total in any case (IRS, 2011a). The cost of child care for most working families easily exceeds $3,000 to $5,000 and, for nearly all, exceeds the $1,000 child tax credit. The average cost of care for a child not yet in school ranges from $4,630 to $18,200 per year (National Association of Child Care Resource and Referral Agencies, 2011). As with the Child and Dependent Care Benefit, women who use a patchwork of formal and informal child care options may not be able to report the Social Security numbers of the people who have helped care for their children. In order to benefit from a dependent care savings account, employers must provide their employees with pretax accounts for dependent care. There is usually a limited enrollment period, and employees who miss the cutoff date cannot receive the benefit. In 2000, only 12 percent of wage earners used flexible spending accounts. Dependent care savings accounts benefit employees with more stable long-term employment arrangements. Tax deductions are primarily available for higher income families who have more complicated taxes and are eligible for more than the standard deductions. At minimum, families must have enough income to enable them to take such a deduction, and most low-income families do not. As a result, working poor women and families are less likely to be eligible for this benefit. Current tax policy that supports care for children provides minimal benefit to very low-income families and more benefit to the middle and upper classes who have substantial tax liabilities. In this way, it may operate as a mechanism shifting the cost of care onto the poor (Sered, 1995).

Federal tax expenditures make up a significant portion of the money allocated for child care in the United States. In 2009, $5.14 billion were allocated toward the Child Care and Development Fund and $6.366 billion were allocated toward Head Start.[1] The majority of that money paid for services to children living in families that fell under 200 percent of the U.S. poverty line (only 5 percent of CCDF and 9 percent of Head Start money went to families earning more than 200 percent of the federal poverty line). At the same time, the child tax credit accounted for $50 billion, of which $24 billion was the refundable portion and $26 billion was nonrefundable. Approximately 87 percent of those benefiting from the refundable portion fell below 200 percent of the federal poverty line, as did 10 percent of those benefiting from the nonrefundable portion. The dependent care tax exemptions accounted for $34.268 billion dollars, 81 percent of which went to families earning more than 200 percent of the federal poverty level (Vericker, Isaacs, Hahn, Toran, & Rennane, 2012). These figures show that the federal tax exemptions and credits are much larger than federal money allocated to CCDF and Head Start combined.

Another way that the tax code has been able to supplement the cost of care is by providing tax exempt status to nonprofit organizations that provide child care (Buehler, 1998). This benefits only families whose children who are in institutional care settings and may disproportionately benefit religion-based care. Ironically, in many states, these care settings are excluded from licensure requirements. In addition to available federal tax benefits, twenty-eight states also offer child care tax credits to low-income households. These credits range from $330 in Maryland to $2,310 in New York (National Women's Law Center, 2012). In most cases, these credits are quite small in relation to the actual cost of care that most families incur.

Last, some might consider child care a business expense because parents cannot work if they must care for young children. In 1939, in the case of *Smith v. Commissioner* (40 B.T.A. 1038 [1939], aff'd, 113 F.2d 114 [2d Cir. 1940]), the Supreme Court determined that child care cannot be classified as a business expense, based on the rationale that it is not directly related to work. This case is current law. Though perhaps access to child care was misunderstood by the men on the court in 1939, it is clear that today access or lack thereof affects most parents' ability to work.

The Child Care Development Fund/Block Grant

Though tax credits and deductions are available for all taxpaying U.S. residents with children, the major federal programs that directly fund child care and early childhood education target children in poverty (i.e., Head Start and the Child Care Development Fund). The CCDBG, together with the Social Security Act, provides federal funding for the Child Care Development Fund (CCDF) (Smith, 2012). Because child care has been framed as a private concern, public policy has primarily addressed child caring for the vulnerable (e.g., low-income children and children with special needs). These programs follow a "less eligibility" model, which is designed to discourage childbearing among those of low socioeconomic status. The perception that publicly funded child care is a problem for low-income families (who are less likely to vote) may make it more vulnerable to cutbacks during funding debates. Funding can be more easily cut for child care than for other, more universal programs such as Social Security or Medicare. Despite (or because of) such a focus on poverty, the needs of the most economically vulnerable are not met.

The Child Care Development Block Grant Act of 1990 (CCDBG) has a fivefold stated purpose:

1. to allow each State maximum flexibility in developing child care programs and policies that best suit the needs of children and parents within such State;
2. to promote parental choice to empower working parents to make their own decisions on the child care that best suits their family's needs;
3. to encourage States to provide consumer education information to help parents make informed choices about child care;
4. to assist States to provide child care to parents trying to achieve independence from public assistance; and
5. to assist States in implementing the health, safety, licensing, and registration standards established in State regulations. (Pub. L. No. 112-74)

Irrespective of its broad-based goals, throughout most of its history CCDBG monies have focused on moving women from welfare into the low-wage workforce. The program explicitly targets funds to those at or below 85 percent of the state median income. An examination of how the different states spent their CCDF monies in 2012 demonstrates that a small percentage of the budget is focused on quality care and the bulk on direct service, despite the declared mission indicated in the legislation (U.S. Department of Health and Human Services, Administration for Children and Families, n.d.). These data also indicate that while most states use all available funds, some do not take full advantage of the funds provided. Given high poverty rates and the expense of child care across the country, one wonders why these funds are not being fully used. Research on usage and eligibility that we cite below suggests that this might stem from lack of providers, low eligibility thresholds, or a lack of awareness on the part of those entitled to these benefits and social service agency workers regarding the availability of child care benefits.

The focus of moving women from welfare to work was clear during the Clinton administration when President Clinton signed the Personal Responsibility and Work Opportunity Reconciliation Act (PRWORA) into law, against the protests of some vocal Democrats in a Republican-majority Congress, but otherwise to much public approbation. Following the 1996 changes to public assistance, three federal child care granting agencies were combined to create the CCDF, which is funded by the CCDBG and Social Security Act funding for Temporary Assistance for Needy Families (TANF), a program to support child care for low-income families. As a result of this legislation, states can transfer up to 30 percent of TANF funds to their allocation of CCDF money, most of which subsidizes child care for low-income parents.

The 1996 increase in CCDF funds was primarily directed toward moving women off of welfare by funding child care to allow women to fulfill their work obligations without jeopardizing their children's safety. Funding increases were incorporated with changes to public assistance that replaced Aid to Families with Dependent Children with TANF. The rhetoric and the mandates of policies such as TANF assert the value of work outside of the home. TANF regulations generally require women to work in order to be eligible for financial assistance (PRWORA, 1996), regardless of whether they are able to secure affordable and appropriate child care. Children in poverty are the most vulnerable to the U.S. gap in child care policy.

The slight increase in CCDF funding was a small concession to help make the TANF work requirements possible. The work requirements, however, raised a number of concerns about the availability and cost of child care for low-income working families, particularly single-headed families, even with the cushioning effects of the additional child care funding. Early assessments of PRWORA predicted a rise in unmet child care as a result of the increased requirements to work in the paid labor force, coupled with increasing state control over child care funds. Some people worried that states would not increase child care slots and that the leeway granted to them would result in fewer options for low-income working parents (McNeil, 1999). Indeed, initial reports showed this to be true. States used the discretion granted under PRWORA to limit eligibility criteria, making it *more* difficult for many women to access CCDF funds, especially when they needed to rely on nontraditional child care such as care provided by friends or family or during night-shift work (Vesely & Anderson, 2009). Soon after the implementation of TANF, McNeil (1999) found that people with lower incomes had higher rates of second and third shift and weekend employment, for which child care is more difficult to find. In addition, she reported a positive relationship between income and child care adequacy and significantly higher percentages of low-income women reporting that the cost of child care was problematic.

Despite an increase in funding with the 2002 reauthorization of TANF and a rise in the income eligibility criteria from 75 percent to 85 percent of the state median income (Lynch, 2010), women still experience difficulty accessing child care. In a qualitative study of forty-five TANF beneficiaries from a range of locations and geographic densities, Zippay and Rangarajan (2007) found that all recipients relied on what they call "packaging." Packaging involves combining multiple child care arrangements, many of them informal, to provide care. It is largely used due to a lack of affordable, consistent, and appropriate child care. Like McNeil, Zippay and Rangarajan (2007) found that many of the recipients worked nontraditional hours or shifts, which made it more difficult to find child care. Some states provide subsidies for child care arrangements that are operating legally, such as family day care arrangements, which may be exempt from some state licensing. The conditions and types of unlicensed child care that are legal and eligible for reimbursement vary by state (Zippay & Rangarajan, 2007).

More recently, funds have been allocated to begin to address quality and education standards (the fifth CCDBG goal). In 2000, $5.3 billion in federal money was contributed to this fund to help subsidize child care for low-income parents, but only 4 percent of this $5.3 billion was set aside to ensure quality improvement. While funding remained flat from 2006 to 2008, the Obama administration raised the funds to the CCDF in the American Reinvestment and Recovery Act in 2009. These additional funds were targeted to address quality and educational standards and were kept at the increased level in 2010 (Lynch, 2010; Lynch & McCallion, 2010). States' flexibility continues to be an important component of the law. In the latest iteration of the law, which increased attention to quality, states have full discretion to determine how to direct quality improvement money from the CCDF, but, historically, little has been done to monitor these efforts (Government Accounting Office, 2002). Though introduced on several occasions, CCDBG has not yet been reauthorized. The most recent reauthorization effort was a Senate bill introduced on June 11, 2013 (Vucic, 2013).

Head Start

Head Start is a comprehensive child care program. It is not really "child care." Like the CCDF, Head Start provides care predominately for families living below the poverty line (75 percent). Of participants, 90 percent must be at or below the poverty line and 10 percent of spaces are reserved for children with disabilities (Hamm, 2006). Though the program was legislated to serve three- and four-year-olds, 71 percent of attendees were enrolled for only one year. The program serves only about half of those who are eligible (Hoffman, 2010; Styfco, 2006; Zigler, 2009). Some Head Start programs provide full-day care and others only partial-day, depending on the state and/or locality (Melmed, 2008). In 2005, only

19 percent of Head Start beneficiaries attended programs lasting at least eight hours (Hamm, 2006). In Fiscal Year 2012, 45 percent of children were in programs for six or more hours per day, five days per week (U.S. Department of Health and Human Services, Administration for Children and Families, 2013a). In 1994, Early Head Start began to provide services to children from birth to age three (Hoffman, 2010) but only a small proportion of children and families can access this benefit. Fewer than 3 percent of babies who are eligible for Early Head Start receive services (Melmed, 2008).

Funding for Head Start began in 1965 with $96.4 million, and the program enrolled 651,000 children. The program was expanding to serve more children and provide more services, albeit with some controversy, across Democratic and Republican administrations through 2006, when it was funded with $6.8 billion and served 905,851 children. That year, it experienced its first ever funding cut of 1 percent, slated for fiscal year 2007 (Haxton, 2007). Funding remained flat through 2009, when it began to increase slightly and was funded for fiscal year 2010 at $7.235 billion, which included a $2.1 billion appropriation by the American Reinvestment and Recovery Act in order to serve more families (Administration for Children and Families, n.d.). Funding for Head Start has continued to increase slightly during the Obama administration. In 2012, $7.969 billion, a $409 million increase from 2011, was allocated for Head Start programming (U.S. Department of Health and Human Services, 2012).

Spending for Head Start has been challenged at both the federal and the state levels, and debates have been bitterly partisan, revealing splits not only around recent economic woes but also about the proper role of women. In one of the more blatant attacks on Head Start at the local level, commissioners in one Maryland County minimized the widespread economic necessity that drives not only single women but also women in dual-earning households to work, necessitating child care. Republican Commissioners Smith and Delauter of Fredericksburg County justified the total elimination of county support for Head Start as a mechanism to promote marriage and exhort women to stay home to raise young children:

COMMISSIONER C. PAUL SMITH (R): I think it's very significant that we did make this marriage week announcement today, because that is the best long-term way to help our children, as marriage is strengthened in our community. As many of you know, I had a lot of kids, and my wife stayed home, at significant sacrifice, during those early years, because she knew she had to be with those kids at that critical age. I know everybody isn't able to survive doing that, but clearly, as we can strengthen marriage we can decrease the children that we have to reach.

COMMISSIONER KIRBY DELAUTER (R): My wife, college educated, could go out and get a very good job. She gave that up for 18 years so she could stay home with our kids, we had to give up a lot to do that. I agree again with Commissioner Smith, you know, the marriage thing is very important. I mean, education of your kids starts at home, okay? I never relied on anyone else to guarantee the education of my kids. (cited in Garofalo, 2011)

At the national level, wrangling between President Obama and Republicans in Congress has been heated, with President Obama criticizing Republicans for making a grave mistake in scaling back early childhood investment (Wilson, 2011).

The Family and Medical Leave Act and State Leave Policies

The Family and Medical Leave Act (FMLA, 1993) provides twelve weeks of unpaid leave during the twelve months following the birth or adoption of a child as well as for other health or family care responsibilities. This leaves the United States far behind the rest of the industrialized world. In 2000, a survey conducted by the U.S. Department of Labor found that 88 percent of those who needed family leave and were technically eligible were unable to afford to take the leave. Despite the passage of the FMLA in 1993, Waldfogel (1999) and Han and Waldfogel (2003) found no change in employee leave coverage and usage. Baum (2006) found that, interestingly, despite the fact that there was no increased usage, passage of the law did lead some employers to increase the availability of leave to parents, particularly to men, who prior to the passage of the FMLA were ineligible for unpaid leave. Men and women, however, continue to experience what the Center for WorkLife Law refers to as family responsibility discrimination (FRD).[2] Approximately 11 percent of the 2,100 FRD cases from 1998 to 2009 in the Center for WorkLife Law database were filed by men. In over half of these cases, the court found in favor of the employees, which study authors indicate is a higher success rate than for other forms of employment discrimination cases (Calvert, 2010).

The result of nearly a decade of debate and compromise prior to its passage into law, the FMLA is limited in a number of important ways. First, it is not universal; approximately 60 percent of the U.S. workforce is employed by organizations that are covered under the FMLA (Klerman et al., 2013). However, as noted in Chapter 3, not all employees who work for employers covered under the legislation work the required number of hours to qualify for benefits under the law. Employers who are covered by the FMLA can deny someone leave if that person's salary is within the top 10 percent of the agency's payroll and his or her leave would be "substantial and grievous" to the company. Wisendale (2003) notes that the U.S. policy differs from those of other industrialized countries because (1) it is unpaid, (2) it is broader than new parent leave because it covers medical care for a parent, spouse, or child, and (3) it is limited to employers of over fifty workers.

A major hurdle that prevents many eligible low-income and middle-income women from taking advantage of the FMLA is that it does not require that the employer or the state pay any portion of the employee's salary. This means that the employee taking leave must have alternative sources of income or savings. A report published for the Department of Labor based on a 2012 survey found that 6.1 percent of both eligible and ineligible employees surveyed who needed leave were unable to take it, nearly triple the 2.4 percent reported in 2000 (and double the figure of 3.1 percent reported in 1995; Klerman et al., 2013). Women who can afford to take advantage of FMLA may "choose" not to for fear of retribution from their employers. Indeed, research shows that FMLA protections are most likely to be invoked by women who have sufficient power in the employment relationship to do so (Albiston, 2008). Low-income women in unstable jobs who have little or no financial cushion are likely among the least powerful vis-à-vis their employers. Of women leaving TANF, 62 percent (many of whom may not be covered by FMLA) received less than two weeks of paid leave including both sick leave and vacation time (Heymann, 2000). This indicates that women leaving TANF have virtually no paid leave to take care of their own or their family care needs.

Two congressional follow-up reports on the FMLA have been produced. A third technical report commissioned by the U.S. Department of Labor and conducted by Abt Associates was released on September 7, 2012, and updated on February 4, 2013 (Klerman et al., 2013). The first report was prepared by the Commission on Leave, which was established as part of the original FMLA legislation in 1995. The Commission on Leave found that a strong majority of covered workplaces had changed their policies in compliance with the FMLA, but that only a minority of workplaces that were not covered by the FMLA (perhaps unsurprisingly) offered parental leave or leave to care for a sick family member (42 percent and 32 percent, respectively). A second survey conducted in 2000 found that despite the passage of time, uptake of the FMLA remained extremely low, at 16 percent, up only 0.5 percent from 1995 (Cantor et al., 2001).

In 2009, the federal Healthy Families Act was proposed, which would have guaranteed employees one hour of sick leave for every thirty hours of work for up to seven days a year (Greenhouse, 2009). This bill never made it out of committee (HR 2460). The first successful expansion of the FMLA was signed into law in 2009 by President Bush as part of the National Defense Authorization Act. Congress added protection of airline workers and caring needs that arise when family members are on active duty in the armed forces (Martin, 2009; Mayer, 2011). The coverage for individuals on active duty or pending active duty is up to twenty-six weeks (longer than the twelve weeks that others employees are entitled to, and under Department of Labor regulations, the coverage includes not only child care but also financial and legal arrangements, rest, and recuperation (Martin, 2009). They further permit leave for a designated next of kin when the service member is activated, which would allow another person to use the leave in circumstances where the service member cannot, such as in caring for the service member's sick child or parent (Martin, 2009).

This FMLA expansion had bipartisan support in Congress. It passed quickly and without contention (Karin, 2009). The primary impetus for the bill was support for service members and their families during wartime. Such supports help encourage military service and ease its burden, as the protracted engagements in Iraq and Afghanistan heavily taxed the growing number of veterans, reservists, and National Guard members and their family members who are in the civilian employment sector. Expansion of the FMLA for service members also acknowledges the caregiving role that service members play, particularly with the increasing number of women serving their country. According to Karin (2009), the swift passage of this expansion was also due to renewed work-life balance concerns that garnered congressional and White House support in the early years of the Obama administration.

From 1995 to 2000, the percentage of employers for whom the FMLA was mandatory remained steady at 10.8 percent. In 2012, though 16.6 percent of employers reported that they were covered, the study researchers estimated that only 9.4 percent actually fit the description of entities legally required to comply with the FMLA. Of employers, 29.7 percent reported that they were unsure if they were covered by the FMLA. From 1995 to the present approximately 59 percent of workers have been covered by the FMLA (Klerman et al., 2013; U.S. Department of Labor, 2000). Between 1995–2000, there was a significant increase in leave taking under the FMLA, from 11 to 18 percent, reported by employees, with leave taking more common in larger workplaces. In 2012, 13 percent reported taking leave for FMLA-related reasons, 16 percent for whom the leave was legally required and 10 percent for whom it was not. This suggests that the legal mandate increased the availability of leave. In 2013, most employees who took leave took only one leave in a year, generally for 10 days or less. Ninety percent reported that they returned to work with the same employer. Of those who did not, 20 percent indicated that they could not return because of a continuing health condition and 25 percent reported that they were laid off. Most others indicated no specific reason for nonreturn (Klerman et al., 2013).

The data indicate that two of the major concerns raised in opposition to the FMLA did not materialize. These concerns were that employers would have to hold places for employees who would not return and that employees would abuse the FMLA. Despite these concerns, 90 percent of workers in 2012 who took leave reportedly returned to their employers, and an even larger percentage indicated reasons for use that could not be seen as taking unfair advantage of the law (Klerman et al., 2013). In 2000, child-care-related concerns formed the most common reasons for taking leave, with 24.4 percent using the FMLA to care for a newborn, a newly adopted child, or a placed foster child, 13.5 percent to care for a sick child, and 10.9 percent for maternity-related reasons (U.S. Department of Labor, 2000). However, in 2012, 57 percent took leave for their own health-related reasons, 19 percent to care for a close relative (parent, spouse, or child), and 22 percent to care for a new child. Some people may not take advantage of the FMLA due to a lack of knowledge. In 2012, only 66 percent of covered workplaces reported "allowing leave" for all FMLA-covered reasons. Only 66 percent of workers had heard of the FMLA in 2012 (an increase from 59 percent in 2000). In 2012, only 70.9 percent of those working in agencies covered by the FMLA had heard of it (Klerman et al., 2013).

The U.S. Department of Labor also reports on employees who do not take leave, despite having an FMLA reason for doing so.[3] Researchers speculated that this may have been the result of a difficult economy. Of those unable to take needed leave, 65 percent were women, and 16 percent of leave-needers needed it to care for a newborn or a newly adopted or placed foster child. In 2000, 19.6 percent reported needing leaves to care for a sick child. In 2012, this figure was not reported. At that time, 34 percent of leave-needers reported wanting leave to care for a parent, spouse, or child. The reasons for not taking leave included fear of loss of job (17 percent), advancement (1.9 percent), lack of eligibility (2.6 percent), employer denial (6 percent, down from 20 percent in 2000), affordability (53.3 percent, down from 77.6 percent in 2000), and the sense that work is too important (3.7 percent, down from 40.8 percent in 1995). In 2012, 30 percent reported "other reasons."[4] The majority of leave-needers who were unable to take leave were from families with incomes below $35,000, had children, and were nonwhite. A greater percentage of those who needed leave but were unable to take it were from single-parent homes than two-parent homes. Of those who could not take leave, 65 percent reported finding someone else to take over their caretaking responsibility. From 1995 to 2000, the Department of Labor (2000) reported a significant closing of gaps between covered and uncovered workplaces in terms of FMLA-related leave. This gain continued to increase into 2012. In 2000, 65.7 percent of noncovered employers offered up to 12 weeks of unpaid maternity leave, with the overwhelming majority of them continuing to cover health benefits and to hold the employee's job. By 2012, 75.9 percent reported offering up to 12 weeks of unpaid maternity leave (Klerman et al., 2013). This may be an indication of a cultural shift that was brought about by the passage of the FMLA.

Of those who took leave for FMLA-related reasons, 48 percent reported receiving full pay and 17 percent reported receiving partial pay. With leave over 10 days, pay was less likely. Generally pay was provided as a result of sick leave, vacation time, or personal time. Half of all leaves were for 10 days or less. In 2012, the two most frequent reasons that were reported for returning to work were no longer needing the leave (e.g., returning health) and inability to afford to continue to take leave (Klerman et al., 2013).

A 2007 report on the FMLA was prepared for the Department of Labor on the basis of over fifteen thousand comments by employers and employees of their experiences with the FMLA over the fourteen years of its existence (Lipnic & DeCamp, 2007). Comments were generally positive, and the law was viewed as an important, if sometimes insufficient, support. Employer concerns were greater in certain sectors, where work was often more time-sensitive (such as transportation). While the most frustrating employer theme was around intermittent leave for chronic health conditions, all stakeholders reported frustration with the current medical certification process. The report outlined the responses as characterized by three main themes:

> (1) gratitude from employees who have used family and medical leave and descriptions of how it allowed them to balance their work and family care responsibilities, particularly when they had their own serious health condition or were needed to care for a family member; (2) a desire for expanded benefits—*e.g.*, to provide more time off, to provide paid benefits, and to cover additional family members; and (3) frustration by employers about difficulties in maintaining necessary staffing levels and controlling attendance problems in their workplaces as a result of one particular issue—unscheduled intermittent leave used by employees who have chronic health conditions. (Lipnic & DeCamp, 2007, iv)

A study ($N = 377$) conducted by the Society of Human Resource Managers of their FMLA-covered members found that 59 percent reported that their organization provided leave *beyond* the FMLA requirements, such as paid leave or leave for noncovered concerns such as parent-teacher conferences or leave for ineligible employees (Burke, 2003, p. 2).

Information on leave policies in workplaces that are not covered by the FMLA is hard to find and varies widely. What is available indicates that there continues to be a large gap between need and the availability of leave as well as the ability of parents to take leave, even if it is offered. Business and Legal Resources (BLR) and the HR Advisor conducted a survey of family leave practices in the summer of 2011 (BLR, 2011). Of the 902 companies that responded, slightly under 80 percent were employers with fewer than 500 employees and 84 percent were mandated to provide FMLA benefits. In reporting on child care benefits, 56 percent of the companies provided some form of "childcare assistance to employees, most commonly flex time or leaves of absence" (BLR, 2011, p. 2). Only 14 percent of the companies provided *paid* leave for child care, and only 29 percent provided unpaid leave. Of the companies, 70 percent allow employees to use sick leave to care for a sick child (or spouse or parent) (BLR, 2011).

The Institute for Women's Policy Research examined maternity leave policies of the "Top 100" employers ranked in Working Mother's annual survey in 2012. As the name indicates, these are companies that are considered to be among the most family-friendly in their culture and policies, and maternity leave is often considered a minimum or threshold family benefit, meaning that this report represents the "best of the best." The list also likely combines covered and noncovered workplaces and employees, and thus some would be required to provide FMLA leave under law. While most provided some paid leave, only 14 percent of the companies provided twelve weeks of paid leave, another 8 percent provided between eleven and twelve weeks of paid maternity leave, and 19 percent provided only one to two weeks or less of paid maternity leave. Of the companies, 43 percent provided at least seven weeks of paid leave (Hegewisch & Hara, 2013). This represents no significant differences from the 2006 survey (Lovell, O'Neill, & Olsen, 2007).

The emergence of state policies suggests that the federal policies do not provide caretakers with the ability to take the leave that they need under the protection of federal law. Many states have designed their own leave protections, often extending benefits to smaller businesses or allowing more than twelve weeks of leave (see Table 5.1 for a description of selected state policies). In 1999, President Clinton issued federal regulations that became effective in 2000 permitting states to experiment with unemployment insurance to pay for FMLA leaves (Birth and Adoption Unemployment Compensation Rule, 1999). These regulations were repealed by President Bush in 2002 (U.S. Chamber of Commerce, 2003). Maine,[5] Minnesota,[6] Oregon,[7] and Vermont,[8] as well as the District of Columbia,[9] provide FMLA benefits to employees who work in organizations that employ fewer than fifty employees.[10] Minnesota[11] and Vermont[12] allow employees who have worked less than full-time to receive unpaid family leave (thirty hours per week in Vermont and twenty hours in Minnesota). The state of Connecticut allows new parents to take twenty-four weeks of leave over two years,[13] and the District of Columbia allows new parents to take sixteen weeks of unpaid leave within two years.[14] Oregon allows twenty-four weeks, twelve weeks of parental leave and twelve weeks of family leave.[15] Other states, such as New York (1949), Hawaii (1969), Rhode Island (1942), and New Jersey (1961), also require that women be eligible for disability payments when pregnant (if applicable) and fol-lowing childbirth. The latter policies amount to paid maternity leave for pregnant women and women who give birth to children but exclude both men and adoptive parents.

California[16] was the first state to provide paid family leave insurance. The states of Washington,[17] New Jersey,[18] and Rhode Island have recently followed, though the implementation of Washington's legislation has been postponed. New Jersey legislation provides up to six weeks of paid leave at two-thirds of an employee's salary, up to $524 a week, to provide care for a sick relative or a new child. This policy is also paid for by a payroll tax.

Rhode Island's paid family leave policy will begin a phased in imple-mentation in January 2014, initially providing workers with four weeks of paid leave. In 2016, paid leave will be provided for up to eight weeks. To fund this leave, approximately 80 percent of the workforce will contrib-ute a payroll tax of approximately 83 cents per month (AFL-CIO, 2013; WPRO Newsroom and the Associated Press, 2013). The state of Washing-ton separates family leave for the birth of a new child or adoption from the leave that is available to care for a sick child, spouse, or parent and allows paid time off to care for sick relatives.[19] However, these policies are not widespread. Advocates in other states or localities are also working to expand paid family leave.

Despite the development of limited paid leave policies for women in California, Washington State, and New Jersey, obviously people cannot

Table 5.1. State Leave Policies

State	Covers people who work in agencies with fewer than 50 employees	Leave for more than 12 weeks in a year	Paid leave for childbirth or adoption	Disability coverage for childbirth	Covers workers who are less than full-time
California[a]		Up to 12 weeks parental leave and up to 4 months maternity disability	55% salary replacement from $50 to $840 a week paid for by a payroll tax; for men and women to care for seriously ill child or spouse or bond with newborn for up to 6 weeks		
Connecticut[b]		24 weeks within 2 years			
District of Columbia[c]	Employers with 25 or more employees	16 weeks in 2 years	For 100+ employees, 1 hour per 37 hours worked, up to 7 days. For 25–99 employees, 1 hour per 43 hours worked, up to 5 days. For fewer than 25 employees, 1 hour per 87 hours worked, up to 3 days		
Hawaii[d]	Employers with 25 or more employees			Up to 4 weeks paid if employer has a policy including paid leave	
Maine[e]	Employers with 15 or more employees				
Minnesota[f]	Employers with 21 or more employees must provide 6 weeks paid leave				20 hours a week

State	Covers people who work in agencies with fewer than 50 employees	Leave for more than 12 weeks in a year	Paid leave for childbirth or adoption	Disability coverage for childbirth	Covers workers who are less than full-time
New Jersey[g]			6 weeks paid leave at two-thirds salary, up to $524 a week to care for a new child or sick relative, paid for by a $33 annual payroll deduction	4 weeks disability before pregnancy and 6 weeks after—this counts against FMLA leave but not 12-week entitlement to care for newborn child	
New York[h]				6-8 weeks	20 hours a week
Oregon[i]	Employers with 25 or more employees	24 weeks—12 weeks of parental leave and 12 weeks of family leave		Up to 12 weeks pregnancy-related disability leave including prenatal appointments and care	

This chart does not include state leave up to 40 hours that is available for families to attend school conferences and/or attend to their children's (or other family members') medical needs. Much of this leave is subsumed under the Family and Medical Leave Act (FMLA), and all is unpaid. Though the authors recognize that this type of mandatory requirement can be helpful to families of older children, particularly those who work in low-wage or service positions, we feel that because this leave is generally unpaid and does not extend for a significant amount of time, it is mostly symbolic. Several states, such as Illinois, Maine, Massachusetts, Minnesota, North Carolina, and Rhode Island, provide such leave (National Conference of State Legislators, 2008).

a. California Family Temporary Disability Insurance, SB 1661, Cal. Unemp. Ins. Code §§ 3301–3306 (2002).

b. Connecticut Family and Medical Leave Act, Connecticut Code Sec. 29 CFR § 25.8 31–51 (1996).

c. D.C. Accrued Sick and Safe Leave Act of 2008, Act 17-0324, Proposed Rule Chap. 32 DCMR DC Regulations (December 19, 2008); D.C. Code Ann. §§ 32-502 to 32-517.

d. Haw. Rev. Stat. § 398-4 (2003).

e. 26 Me. Rev. Stat. Ann. § 843 (1999).

f. Minn. Stat. § 181.940 (Subd. 3) (2013).

g. New Jersey Temporary Disability Benefits Law, Pub. L. No. 1948 c110 (43: 21–26) (2008).

h. New York Worker's Compensation Law, Article 9 Disability Benefits § 201 (1949, 2007).

i. Or. Rev. Stat. § 659.470-494 (1995).

leave newborns unattended after five to six weeks of paid leave or up to twelve weeks of unpaid leave, and therefore even the most generous leave policies do not address ongoing child care needs over the long term.

California family leave insurance provides up to 55 percent salary replacement from $50 to $840 a week for six weeks (as of 2005) when a new child is born or adopted or in order to care for a seriously ill parent, spouse, or child. This leave is given in addition to disability insurance provided to pregnant women and for women who have just given birth. It is funded by a payroll tax.[20] The debates around the California and Washington paid leave bills are instructive. The landmark California legislation was a product of bipartisan efforts. According to activist Noreen Farrell (2012), it was "supported by a broad coalition of advocates, unions and community groups and passed with strong support from Democrats and Republicans." Despite bipartisan support, business groups firmly opposed the legislation, and the debates surrounding it were contentious (Jones, 2002). In the hard-fought advocacy effort that led up to the legislation, unions had a role in reframing the policy as one that was beneficial to families, rather than one that was designed to benefit women. The policy was also designed to benefit families regardless of income, rather than targeting low-income households. Some believe that the universal framework that made it more broadly appealing when originally passed may also garner broader support for the policy in the future (Lester, 2011).

In an analysis of newspaper, television, and radio reporting on the debates over the proposed policy, Dorfman and Lingas (2003) found that most of the positive framing of the California legislation centered on the importance of parent-child bonding or the resolution of work-family conflict. These were often illustrated by poignant anecdotes of mothers and young children. The opposition framing did not contest the underlying values that drove the policy, but rather portrayed it as bad for business (Dorfman & Lingas, 2003, p. 9). The support of some businesses for the legislation and anecdotes of successful implementation of similar workplace policies undermined the general business opposition.

Dorfman and Lingas suggest that advocates elsewhere can learn from California's experience. Indeed, the tactic of gaining support from within the business community was also used during testimony for the FMLA, where business interests testified on both sides of the debate. The framing of the policy as one that promoted family values, bonding, and resolving untenable dilemmas was written into the preamble of the California legislation. These frames resonated with Californians and were able to supersede the arguments of businesses that opposed the legislation, many of which were founded on future projections. Dorfman and Lingas also found that when opponents became overly contentious around details, they were viewed negatively. While it is important to engage with details and address feasibility of any policy, advocates must not let discussion of details eclipse a value-based framing of the issue.

Washington State passed paid family leave legislation in 2007, to be implemented in October 2009. This program will provide $250 a week for up to 5 weeks for the parents of a new child (either a newborn or adopted child) and applies to all employees working for companies with at least twenty-five employees who have worked at least 680 hours in the past year (Hollo, 2012). However, as a result of the current recession and a large state deficit, Washington postponed the implementation of the Family Insurance and Medical Leave program until 2015. As part of the ongoing debate, a bill to repeal that act, with some Democratic support, was introduced to the 2013 state legislature (Connelly, 2013). In response, supporters of the program introduced a "dueling bill" to expand the legislation (LaCorte, 2013). The Senate budget did not ultimately include cuts to the program, despite calls for cuts by the governor and cuts to many other state programs. According to Washington Policy Watch, a progressive advocacy group, this was due to grassroots opposition: "after the strong show of public support for paid leave policies, apparently Senate leaders thought better of undermining protections for working families" (Watkins, 2013).

Laughlin (2011) reviewed maternal employment and leave taking from 1960 to 2008. Her findings "suggest that for women who plan to return to work after having their child, many work as long as possible into their pregnancy in order to have more leave, both paid and unpaid, available to use once their child is born" (p. 10). Women are strategic, and take advantage of workplace and legal policies to maximize family time. From 2006 to 2008, 41 percent of women used unpaid leave to care for children and 36 percent of women used paid leave. Many women used these in combination. These limited policies often require women to rely on the kindness of employers to address their needs. Although some research has suggested that women who work for employers who provide greater benefits than those required by law use fewer sick days and are more likely to return to their employment after taking family leave, most employers have been slow to the adapt to the needs of mothers in the paid workforce (Milkman & Appelbaum, 2004).

Conceptualizing Care as a Universal Rather Than "Unusual" Need

In this chapter, the policies we have reviewed depict a U.S. child care policy landscape that appears to be predicated on a particular "causal story." The causal story is that parents' need for child care is an unusual, unexpected, or temporary condition. That means that the U.S. policies are about emergency care: when one has a temporary need to care for oneself or a sick family member, for the extremely needy, or for a very short time when a child first comes into a family.

The very limited nature of the FMLA protection and child care funding provided under CCDF suggests that it is only in aberrant situations that one's family care responsibilities interfere with one's ability to work. In "normal" situations, families are expected to provide care for each other, and this cannot be an obstacle to workplace performance. Though some minimal tax benefits are available to help pay for child care, they are clearly insufficient, cannot be paid to someone who does not want to report this minimal income to the IRS, and do not address the quality of care that children receive. Eligible employees who need more than the twelve weeks of leave provided under the FMLA after a child is born can be fired. Employees experiencing a child care crisis, such as a sick child who cannot be left unattended, and cannot go to work can be fired. Employees who work for employers with fewer than fifty employees can be denied leave and are unprotected by the FMLA. For eligible employees without independent sources of financial support, the FMLA's unpaid leave is likely not a feasible option.

Low-income women may still be eligible for state child care assistance after five years but cannot receive TANF cash benefits. In addition, many single mothers who work at low-wage jobs have irregular hours, making it more difficult to find child care. Those who cannot find child care often lose their jobs as a result of not going to work, or must leave a child unattended or in an unsafe situation. Child care is an ongoing and not a temporary need, though it has not been defined by U.S. federal policies as such. Beyond leave policies, financial benefits such as child care subsidies and tax benefits are extremely limited. They do not provide sufficient benefits for low-income families who still scramble to find affordable care or for higher income families who receive a small fraction of support in relation to child care fees that they pay to enable them to work. In the next chapter, we examine the continuing child care problems faced by U.S. families within the current policy framework. We then describe more comprehensive programs that exist in the United States and elsewhere that can serve as models to address current policy limitations.

6

Women and Child Care

According to the Project on Global Working Families' scale of family support policies (Heymann et al., 2007), the United States was one of only five countries, out of 177, that provided no guaranteed paid leave to women bearing children. In 66 of the countries surveyed, fathers were entitled to paid parental leave; in 31 of these countries fathers were also eligible for fourteen or more weeks of paid leave. As a result of the limited public policy in the United States, the private sector has been left to establish policy.

This chapter explores the extent of U.S. problems with the provision of child care as well as public opinion regarding beliefs about government's role in developing a solution. While we explained existing policies in the prior chapter, here we review the needs that such policies leave unmet. We then review programs that could be used as models for the United States to better meet the needs of children and families, including European models as well as U.S. demonstration programs.

Women, Work, and Child Care Needs

Women have always worked largely for economic reasons (Golden, 1990). Though women's rights groups in the 1960s and 1970s helped reframe gender roles and, thus, enabled women to enter many professions such as law, medicine, and business that had traditionally been male domains, gaps have remained in the way that the larger societal structures address the balance between work and family. Men who had held "family-wage" jobs traditionally had wives to care for their children. Women entering such jobs were told or believed that they could have it all—careers and families. However, this left no one at home to care for the children and required families to find private solutions to address their child care needs (Eichner, 2012; Williams, 2010). Many middle- and upper-class women who choose to take a few years off to care for young children find it difficult to return to their careers when their children begin school because it is perceived that they have become deskilled or are not as committed to their careers as are men. Women who temporarily leave the labor force for two years or more to take care of their young children often experience lifelong financial penalties (Avellar & Smock, 2003, Crittenden, 2002). They not only have lower pension contributions but also, on average, earn less than women who have no children and men (regardless of whether or not they have children) for the rest of their careers (Budig & England, 2001).

In 2013, 47 percent of the U.S. labor force was composed of women. Of primary earners, 40 percent were mothers, 37 percent of whom were part of married couples and 63 percent of whom were in single-parent households. Of married women, 15 percent earned more than their husbands (Wang, Parker, & Taylor, 2013). In 2010, full-time salaried women earned on average $82 for every $100 earned by a man. (U.S. Department of Labor, Bureau of Labor Statistics, 2011). In 2008, women with children made an average of 73 cents on the dollar that men with children earned, while women without children earned 86 cents for every dollar that childless men made (U.S. Department of Labor, Bureau of Labor Statistics, 2011). In 2009, full-time employed female workers earned 77 percent of what men earned. In 2010, full-time, year-round-employed women workers who were not self-employed earned, on average, 19 percent less than men (DeNavas-Walt et al., 2010). Controlling for almost all possible variation in employment, women who have children still earn 2.5 percent less than other women, and men who have children earn 2.1 percent more than men without children (Government Accounting Office, 2003).

The income that women earn is often necessary for the family's economic well-being. In 2010, 58.6 percent of women were in the paid labor force. Among married couples, 55.3 percent of both partners were in the labor force. In married families, women contribute approximately 37 percent of their family's income, and in single-parent, female-headed families women are often the primary financial support for their children. Furthermore, 61 percent of women with children younger than three are in the paid labor force (U.S. Department of Labor, Bureau of Labor Statistics, 2011). An analysis of median family income for married households from 1979 to 2000 found that family income has risen *only* as a result of women's paid labor. It is particularly necessary for low-income women to work as their salary contributions often keep their families out of poverty (Mishel, Bernstein, & Allegretto, 2005).

Inadequate child care is not a class-based concern. Even congressional staffers have trouble obtaining adequate child care for their children (Lovely, 2010). Only a handful of states and private employers provide some paid parental leave or child care. There remains a wide gap in leave availability among women with different levels of educational attainment. While the percent of women who have access to some paid leave went from 27 percent in 1966 to 66 percent in 2008, the percentage of those lacking a high school degree who have access to paid leave remained a steady 18 percent from 1966 through 2008 (Folbre, 2008).

Women's unpaid care for their own children is not quantified and is virtually absent from U.S. public discussion (Palley, 2010). Our current workplace structure seems to indicate that men and women without children deserve higher pay because they can be more committed to their paid employment. However, this argument makes sense only if one ignores the societal value of children and hence child care (Crittenden, 2002). The crises of societies with large population declines show us that, as a society, we need women to have children (Russell, 2011). Data on brain development, workplace achievements, and criminal justice outcomes (among others) also indicate that the work of child caring must be done and done well.

Although most U.S. parents are not at home providing primary care for their young children, the United States spends less than a half of 1 percent of the federal budget on child care (Boushey, 2007). In 2002, the National Survey of America's Families indicated that over 40 percent of all children under age five spent at least thirty-five hours a week in care with someone other than their parents (Capizzino & Main, 2005). These trends have continued. The 2005–2009 American Community Survey data (collected by the U.S. Bureau of the Census) illustrated that children younger than five whose mothers work spend an average of thirty-five hours a week in child care (National Association of Child Care Resource and Referral Agencies, 2011). Most children receive some nonmaternal care by the age of six months (National Institute of Child Health and Human Development [NICHD], 2006). The average child has spent approximately twenty-seven hours in child care per week in the first four and a half years of his or her life (NICHD, 2006). Approximately half of all children under three spend twenty-five hours a week in care with someone other than their parents (Drummond & Seid, 2001).

As a result of unpredictable hours and the unstable nature of their work as well as the high cost of formal child care, low-income families often must rely on informal child care arrangements that are more likely to be unsafe and unreliable than formal child care (Fuller, Loeb, Strath, & Carrol, 2004; Henley, Shaefer, & Waxman, 2006). Other families work alternate hours and pass off their children to family members in a "tag-team" approach, limiting the amount of family time in order to cope with unaffordable and inadequate child care options. Limiting time spent together as a family reduces parents' satisfaction with family life (Grosswald, 2004). Older siblings may also miss school to care for their younger brothers or sisters, in the absence of affordable options for low-income families (Shdaimah, Bryant, Sander, & Cornelius, 2011).

In some states, as a result of funding cuts, single mothers are now finding that they cannot obtain child care assistance to work and must quit their jobs and rely on public assistance (Goodman, 2010). Roll and East (2012) have described some of the many bureaucratic hurdles faced by low-income women in accessing and using child care subsidies as well as problems created by the "Cliff Effect." This occurs when increased earnings cause families to lose their child care subsidy, which, then, causes an overall reduction in income for families who are already at the poverty level. Their study documents how this creates perverse incentives for women to forgo raises and additional hours in order to survive in ways that also ensure a supply of low-wage workers (Roll & East, 2012).

Public Opinion Regarding Public Funding for Child Care

A pluralist perspective (Dahl, 1998) suggests that the reason there is no universal child care policy in the United States is that there is no public will for such a policy. Indeed, data from public opinion polls in the United States in the 1990s and early 2000s suggested that most people thought that parents should be the primary influence on families and that it is preferable for mothers to stay home with their children, particularly children ages zero to three (Bostrom, 2002; Farkas, Duffett, & Johnson, 2000; Opinion Research Corporation International, 1999; Robison, 2002; Sylvester, 2001; Wang et al., 2013). However, a recent Pew survey indicates that only half of Americans (51 percent) believe that children are better off if their mothers stay home and 79 percent reject the idea that women should return to their more traditional roles as stay-at-home mothers (Wang et al., 2013). This indicates that perhaps there have been some recent changes in public values regarding care for children. Two recent telephone surveys of nationally representative samples (comparable numbers of men and women and of Independents, Democrats, and Republicans, which was geographically representative) found that a large majority of Republicans, Democrats, and Independents favor national legislation to support paid family leave and sick days (First Five Years Fund, 2013; National Partnership for Women and Families, 2012).

As we know from the data on working women and placement in child care, most American parents will remain unable to stay home to care for their children unless the United States adopts more generous and universal leave or family support policies that would enable them to do so. Perhaps this is why the most recent survey data *also* suggest that the majority of parents and grandparents support increasing taxes to improve both the quality and the affordability of child care (NACCRRA, 2008c). In a 1998 Pew Survey (Pew Research Center for People and the Press, 1999), most respondents (74 percent) favored increased public spending to assist poor women to provide child care for their children. This may be explained not only by the lack of affordability of care, but also by beliefs that requiring parents to work is more important than parental care duties, particularly for low-income families. Another recent survey found that most people believed that it was preferable for poor parents to work rather than stay home to care for children (Farkas et al., 2000).

The 2000 Public Agenda survey (Farkas et al., 2000), which was based on nationwide random phone calling of 815 parents of children younger than five and 444 parents of children aged six to seventeen found that 57 percent of parents believe that parents of children younger than five work to make ends meet and 87 percent believe that mothers who work outside the home can be just as committed to their children's care as stay-at-home mothers. Also, 82 percent of all parents reported that they thought day care was a necessary alternative to home-based parental or family, friend, and neighbor care. In other words, regardless of parents' preferences or beliefs about parental care, reality often dictates that families pay others to watch their children (NACCRRA, 2008c).

Working women under forty thought that child care was the second most important policy issue in the U.S. after health care. It was the third most important issue for Asian American, Hispanic American, and white women of all ages (AFL-CIO, 2006). Another poll found that most people would be willing to pay higher taxes in order to support early childhood education programs and after-school programs (Opinion Research Corporation International, 1999; Pew Research Center for People and the Press, 1999).

In a study of 3,000 randomly selected adults including 1,066 parents, a Zero to Three (2000) poll found that 80 percent of parents of young children and 80 percent of adults surveyed supported paid parental leave. Furthermore, this survey found that 73 percent of parents and 65 percent of all adults support government assistance to help parents pay for child care (Zero to Three, 2000). Most agreed that expanding disability or unemployment insurance would be a good way to do this. Furthermore, in a national survey completed by the Institute for Women's Policy Research (2010), 81 percent of women and 71 percent of men supported laws to provide paid leave for new parents. Approximately three out of four voters also supported laws that would improve both the quality and affordability of child care. Moreover, 81 percent of Democrats, 63 percent of Republicans, and 71 percent of Independents supported laws to improve the quality and affordability of child care and after school care. Approximately two out of three voters supported laws to provide paid sick days, which may be used not only for parents who become ill but also to care for sick children. In all, 40 percent suggested the leave should be for three months or less, 25 percent suggested that it should be between four to eleven months, and 33 percent suggested that it should last one year or longer. These survey results indicate that the majority of Republican, Democratic, and Independent voters see a role for government in supporting child care and leave policies.

The availability of quality, affordable child care seems to be decreasing rather than improving. The National Women's Law Center reports that in 2011, families overall were faring more poorly than they were a decade ago. As a result of state budget shortfalls, state support for child care further declined in 2012. In 2011, eleven states reimbursed child care providers at the federally recommended level (75 percent of the market rate). By 2012, this was reduced to one state. By February 2012, in twenty-three states, eligible children were being denied child care assistance; some were placed on waiting lists, while others were simply turned away. According to the National Women's Law Center twenty-seven states had child care policies that left families worse off in February 2012 than they had been in February 2011 (Shulman & Blank, 2012).

The popular press has recently focused on the impact of sustained budget cuts to child care programs at the local level, documenting growing shortages of assistance in the face of rising need, particularly for parents in low-wage jobs (Goodman, 2012). The emphasis on the simultaneous vulnerability and deservingness of working parents and their children in a struggling economy pervades popular media reports and echoes the framing of child care needs in the legislative testimony we reviewed in Chapter 3. Like other accounts, Dvorak (2010) notes the irony of the "mixed message [that Washington, DC] is sending . . . asking folks to stay employed or get a job in this horrendous market, while taking away the crucial tool that allows that to happen: affordable child care." Child care is described as an important support, without which families cannot go to work. Cuts were ubiquitous across the federal and state levels during the most recent recession (Tavernise, 2011).

The State of Nonparental Child Care

If people have children and are unable to take leave from work to care for them, these children are often cared for in nonparental child care settings. Much of this care is unlicensed and unregulated. As a result of the large numbers of children needing nonparental care in the past thirty years, the child care industry in the United States has grown at a tremendous pace. In 1982, there were 30,800 child care centers in the United States, but by 1997 there were 62,000 (Fuller et al., 2004). Though the number of centers has more than doubled since the early 1980s, there has been uneven growth, with more centers being developed in suburban areas, where there is less expensive real estate and parents who can pay fees, and in low-income communities that receive government support (Blau, 2001; Fuller et al., 2004). Fewer than 30 percent of child care workers are employed by formal child care centers. In 2010, the average annual wage for center-based child care workers was just over $19,000, reflecting the low pay and part-time nature of much of this employment (U.S. Department of Labor, 2010b). The size and extent to which the structures are formalized, as well as the quality of care that is delivered, largely depend upon community economic differences (Fuller et al., 2004).

Lack of child care regulation affects families at every income level. However, as previously noted, it is particularly acute for low-income families with limited resources who are often forced to choose between work needed to feed and house their families and settings that they know are low in quality or unsafe (Chaudry, 2004). The federal government has done virtually nothing to regulate this industry, and the records of states are poor. Three issues are generally raised in the discussion about child care in the United States: quality, affordability, and availability.

Quality

Research on brain development and the association between quality early education and care and individual and societal benefits underscores the need for public policy that views child care from the earliest years as a social good worthy of investment (Zigler & Hall, 2000). Successful programs have focused on both academic and social skills (Heckman, 2008). Child care can be divided into three categories: custodial, developmental, and comprehensive. Custodial merely keeps children safe while their parents cannot be with them. Developmental care is designed to provide them with both custodial care and appropriate developmental opportunities. This type of care is often synonymous with quality care. Comprehensive care addresses physical, social, emotional, and family support and mental health care needs of children and is generally provided to at-risk youth (Zigler et al., 2009). Successful programs have included components such as home visiting and follow-up after preschool (Heckman, 2008).

This section discusses the elements of child care that are essential to make it "quality care" and presents successful European policies that have often been considered ideal. This is followed by a discussion of exemplary child care programs in the United States provided by the U.S. military, public/private partnerships, and some prominent corporations. There are several different models that could be successfully used to address U.S. child care deficits. They all require money for care providers and infrastructure as well as standards and oversight to ensure high-quality care from both home care providers and center-based care providers. Improving the quality of early education and care in the United States cannot be done "on the cheap," but the payoff will be lasting: this would be money well spent.

Evidence from preschool programs throughout the United States and elsewhere shows that they can help students develop social and emotional skills, which are key elements of school readiness, to prepare them for kindergarten and beyond (Boyd et al., 2005). Children from all socioeconomic statuses benefit from early education, but the benefits are more pronounced among lower-income children. The benefits of early childhood investment over the life course have been borne out by longitudinal research with children enrolled in the Perry Preschool Program (Belfield, Nores, Barnett, & Schweinhart, 2006) and the Syracuse University Family Development Research Program (Yoshikawa, 1995). High-quality, intensive preschool programs have been shown to decrease poverty (Duncan, Ludwig, & Magnuson, 2007).

Research on child care identifies several key elements of quality care. They include specialized teacher training and physical space. Teacher interaction is also important. "[C]hildren in better quality programs had more positive interactions with their teachers (caregivers), while children in poor quality programs spent more time in unoccupied behavior and in solitary play" (Vandell, Henderson, & Wilson, 1988, p. 1287). In order for this to occur, there needs to be a sufficiently low child-staff ratio. Findings from studies of programs that target at-risk youth found that "[t]he programs with the largest initial effects on learning and development tended to be those that provided the greatest quantity of services (operating for more hours per year and continuing for more years) with high staff-to-child ratios (e.g., 1 to 3 for infants, 1 to 6 at ages 3 and 4) and highly qualified staff" (Bowman, Donovan, & Burns, 2000, p. 131).

Specialized early education training has also been associated with higher quality care (Whitebook, Howes, & Phillips, 1990). Highly qualified staff are those with education and training related to child development. In a comprehensive review of the research on quality early education programs, the National Research Council noted that multiple studies had identified that "[t]he professional development of teachers is related to the quality of early childhood programs, and program quality predicts developmental outcomes for children." Formal early childhood education and training has been linked consistently to positive caregiver behaviors. The strongest relationship is found between the number of years of education and training and the appropriateness of a teacher's classroom behavior (Bowman et al., 2000, p. 309).

An NICHD (2006) study that tracked children from early child care settings until kindergarten found that children who had been in center-based care exhibited better language and cognitive development than did other children. Children in high-quality care had better cognitive and language skills than those in low-quality care. In a review of the literature, Burchinal (1999) found that across studies, family characteristics, such as parental income and single parenthood, were more predictive of child developmental outcomes than the type and amount of child care the child received.

Despite the importance of early childhood education, approximately 40 percent of children are in care that does not meet minimum educational adequacy standards (Melmed, 2008). Moreover, most care for children who are under school age is provided, as noted above, by nonrelatives in the homes of child care providers (Hamm et al., 2005). As noted earlier, even identifying the extent to which quality child care exists is a challenge because so much care is unregulated (Hamm et al., 2005). NACCRRA reports note that few states have standards linked to quality child care and oversight of existing standards is quite limited (NACCRRA, 2006b; NACCRRA, 2008a). Many states that currently use child care standards limit their quality evaluation to care for children between two and a half and five years old (Matthews & Schumacher, 2008; National Infant and Toddler Child Care Initiative and Zero to Three, 2008). As of 2008, only six states include infant and toddler care in their quality standards (National Infant and Toddler Child Care Initiative and Zero to Three, 2008). Many educationally focused programs are only two to three hours a day. As a result, parents needing to provide care for their children for full days often cannot enroll them in developmentally appropriate programs. Barnett, Hustedt, Hawkinson, and Robin (2006) estimate that only 25 percent of early childhood education programs are full-day programs. This means that many families must make child care arrangements for the time that their child is not enrolled in a developmentally appropriate programs.

A strategy that is being used at the state level in all forms of early childhood programs is a system that rates programs using one to five stars depending on the quality as measured by outside evaluators. The Quality Rating and Improvement System (QRIS) was created by the National Child Care Information and Technical Assistance Center (NCCIC) in 1998. It "is a systemic approach to assess, improve, and communicate the level of quality in early and school-age care and education programs" (Administration for Children and Families, 2013, p. 1). As of April 2011, there were twenty-five states fully accredited by the NCCIC.

The building blocks of a statewide QRIS consist of (1) a series of graduated standards, built on the foundation of child care licensing requirements; (2) accountability and monitoring processes to determine how well programs meet QRIS standards and to assign ratings; (3) program and practitioner outreach and support, including support for providers, such as training, mentoring, and technical assistance, are included to promote participation and help programs achieve higher levels of quality; (4) financial incentives, such as tiered subsidy reimbursement, which pays a higher reimbursement rate to providers who care for children from families who receive CCDF subsidies and meet standards beyond minimum licensing; and (5) parent/consumer education efforts (QRIS Definition and Statewide Systems; NCCIC, 2009).

The standards include family involvement, staff training and credentials, the learning environment, as well as leadership and management skills of the care provider or agency. Each criterion is measured by a scale using information from the care provider and independent evaluators (Matthew & Schumacher, 2008; National Infant and Toddler Child Care Initiative and Zero to Three, 2008; New York State Council on Children and Families, 2009). These ratings may help researchers determine the extent to which quality care is available in various localities for infants and toddlers. Star ratings should help parents make child care choices. However, they can work in this way only if parents have the ability to make choices about child care because they can afford to make them and they are available. We know that in many places, options are neither affordable nor available. Children who are not in licensed programs, often because their parents cannot afford to pay for them, may remain in low-quality care or relative care, which may or may not be low quality (Child Care Aware of America, 2012; New York State Council on Children and Families, 2009).

The QRIS is managed through the U.S. Department of Health and Human Services, but the funds are distributed to individual states. Each state has its own system name and website. Individual state systems follow federal guidelines but create distinct procedures and policies to fit local circumstances. For most states, participating in the QRIS is voluntary; however, North Carolina, New Mexico, and Oklahoma have made it mandatory for all child care facilities to meet the first level of the QRIS to become a licensed center. In addition, in Oklahoma and Wisconsin, it is mandatory for facilities that serve children receiving subsidies to meet higher levels of the QRIS standards to obtain funding (S. Fischer, interview, September 23, 2011). As of 2009, twenty-three states and three counties (two in Florida and one in California) participated. Twenty of these sites had programs that were fully voluntary; the other six were partially voluntary (Tout et al., 2010).

There are many incentives for child care facilities to participate in the QRIS. Along with professional development opportunities and regular evaluations and assessments, there are financial incentives available to participating facilities. While incentives vary from state to state, all have some kind of financial incentive system in place (Mitchell, 2012). These include tiered subsidy reimbursement based on the QRIS level (the most common financial incentive); quality grants, bonuses, and awards for program improvement and professional development; low- to no-interest loans linked to quality rating; scholarships for higher education, training, and professional development for child care facility staff; wage supplements, which serve as salary incentives for child care teachers and staff based on experience and level of education; and tax credits for parents.

While the federal government encourages states and facilities to utilize the QRIS, because the participation in the QRIS is voluntary in most states, there are no real consequences for nonparticipating facilities to meet QRIS standards. However, if participating programs do not maintain the required standards, they lose their financial incentives. Moreover, facilities that do not meet minimum requirements for licensing will lose their license and could incur fines (S. Fischer, interview, September 23, 2011). States have strongly promoted participation in QRIS. One of the missions of this program is to inform parents and the community about the child care facilities that are high functioning. Therefore, most states publish ratings on websites that provide information for parents when choosing a child care facilities (S. Fischer, interview, September 23, 2011).

Availability and Affordability

Child care, particularly quality child care, is very expensive. NAC-CRRA (2011) found, based on information provided by state Child Care Resource and Referral Agencies and state Child Care Offices, that the average cost of center-based infant care for the 2010–2011 year ranged from $4,630 in Mississippi to $18,200 a year in Washington, D.C. (slightly lower for home care) and between $3,900 and $14,000 for a four-year-old in center-based care (again slightly lower for family child care) (NAC-CRRA, 2011). Accounts of child care costs in particularly pricey markets, such as New York City, suggest that it can cost much more (Quart, 2013). Care for infants was the most expensive, largely due to the need for more staff to comply with optimal staff-child ratios. Several studies have indicated that parents of young children, particularly poor and working-class parents, struggle to find affordable quality care (Melmed, 2008; NACCRRA, 2006a). As noted earlier, despite these needs, when adjusting for inflation, federal funding for child care declined between 2002 and 2007 (Shulman & Blank, 2007). Accounting for inflation, this funding remained essentially flat between 2007 and 2012 (Shulman & Blank, 2012). Funding for children, including funding for early education and child care, has continued to drop (Isaacs, Edelstein, Hahn, Toran, & Stuerle, 2013). At the same time, child care costs have risen faster than wages (Boushey, 2007). The high cost of care coupled with declining support means that low-income families are particularly hard hit. An analysis of 2005 census data found that families with children younger than six living below the poverty line spent 32 percent of their income on child care, whereas families making 200 percent of the poverty line spent 18 percent of their income on child care (Smith & Gozjolko, 2010). Several studies indicate that low-income parents struggle to find afford-able quality care (NACCRRA, 2012) and that the supply is particularly inadequate in poor and rural areas (Shumacher & Hoffman, 2008).

State child care funding is heavily dependent on the economy. When inflation is considered, federal money for child care assistance from the CCDBG declined between 2001 and 2012 (Shulman & Blank, 2012). Between 2003 and 2005, the Government Accounting Office (2010) found that nineteen states had reduced eligibility for state child care assistance for the working poor since 2001, eight increased assistance, and eight made changes that both increased and decreased assistance. This was true despite the increasing number of children living in poverty. In 2005, 8 percent of children were living in families with incomes that were below 50 percent of the poverty level (approximately $20,000 a year for a family of four), 19 percent with incomes below the poverty line, and 40 percent with incomes below 200 percent of the poverty line. Yet, only 30 percent of low-income families with children in center-based care and only 16 percent of those with children in in-home care received federal or state subsidies to help fund the cost of care (Glynn, 2012). Furthermore,

in 2011, 30 percent of children receiving CCDBG funding were in unlicensed care (Child Care Aware of America, 2012). Between 2001 and 2010,
many states increased their income eligibility limits for state child care
assistance, largely to keep up with inflation. Nonetheless, the increases
in sixteen states did not keep up with inflation. In two-thirds of states,
eligibility remained less than 200 percent of the poverty line. In addition,
in 2012, twenty-three states had waiting lists or were no longer accepting
applications for eligible applicants (Shulman & Blank, 2012). In seven
states, they reduced the number of families who were eligible by lowering eligibility requirements, and eligibility for child care supplements
remained the same in fourteen states despite inflation (effectively lowering it). In twenty-seven states families fared worse in terms of their
eligibility for child care assistance in 2012 than they did in 2011, whereas
in seventeen states they fared better (Shulman & Blank, 2012).

Cost-Benefit Analysis of High-Quality Care

Voluminous research addresses the social benefits of high-quality child
care. Other research identifies the availability of quality child care as
an asset for businesses. For example, a recent Presidential Report that
included a significant review of research conducted on work life policies
noted that flexible work arrangements lead to increased worker productivity and reduced worker turnover and help recruit highly skilled workers (Romer, 2010). Economic justifications for government support of
child care and early education in what Prentice (2009) calls the "invest-
ible child" have garnered some support among the business community
and created alliances among unlikely advocates.

There is also little debate that it is less expensive to provide quality
care than to pay for foster care or incarcerating children in the juvenile
justice, or, ultimately, the adult criminal justice system (Katner, 2010). It
is well established that brain development in the early years is a crucial
foundation for childhood education as well as the life course (Schonkoff
& Phillips, 2000). Brain development at this stage can enhance or limit

cognitive abilities as well as social and emotional development in ways that can have an impact not only on learning but also on psychosocial functioning. According to Shapiro and Applegate (2002), "The neurobiological substrate of the capacity for affect regulation is strongly shaped by the quality of the infant's interpersonal world" (p. 108). Individual and societal benefits accrue not just from increased potential and capacity of future citizens, but also from a reduction in delinquency and crime. Katner (2010) reviews well-documented literature dating from as early as the 1990s, including evidence compiled by the U.S. Office of Juvenile Justice and Delinquency, showing that quality early childhood education is correlated with lower rates of delinquency. Early childhood investment can reduce costs associated with crime and the need for rehabilitation and treatment (Heckman, Grunewald, & Reynolds, 2006). Investment in early childhood education may also indirectly reduce delinquency through other factors such as school readiness, language acquisition, school attainment, and mental health (Katner, 2010).

Some have questioned the consistency of the reported benefits of early education and care, although many attribute variability of program achievements to uneven quality and lack of minimum universal standards of U.S. child care. In an attempt to address this question, Esping-Andersen and colleagues (2012) examined child care in relation to outcomes in Denmark and the United States. Their findings regarding Denmark, where child care is highly utilized (85 percent of children younger than six are enrolled) and is provided according to a relatively uniform and high standard of care, provide support for the benefit of early care *when quality can be ensured.*

Nobel prize winner James Heckman's research (Heckman, 2008; Heckman, Stixrud, & Urzua, 2006) suggests that investing money in early childhood programs reaps greater benefits than do programs aimed at school-age children, which in turn reap greater benefits than job training programs. Heckman's analysis, which is depicted graphically in Figure 6.1, suggests that public investment in child care and early education would reap large long-term economic benefits for the country as a whole.

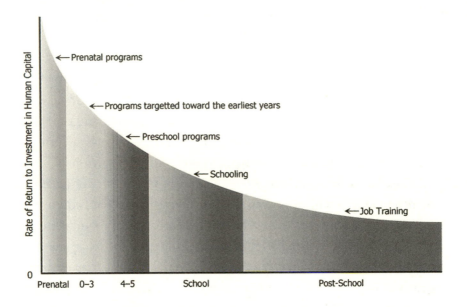

Figure 6.1. Return on Investment in Learning.

Public dollars spent on children are not in line with what we know about childhood development, however, with the most per capita spending at both the state and federal levels targeted to programs, generally, that serve children ages six to eleven, and the least to programs serving children ages zero to two (Macomber, Isaacs, Vericker, & Kent, 2010). This indicates a lack of attention to evidence that should be informing public policy.

Models for Providing Affordable Quality Child Care

Since the groundbreaking initial work of Kamerman and Kahn in 1981, many researchers have explored comparative policies. We do not provide a comprehensive picture of all possible child care regimes; instead, in this section we draw from the excellent and thorough extant literature that provides a rich comparative perspective. In our review of programs outside of the United States, we focus primarily on countries with advanced industrialized economies. In the first section, we present brief overviews of countries with more robust social safety nets that may have what are considered to be ideal programs. Then, we present overviews of countries with more market-driven philosophies that are often considered more similar to the United States. We also explore successful programs in the United States such as Educare, a public-private partnership, and care provided to children of parents serving in the U.S. military. We provide this section, in part, to make the point that there are many models of more expansive policies from which to draw inspiration.

Most Western European countries provide much greater social benefits than those that are provided in the United States. Maternity leave and child care are no exceptions. In 2000, the International Labour Organization, a part of the United Nations, developed an international standard for maternity leave including fourteen weeks of paid leave, with at least two-thirds pay. By 2007, all Western European countries other than the United Kingdom and Norway exceeded the standard. The United States did not (Russell, 2011).

France, Sweden, and Denmark

France, Sweden, and Denmark provide excellent models for universal quality systems. In these countries, parents are supported to stay home with their children, given sick insurance to care for them, and provided with the option of publicly subsidized child care. The goal of the Swedish program is to both encourage child development and enable parents to balance work and family. Parents together receive 480 days of paid parental leave, which may be used up until a child reaches the age of eight. Two months of this leave is set aside for fathers. Sweden has seen an increase in fathers' use of parental leave since it created a tax incentive that favors more equal distribution of parental leave in 2008 (Ploug, 2012). Children ages one to eleven are guaranteed spaces in quality child care. Of child care, 90 percent is public, and in 2002 the maximum fee that families were asked to pay was 1 to 3 percent of their monthly income. Such fees are waived for low-income families. Parental fees cover only 9 percent of the operating costs of child care facilities, and the rest are paid by national funds drawn from taxes. Of all workers who care for children ages one to six, 50 percent must have university degrees, and the others must have postsecondary certificates (Clearinghouse on International Developments, 2009; Organisation for Economic Co-operation and Development [OECD], 2006). In 2006 (the most recent data that were available in English), the cost of this child care was equivalent to 1.9 percent of Sweden's GDP (OECD, 2006).

In France, women receive at least six weeks prior to birth and ten weeks after birth of 100 percent paid maternity leave (they receive more for additional children). Men receive between three and eleven days of paid parental leave. Mothers receive monthly allowances that are means tested, but 90 percent of all mothers are eligible. Women can take up to three years leave (and sometimes four when the child has health problems) and return to their previous job or its equivalent.

France does very well on indicators of work-life balance compared to other OECD member countries. In a review of France's placement on common work-life balance indicators, the OECD (2011) reports, "Fertility is above the OECD average and close to the replacement rate of 2.1 children per woman; the employment rate of women aged 25 to 54 is above the OECD average, and 80 percent of them work full-time; and despite a recent slight increase, child poverty concern 8 percent of children aged from 0 to 17 and is well below the OECD average (12.75 percent)." While there is still an imbalance in women's share of unpaid activities, and higher opportunity costs for women who have children (OECD, 2011), France is considered a leader in labor force policies that work toward promoting equality and child and family well-being.[1]

France has combined its family-friendly leave policies with an impressive array of subsidized child care options from infancy. These include nurseries, home-based care provided by registered child minders for one to three children, and crèches, which are child care centers that are run by the municipal council or a voluntary-sector organization, by parents, or in a registered child minder's home (Embassy of France, n.d.).

France also has standards for quality. The initial training requirements in France for caregivers for children younger than three is a nurse mid-wife degree and a year of specialized training. Teachers for children ages three and four must have a bachelor's degree and twenty-seven months of additional training. Of instructors in early education and child care settings, 75 percent have early childhood degrees and the other staff must hold certificates. For children zero to two, there is a one to five staff to student ratio; for ages two to three, there is a one to eight staff to student ratio; and for children three to six, there is a twenty-five to one staff to student ratio (Office of Economic Development, 2010). Funding for child care has not declined in France, despite economic woes. Funding "toward collective childcare facilities have risen steadily over the last decade and despite an overall background of cost containment in other public services the system of public crèches has suffered no cutback in funding" (Fagnani, 2012, p. 511).[2] In fact, President Sarkozy's 2009 proposal to reduce the three-year leave to one year, while increasing the benefit levels paid during leave, was met with strong opposition (Fagnani, 2012).

Public spending on day care in Denmark is the highest of any OECD country (Esping-Andersen, 2009). Denmark has a three to one ratio for child care (care for children younger than three) and seven to one for preschool. All teachers receive early childhood training. As a result, 85 percent of one- to two-year-olds are enrolled in Denmark's day care programs. In Denmark, parents have the right to be absent from work on the first two days of a child's illness, at which time it is presumed that they can arrange for the child's care if more time is necessary (Ploug, 2012). Based on the differences in earnings that mothers who are not forced to exit the labor market as a result of their inability to find appropriate child care make to the tax system, these women actually end up paying for the care that their children receive in tax payments. Over their lifetime, they contribute more to the tax base for the country than it costs to provide their children's care (Esping-Andersen, 2009). Esping-Andersen's (2009) analysis demonstrates that the cost of caring for children is not significantly higher in France and Scandinavian countries than in the United States. Rather, the distribution of the cost or who pays for the care is simply different. Where the public sector pays for a significant portion of the care, the quality of care is generally higher for all children and resources are more equitably distributed.

Care policies may be popular in Europe not only because they are needed by families but also because they satisfy other concerns. The introduction of flexible and part-time work that allow for caring, largely carried out by women, also allows more jobs to be spread out among more people. This is helpful for those seeking work when employment opportunities are narrowed, and it is also helpful for employers who prefer not to take on full obligations toward employees but prefer more flexible arrangements (Morgan, 2009). Such policies may also encourage women to bear children at a time when birth rates are of concern to many European countries (Grant et al., 2004).

The findings offer a cautionary note to advocates of paid care in the home. The development of paid care leaves in different welfare regimes may reflect their appeal to political elites at a time of high unemployment and fiscal pressures on the welfare state. Efforts to remunerate caregivers of young children have also been driven by forces seeking to reinforce traditional gender roles in the home. These policies also have popular appeal in countries where there are constituencies that favor maternal care of young children. Though the policies are often couched in the language of choice and helping parents balance work and family, the underlying goal of care leave policies has been to value and support full-time female caregivers (Morgan, 2009, p. 51).

Leave policies may not always support women's equality in the workplace. Using the Luxembourg Income Study to compare twenty-one countries across Eastern and Western Europe, North America, Israel, and Australia, Misra et al. (2011) found that parental leave policies are positive only when such leaves are not too long. Moderate leaves were considered to be forty to ninety weeks. Both very short and very long leaves were associated with a maternal wage penalty. Morgan (2009) suggests as an example of how this works that in the gender-segregated labor markets in Norway private employers hesitate to employ women because they assume that women will take long maternity leaves (which are guaranteed by law). For these reasons, it is not surprising that European center-right and conservative parties have supported and promoted such policies (Morgan & Zippel, 2003). The motivation of gender equality and the influence of feminists have played only a limited role in shaping family policy. Such policies are often framed more along the lines of work-family life balance or care for children rather than the achievement of gender equality and are often structured to match this framing and reflect the underlying motivations, which combine family goals with other economic and social concerns.

Commonwealth Countries: England and Canada

England. It has been argued (Esping-Andersen, 1999) that the United States and countries such as France and Sweden have different welfare regimes making comparison and potential adoption of such welfare state child care policies unrealistic. However, countries such as England and provinces such as Quebec, Canada, have market-based economies that are not as welfare focused as those of France and Sweden and may therefore make them more realistic comparisons. Kunin (2012), an elected official and longtime political actor, suggests that countries such as Canada, England, and Australia would more likely be accepted as models for the United States as their political philosophies and approach to the benefits and the social safety net more closely mirror those of the United States. She suggests that child care reforms in countries such as England were motivated or rationalized on pragmatic rather than moral or philosophical grounds. According to Waldfogel (2010), in the late 1990s the New Labour Party was focused on addressing inequality associated with poverty. As a result, their policies were responsive to scientific evidence regarding the importance of early development in addressing this inequality. In 2004, the government established a ten-year child care strategy focusing on both parental choice and improved child care options. Because of concerns regarding the quality of early care, the government extended maternity leave to cover the first year of a child's life (Waldfogel, 2010). This may also have more appeal for U.S. policymakers as it speaks to business and government interests rather than being predicated on more contestable moral values such as women's equality or the role of the state. Prior to the introduction of their comprehensive child care systems, England and Quebec also faced fragmented early childhood systems. Nonetheless, they have been able to improve their systems and provide models that may be more easily adapted in the United States.

Beginning in 1999, new mothers in England were provided with twenty-six weeks of guaranteed maternity leave (Maternity and Paternity Leave Regulations, 1999). Over time, this leave has become paid and been extended. At present, women who have or adopt children in the United Kingdom can receive 90 percent of their regular salary pay for the first six weeks of leave, and for the following thirty-three weeks they are entitled to receive up to £123.06 a week (Criscione, 2011), after which they can take unpaid leave for the rest of the year (an additional twelve weeks). Fathers are also eligible to receive two weeks' statutory paternity leave to be taken within fifty-six days of the birth, for which they receive £136.78 a week or 90 percent of their weekly earnings, whichever is less (British Government, 2013). In addition, parents with children younger than six, or children with disabilities under eighteen, may apply to their employers for the right to work flexibly and their employers must seriously consider these requests (Employment Act 2008). This requirement potentially enables more flexible workplaces. Beginning April 3, 2011, mothers will be able to transfer the second half of their twelve-month entitlement to the father, providing them with up to a maximum of six months of leave (Criscione, 2011). In 1999, Britain also established a parental leave policy enabling either mothers or fathers to take up to three months of unpaid, job-protected leave for child care or other family emergency circumstances (Waldfogel, 2010).

British initiatives to improve care for children younger than four began in the late 1990s. In addition to flexible parental leave that is offered in Britain, beginning September 1998 free public nursery schools were available for all children beginning at age four. In 2004, they began to include free preschool for three-year-olds. In addition, in 1999, the Sure Start initiative was begun to provide children and families in high-poverty areas with family support and early learning experiences. Localities were afforded flexibility in the design of programs, so programs ranged from drop-in to more formal curriculum-based educational settings. Five hundred programs were established (Halfon, Russ, Oberklaid, Bertrand, & Eisenstadt, 2009).

In 2004 the Children's Act was passed. This act led to the creation of 150 local authorities, called Children's Trusts, which were designed to coordinate children's social, health, and educational services and improve the communication between these sectors and the private voluntary sector (e.g., nonprofits) in an effort to reduce child poverty. It also expanded the Sure Start initiative to the current level of 3,500 programs, one for every community, providing universal early education and care services. It provides fifteen hours of play-based curriculum for thirty-eight weeks a year as well as extended care services for children whose parents work (Halfon et al., 2009).

In 2006, the Child Care Act was passed. This legislation requires local authorities to provide sufficient child care for all eligible citizens through the voluntary and private sectors. Further efforts were made to improve access to information about child care and increase the number of college graduates in leadership positions in the child care field (Halfon et al., 2009).

Waldfogel (2010) explains that the British child care policies were part of a broader social plan to address the poverty in the England. She suggests that the successes were largely the result of politicians focusing media attention on the impact of universal policies rather than benefits being provided to the poor. It is important to note that Britain has a parliamentary government, and as a result it is generally easier for the British to introduce and change laws than is the case in the United States.

Canada. Although Canada does not have a national model child care system and struggles with some of the same challenges as are pervasive in the United States, including a belief by many that child care is the sole the responsibility of parents, each province provides some unpaid maternity and parental leave. Quebec has developed some excellent and successful child care policies and programs.[3] First, mothers may take up to eighteen weeks of unpaid maternity leave as well as fifty-two weeks of unpaid parental leave following maternity leave. Fathers are eligible for five weeks of unpaid paternity leave in addition to fifty-two weeks of unpaid parental leave. Though leave remains unpaid for many, the leave provided in Quebec is much longer than the leave provided in the United States (Halfon et al., 2009).

Quebec also publicly funds over nine hundred child care programs, which are free for income-eligible families receiving social assistance and are available to others at a low cost. "The new child care centers shift the delivery of child care from a market service designed to support parent's labor force participation to a public service that is designed to support children's early learning and development with options that support parents' work schedules" (Halfon et al., 2009, p. 11). In 2009, more than 60 percent of children younger than five in Quebec attended regulated child care programs (Halfon et al., 2009). This is a much higher percentage of children than those who are provided with publicly supported care in the United States (or the rest of Canada).

Existing U.S. Models
The U.S. Military Model

For those who suggest that the high-quality, universal child care that is available in other OECD countries could never be provided in the United

States, the U.S. military provides an example of how it has been done here. As a result of poor-quality child care, excessive cost, and long wait lists that military personnel faced, 1989 saw the passage of the Military Child Care Act. The legislation provided for the development of a systemic model of care for the children of military personnel, which could serve as a model for the rest of the country. Military personnel go to one place to find family child care, child development centers, and care for school-aged children. Military child care must meet Department of Defense certification standards, and child development centers must be in compliance with National Association for the Education of Young Children (NAEYC) accreditation standards. Furthermore, parents pay fees based on a sliding scale, and providers are given subsidies to enable them to provide care for children of parents with low incomes (Pomper, Blank, Campbell, & Schulman, 2004).

The quality of care has been improved upon as a result of inspections and requirements that programs comply with the Department of Defense certification standards. In 2005, 91 percent of military child care centers were accredited by NAEYC, as compared to 8 percent of civilian child care centers. Military child care workers are paid salaries commensurate with the pay of other military personnel with the same amount of education and training. This means that full-time workers receive health benefits, sick leave, retirement benefits, as well as life insurance, and some supervisors earned up to $76,000 a year (Pomper et al., 2004). Child care workers in these programs are well compensated and receive extensive initial and ongoing training, which contributes to the stability of the child care workforce (Pomper et al., 2004). The sliding-scale nature of the programs' cost make them affordable to all parents. In 2004–2005, costs ranged from a low of $43 to $59 per week to a high of $107 to $126 per week, depending on parental income; this equates to approximately 8 to 13 percent of income for lower-income parents and 9 percent for higher-income parents. The armed forces subsidize both family care and center-based care, both of which are licensed and regulated (Pomper et al., 2004). Military child care is an important service, but it is far from perfect. One survey of military families found that while many were satisfied with care, there was a mismatch between needs and available slots (Zellman, Gates, Moini, & Suttorp, 2009). Due to the greater need for infant care and its high cost, there were often waiting lists for such care, while preschool slots were unfilled. The authors of this study suggest that assessing family needs and then modifying programs and resources to align better with these needs would improve on the existing program, which provides a much-needed service.

Public-Private Partnership Models

Educare is a public-private partnership that reportedly provides excellent early childhood education centers. It was originally funded by the Buffett Early Childhood Fund and Ounce of Prevention Fund and has been supported by other foundations including the Bill & Melinda Gates Foundation, the Irving Harris Foundation, the W. K. Kellogg Foundation, and the George Kaiser Family Foundation. The funding for day-to-day Educare operations is provided by Head Start and Early Head Start, which some states and localities supplement with their own child care funding. Private philanthropists build Educare schools and provide ongoing training to staff. They use their resources to "facilitate the flow of public dollars which support day to day operations" of these schools (Educare, n.d.). This is one way to develop the infrastructure that is needed in the United States to support child care.

In Educare models, children have the same team of caregivers from birth until three and then from three to five in order to create continuity of care. The curriculum encourages the development of preliteracy skills as well as social and emotional skills. First and foremost, it seeks to address the lag that low-income children typically have behind their middle-class peers in terms of vocabulary development, which Educare notes on its website is evident as early as eighteen months and increases with age. Parents are included in the program and are given instruction in how to teach their child as well as how to advocate for their child when he or she enters primary and secondary school. These programs include social workers and a host of other professional consultants such as physical therapists, speech pathologists, nurses, and artists.

One of the goals of Educare is to serve as a platform. Educare describes its programs as "showrooms that demonstrate what high-quality, well-implemented early programs can look like [in order to] help to convince policy makers, business leaders and others that investments in early learning make a difference in the life outcomes for even the most at-risk children" (http://www.educareschools.org/about/educare-Platform.php). On its website, Educare notes several instances in which their programs have been used to help successfully lobby states to increase their spending on early childhood programs. For example, Educare of Omaha helped advocates convince legislators to change the Nebraska constitution to note that education begins at birth. Subsequently, the state of Nebraska created a $60 million public-private endowment to expand child care services for children from birth to three years. Educare also highlights that since the opening of Educare of Chicago in 2000, the state of Illinois has increased its early education funding by $172 million.

Several other public-private partnerships have been created, with most focusing on supporting care for low-income children. Many have been used to improve the quality of such care. For example, in New Jersey, the Schuman Foundation, the Lucent Foundation, Johnson & Johnson, and other private foundations provided two years of funding in 1998 and 1999 to provide technical and financial support to help child care agencies serving low-income children meet the standards necessary for state accreditation. As a result of a lawsuit, *Abbott v. Burke* (1990), which addressed educational equity, the state of New Jersey began differential reimbursement for child care serving low-income children, providing higher reimbursement rates for accredited programs. This funding, though short in duration, was used to help improve the standard of early education services provided to low-income children (Mitchell, Stoney, & Dichter, 2001).

Conclusion

In this chapter, we have provided a description of what U.S. children and their families face. Most children do not have a stay-at-home parent, even throughout their early childhood. Whether this is through economic or other necessity or by choice, it is reality. Families in need of child care face several hurdles. They often have trouble ascertaining whether a particular child care arrangement is appropriate and safe. In fact, it is not always clear to parents what criteria they should use to make this determination. Even parents who are able to choose from a variety of arrangements may not be able to afford what they believe is optimal care for their children. Low-income and even middle-income families make difficult choices about how best to support their families and keep them safe. These families sometimes have to weigh getting or keeping a job that keeps them fed, housed, and possibly with medical insurance, with child care that may be less than optimal or that keeps them in a financially precarious situation that can make economic gains marginal or tenuous. A third struggle for many U.S. families is accessibility of child care. There is a dearth of child care options for those who work outside of traditional work hours. Transportation to or distance from child care can also be a hurdle. In addition, as noted earlier, there is a shortage of child care slots more generally (Taylor, 2012). Child care is a concern throughout the world, yet many countries do a better job to assist children and their families than we do in the United States. While Sweden's and France's policies may seem utopian to U.S. child care advocates, more modest proposals such as those implemented in England and Quebec would be an improvement that might be more palatable to the American electorate. If the framing of the U.S. child care problem were expanded to become more universal, home-grown child care policies like the U.S. military's or Educare's might provide the building blocks on which a national policy could be based.

7

Strategic Framing of Child Care

Building on the historical and legislative context that we have laid out, in the next chapters we provide an insider perspective on what it would take to build a child care movement in the United States. We examine why a broad-based movement around child care has not coalesced, despite the recent increase in calls for concerted efforts to address the quality, content, safety, and adequacy of care for preschool-age children starting from birth. The analyses presented in this chapter and the one that follows are based on data from interviews we conducted with key child care advocates to better understand their perspective on what has shaped the actions of organizations, individual advocates, and other stakeholders. Ethnographic techniques, including in-depth interviews, have become increasingly common as tools to study policy (Schatz, 2009). We focused on the perspective of elite advocates who represent different interest groups because their actions and vision are crucial in shaping national and local policy advocacy (Duffy, Binder, & Skrentny, 2010; Hoefer, 2000).

We conducted interviews with twenty-three activists from groups that advocate for policies and programs related to caring for young children.[1] These include nonprofit service provider and philanthropic organizations, unions, and policy institutes. When we originally started data collection, we had hoped to speak with representatives from business groups and organizations that overtly oppose the expansion of government support for families. However, few such organizations were identified by the advocates. We contacted the major business lobbying groups that we assumed, based on their ideological positions, would oppose expanded government intervention into the child care arena. The only opponent to the expansion of national child care policy and family leave who was willing to speak with us was Phyllis Schlafly of the Eagle Forum.

Strategic Framing of Child Care for the Policy Agenda

Advocates, researchers, and funders in our study confirmed what we see in the public policy debates: in the words of Ellen Galinsky, executive director of the Families and Work Institute, "framing is a big issue." Research groups such as the Families and Work Institute have tried to create politically neutral research papers assuming that *facts* will be sufficient to sway public opinion and help create good public policy. However, according to Galinsky, regardless of what the data show, advocates still come up against resistant frames and "if children continue to be thought of as private property and not as a social good, then we are not going to make the investment." She also noted the impact of prevalent work beliefs such as "presence is productivity" and the need to be physically present in the workplace in order to complete job tasks, which shape work-family policy. Such beliefs do not *explicitly* conflict ideologically with the belief that women can work in the paid labor force as they do not explicitly target women. They do not, however, allow for flexible work schedules or part-time work. Statistics regarding women's employment and promotion also show that such rhetoric is often a coded way of undermining support for women's paid employment and women's advancement as the task of child care still falls overwhelmingly on mothers. It justifies lower wages and truncated promotion for women based on assumptions about the quality and productivity of women's work, which are affected by the very arrangements that would allow many families to combine childbearing and paid employment. Until these assumptions change, Galinsky noted, it will remain difficult for flexible workplace policies to take hold. These assumptions may be hard to challenge, because they place assertions about women's work into the realm of individual decision making, obscuring the social and economic forces that inform women's choices and employers' treatment of working parents. Galinsky's concerns echo Morgan's research on European care leave policies that have been supported by conservative and center-right parties that may not be in the best interests of women's equality and career choices (see Chapter 6). They may also be affected by the electorate, which is disproportionately represented by voters older than sixty (Imig, 2006). The views of these voters may be less likely to reflect the realities of today's child care dilemmas than their own experiences, raising children at a time when women were less likely to be involved in the full-time labor force and many more families were reliant on a single wage earner.

The limited number of policies to address the needs of working parents is undergirded by the belief that middle-class mothers should be at home to raise their children. If parents should be raising their own children, then there is no need for the public sector to be involved with child care. According to Steffany Stern of the Partnership for Women and Families, "[M]any policies were written when most families had one working parent and one stay at home parent." Contemporary "policies don't deal with the current situations of families." Many existing policies were passed when there was a public perception that middle-class mothers were at home to care for their children. Though this belief is still held by some, it is not a viable reality for most families. There are also those who do not ascribe to this belief. Many women aspire to careers. Over the past fifty years, society has invested heavily in the education of women through programs such as Title IX. This potentially opens a space for change. However, advocates have apparently not yet been able to build upon changes in women's work patterns and career aspirations to create an opening for child care policy changes.

An additional area of concern is how respondents focus their attention and develop strategies for choosing and presenting their areas of substantive focus, which we examine in the subsequent chapter, to the public and to public policy decision makers. Though this relates to framing, it is broader in that it suggests that different interest groups use different strategies to influence public policy. For example, there is debate among quality care advocates regarding what a quality rating system should include and whether to focus advocacy efforts at the state or federal level. Another example of strategic difference is between those who focus on ensuring support or expanding funding for existing programs such as Head Start, or others, many of which are funded by the CCDF, and those who wish to reframe child care as a family support in an effort to gain more broad-based support.

Four dominant frames are currently being used to address the problems families experience with child care in the United States. Each of these frames involves values and causal stories that are not always explicit but which inform the priorities of advocates. The first frame is that care for children, basically from birth, is necessary to enable the mothers of poor children to work. This belief has been used to support child care programs associated with "welfare" throughout the years, which since 1996 has been administered through the federal program Temporary Assistance for Needy Families (TANF). The second frame is that low-income, disadvantaged children need to receive early education services such as Head Start, beginning at age three, in order to counteract the disadvantages of being raised in poverty. Proponents relying on this frame often refer to fairness claims in the form of "leveling the playing field" or the need for forward-looking investments that ultimately cost less to society as they help to produce more adequately prepared and functioning citizens. The third policy frame, one that has been used to support the development of universal pre-K programs, suggests that all children need to receive early education services beginning at age three or four. Unlike the first two, this frame focuses on all children and often refers to literature showing the importance of developmentally appropriate early education for all. Finally, a less dominant theme mentioned by advocates is that all families struggle to find appropriate child care for their young children. Policies primarily based on the theme of quality and safety, such as the establishment of quality rating systems, have been developed to help parents identify quality care for their children. These policies are grounded in the assumption that parents have the financial ability and range of child care options to be able to choose the care that best meets their children's needs. Another is providing tax benefits for middle-class parents. Imig and Meyer (2007) identify similar frames in their review of prekindergarten policy advocacy. In the section that follows, we describe in detail these four frames.

Help Low-Income Children

Most existing child care policies in the United States focus on children in low-income families. The reason policies have been developed to focus on the needs of low-income children stems largely from the historic role of child care centers as both places to assimilate new immigrant children and places for poor children, whose mothers had to work as a result of some unfortunate circumstance such as the death or desertion of their husbands (Rose, 1999). It is also consistent with Lockean liberal views that unless a person is especially needy (e.g., disabled, widowed, or a minor), government should have no role in providing assistance (Hartz, 1999; Nivola & Rosenbloom, 1999).

Head Start and many state and local level child care programs, many funded by CCDF money, target low-income children. Some respondents suggested that child care policy should be restricted to poverty-based solutions focused on improving the situation of poor children. There are several reasons that the respondents believed that the needs of the poor should be paramount. They ranged from ideological reasons that it is one's individual responsibility to provide for one's own children and that unless one is in dire circumstances, this is not a government concern to the strategic belief that allocation of resources for the poor is less controversial and, therefore, more likely to garner support. Some examples of the ideological perspective include that the "federal role falls on helping those who cannot help themselves" (Sara Lee Todd, senior legislative advocate for the Service Employees International Union) and that there is "more return on investing in those in greatest need" (Susan Hibbard, a consultant for the Build Initiative). John Wilcox of Corporate Voices for Working Families observed that early education and care programs provide maximum payoff for low-income children. This position sees competition for resources and advocates for scarce resources going to those most in need both due to their need and due to the perceived greater benefit to be gained through use of resources to those for whom they will make the greatest difference. Joe Thiessen of Voices for America's Children explicitly noted that benefits to the poor would bring about broader benefits to society "[i]f we improve the system that serves the poorest, ultimately you will help everyone."

Many of our respondents who indicated a preference for starting with the needs of the most vulnerable did not limit their vision, however, to child care for low-income families. The Build Initiative describes itself as a foundation funded initiative to support "state efforts to create comprehensive early childhood systems—coordinate effective policies that address children's health and mental health, nutrition, early care and education, family support and parenting and services to children with special needs" (www.buildinitiative.org). Catherine Graham Hildum of the First Five Years Fund, an organization funded by private philanthropists including J. B. Pritzker, Warren Buffet, the Henry J. Kaiser Family Foundation, Irving Harris, and the Bill & Melinda Gates Foundation, explained that the organization was concerned with the importance of early education: "Our focus is on the most disadvantaged first. Though we believe in universality, we think that first we have to get care for the most disadvantaged in high quality settings."

The view that improving funding for existing poverty-based programs is a first step in developing a solution to address U.S. child care problems is not without its critics. If policies are developed that first address the needs of the poor, those just above poverty or even those in the middle class may not feel invested in supporting the policies since they provide no direct benefit for them (Rose, 2010). Many believe that universal policies, such as social security insurance benefits, have remained stable and even grown because they have a broad constituency with a vested interest in supporting them. Poverty-based programs such as TANF, on the other hand, are often inadequately funded, the first to be sacrificed, and highly stigmatized. According to Danielle Ewen, director of Child and Early Education for the Center for Law and Social Policy (CLASP), much of the advocacy around child care policy focuses on poverty-based solutions. Though CLASP's priority is policy research to benefit low-income children, "our team takes the perspective that our child care system is so broken that we cannot fix it for low-income people if we do not fix it for all." The privatized nature of our current system has led to an insufficient amount of quality care, which many cannot afford or even find and a lack of political focus on the child care concerns because they are viewed by many as private struggles. Policies that exclusively address the needs of low-income families reify the belief that child care, for most, is a private struggle.

Though all of our respondents seemed to recognize that low-income children are at greater risk without access to adequate child care, some identified a need to develop broader based solutions in order to help low-income children. Others thought, because of limited resources, it was necessary to focus on the neediest as a first step toward a more universal vision. Last, some felt that for those who were not poor, the only possible role for government was to ensure quality control. This disjuncture as well as relatively unanimous agreement that despite the universal nature of child care problems in the United States, low-income families suffer the most, has led to both policies and advocates focusing largely on addressing their needs. Fewer people are willing to advocate on behalf of greater universal access to quality child care than on behalf of improving funding largely for existing poverty-based programs in the United States.

Support Low-Income Working Parents

There have always been advocacy organizations that have promoted women's rights and need to engage in paid labor, though, historically, in the United States the ideal was that women should be supported by men. During the New Deal Era, proponents of mother's pensions felt that they were honoring motherhood by supporting pensions rather than creating child care institutions, which would have enabled, even encouraged, women to work out of the home.[2] Of course, these pensions were restrictive and never provided sufficient funding to enable low-income women to leave the labor market (Rose, 1999).

In the 1990s, the Personal Responsibility and Work Opportunity Reconciliation Act ended "welfare as we knew it," replacing the child-support-focused Aid to Families with Dependent Children with TANF, which was designed to incentivize maternal work. Much of the rhetoric surrounding this change suggested that it was not appropriate for low-income women to be paid to stay home with their children since most middle-class women had to work. A major reason some organizations support child care is to enable parents, particularly low-income parents, to work. Organizations such as unions and 9 to 5 are primarily concerned with child care issues as they relate to supporting low-income women in the workforce and unions have also been concerned with protecting the rights of child care workers. For example, Linda Meric of 9 to 5 noted that child care was critical to enable *parents* to get and keep their jobs, seeing child care primarily as a support for low-income working parents. Becky Levin of AFSCME noted that most women with young children who are not in the workforce are less educated and cannot get a job that will provide them with sufficient resources to pay for child care. This limits their ability to become "better parental providers" and ultimately keeps many of these families in poverty. Women may decide to stay home to care for their children because child care costs more than what they would earn if working. Even women who can afford to drop out of the paid labor force to raise children when they are supported by partners are economically vulnerable should their relationships fail and they need to find work. Someone who has left the workforce for a few years is less likely to be hired than someone with a resume indicating recent employment.

As we discuss in Chapter 6, the cost of child care for poor working parents is, in many instances, untenable. This is easily illustrated by looking at the minimum wage and the predicament of a parent earning the minimum wage if she or he has a child or children. A minimum wage job currently pays $7.25 an hour, which is equal to $290 a week or approximately $15,000 a year. A family with two working parents working in minimum wage jobs would earn approximately $30,000 a year. In many states, child care is expensive if a parent is unable to access publicly subsidized care; her or his entire income might need to be allocated to provide child care for two children. This would leave a family with no money for housing, clothing, food, or other needs. Ultimately, this would probably require one parent not to work or for parents to work in shifts. If the family is somehow able to access care, they do not have the resources to be selective regarding the quality of the care that they are able to access. Though family leave could easily be an avenue to ensure that children receive adequate care when they are very small, interview data suggested that most child advocacy groups do not concern themselves with parental leave policies because of the limited amount of time that they cover but, rather, focus on the education and care for older preschool-age children (not infants) believing that that is more palatable to the electorate. This is an artificial division as the needs of working parents cannot really be separated from the needs of their children.

Helen Blank at the National Women's Law Center noted that because U.S. family leave is defined by law as twelve weeks (currently unpaid), many assume "even if we get paid leave, it will only be for 3 months and then, what?" She suggested not that paid leave was unimportant, but that the way we have defined family leave in the United States is so limited that it really cannot be used to address longer-term child care needs. The construction of U.S. national labor support policies such as the FMLA and some state-level sick leave policies as a short-term emergency relief limits their utility as it relates to the long-term care needs of children, which extend far beyond the first three months of life.

Early Childhood Education

In the interviews, there was little discussion of child care without reference to early education. Many of the advocates and policy analysts interviewed for this study have focused their efforts on advocating for educational services, using the language of early education that draws on brain development research, particularly for economically disadvantaged children. Their belief is that if we talk about education, the electorate is more likely to provide greater support for these programs (see also Rose, 2010). One limitation of the education perspective is that it often does not allow for space to talk about child care needs outside of "educational services." Several noted that the Obama administration has pledged to greatly increase funding for early education and some referenced the importance of the Early Learning Challenge grants, which at its peak in 2011 awarded nearly $500 million in competitive funds to encourage states to coordinate early learning systems and to collect data (U.S. Department of Education, 2013a);[3] Obama's rhetoric focuses on education, often to the exclusion of custodial aspects of child care (i.e., in his February 13, 2013, State of the Union Address).

Pew representative Libby Doggett described current, nonpublic data that demonstrate that though the public may support education for three- and four-year-olds, they are still uncomfortable with the idea of children younger than three being in schools or in formal child care settings. According to Danielle Ewen, no one wants to talk about babies being in child care for ten hours a day despite the number of children in such care. Largely as a result of perceived public opinion based on polling results, over the past twenty years early childhood advocates have begun to talk more about early childhood education to the exclusion of care. The goal of foundation-supported groups such as the First Five Years Fund is to get one million more children into early education settings, focusing first on economically disadvantaged children with the ultimate goal of providing universal services. Still, the early education and care community has largely coalesced around the idea that early care programs need to make children "ready to learn." Few of these organizations address children's care needs after the traditional work or school hours or the needs of school-age children both before and after school. As Ewen noted, by focusing on "education," which is usually provided for young children only two to three hours a day, parents are left to figure out what to do with their children the rest of the time that they are working. Parents of school-aged children are also left to establish piecemeal plans for their children because few people work from nine to three or only nine months of the year.

The framing of child care policy as "early childhood education" has been viewed as a preferred strategy by many policy advocates because it has potential to garner support from business groups that may see children as their future workforce and hence be supportive of education but may be more likely to view child care as simply "babysitting." However, since educational programs are generally not designed to meet the care needs of parents, programs designed with this in mind have done little to meet that concern. Becky Levin of AFSCME challenges the disparagement of custodial care, asking, "[W]hat is wrong with babysitting? There is something to be said for knowing that your child is safe when they are with a babysitter." Keeping these questions off the agenda implies that custodial care is less important than education or that it is something to be ashamed of. The failure to talk about children's care needs as a result of their parents' work schedules reinforces care work as work that can be taken for granted, work women are expected to do without reward, support, or acknowledgment of its importance to our society and economy or of the burden it places on women, children, and families.

Universal Care Perspective

The final, less dominant, perspective that there needs to be a broad-based solution for all children irrespective of age or income was articulated by Danielle Ewen of CLASP: "As long as child care is in the market and 60 percent of the cost is carried by parents, we will never get a system that is affordable and accessible. We need to figure out a way to make child care a public good." Defining child care as a public good would mean making it available to everyone, regardless of ability to pay. Public goods are provided outside of the market to all because they are considered a benefit to broader society or because of ethical considerations that income should not be a barrier to access certain goods or services, which include air or public roads. Becky Levin of AFSCME noted that, "[W]hat we have is piecemeal, there is never a perception that [we could develop a policy that would enable] all families and kids to benefit. The whole issue of [government support for] staying home with your child is overlooked in public policy. Sweden gives payments to stay at home parents." Though there are multiple ways to develop a universal care policy such as any of those we reviewed in Chapter 5, as a nation, we have not yet begun to seriously consider any. While many advocates may see the importance of considering a universally available care system, as a group they are far from figuring out how to develop strategies to advocate for universalism. This may, in part, be because they are busy focusing on addressing the needs of low-income children and working women or the educational needs of children. Current advocacy efforts are primarily focused on addressing weaknesses in the existing policy structures rather than looking for a new one.

Many advocates expressed support for universal care.[4] Almost all *also* noted that they felt that the development of a universal child care system was not politically viable. Adele Robinson of the National Association for the Education of Young Children noted, "We don't yet know what to do. . . . [W]e are not very linear, some are starting to think about this— we need to get a better sense of benchmarks and timing. What are some things that go to a universal expectation, what does it take to build that, we are still scratching our heads."

Advocates identified one universal aspect of current child care policy as the advent of state quality rating systems. Though universal quality standards may provide important information to parents seeking care options for their young children, they do not fund the development of more programs that are designed to meet the care needs of families with children. Rather, they help rate the programs in existence. A universal ranking system may be one step toward improving quality standards, but it will not address the needs of those who cannot afford or cannot gain access to the highest quality programs and does not address the needs of those in unlicensed settings (which is the majority of children who are not yet in school). It also does not provide incentives to expand the existing network of child care even for those who can afford to pay.

The Influence of Policy Feedback

As noted by Sonya Michel (1999) in a historical review of national child care policies and, more recently, by Andrew Karch (2010), looking at the development of state-level early childhood education policies, existing policies create constituencies that ultimately affect how early care and education policies are shaped both at the state and national levels. This phenomenon is often referred to as policy feedback (Karch, 2010; Pierson, 1993). Some of the challenges of the existing policies are that many Head Start and pre-K programs are only part-day programs and cannot meet the care needs of parents. Head Start executive director Yasmina Vinci and Helen Blank of the National Women's Law Center indicated that many advocates do not want Head Start to be rolled into other federally supported child care because the current federal and state quality standards for child care are minimal. This leads to differences among constituent groups. Blank explained that current funding for child care is also siloed and divvied up in ways that may make it confusing to legislators. Some funding is federal money with state matching grants, other funding is purely state funding, and still other funding is TANF transfer money. There is also a tension between Head Start and child care because Head Start has more mandates and requires family support that is not provided by more general funding for child care provided through CCDF or through state funding mechanisms (Helen Blank; Yasmina Vinci). In a recent analysis of state preschool and Head Start spending, Karch

(2010) provided examples of Head Start leaders opposing the creation of state preschool programs over concerns that they might adversely affect Head Start enrollment. He suggested that the ability of the Head Start community to influence the spending has a lot to do with the historical role of Head Start in each state and its continuing strength at the state level. In 2006–2007, forty-one states provided public money to support preschool education. Ten states supported both Head Start and preschool programs, thirty supported only preschool programs and one, Oregon, only supported Head Start (Karch, 2010; Rigby, 2007).

The current organizational structure of many child care institutions is threatened by the development of new programs such as pre-K programs when they are connected to schools. According to the principle of policy feedback, new policies build on existing policies. New proposals that threaten existing programs and constituencies are often met with resistance. Pre-K programs are often (though not exclusively) designed to build on the existence of elementary schools. Adding pre-K programs to existing elementary schools threatens the way many child care centers operate. Because of insufficient funding for child care, many formal child care institutions rely on cost shifting, using money received from the care for older children to help supplement the care for younger children. Cost shifting enables these institutions to provide the higher ratio of care to infants and young toddlers that is required by law. These organizations are threatened by the development of pre-K programs in schools because they undermine their economic sustainability of child care centers by creaming off the most profitable programs. Furthermore, most pre-K programs are not designed to replace child care institutions. Many state pre-K programs are limited to three- and four-year-olds and are partial-day programs. Dana Friedman points out that while they may be universally available in theory, they are not always universally funded. Because most are partial-day programs, they also require wrap-around services from child care centers (Becky Levin; Danielle Ewen). As a result of this, and possibly because of some parental preference for private or full-day care, a small percentage of children are actually enrolled in state pre-K programs (25 percent of four-year-olds and 16 percent of three-year-olds participated in these programs in 2009) (Pew Center on the States, 2009).

Keeping Child Care off the Political Agenda

Most of the people whom we interviewed felt that there were really no groups opposing policies to create better care for children. Some, however, such as union representatives and Linda Meric of 9 to 5, mentioned that many probusiness groups, especially at the national level, often opposed legislation that would help working families. Even more, Susan Hibbard, consultant for the Build Initiative, discussed the challenges of creating and sustaining child care policies in the current political climate.

> I'll never forget in Oklahoma when the great work that they were doing was being sort of pushed back and even the Governor's support for it was undermined hugely by this group that started calling Oklahoma a "Nanny State" and that people were trying to turn Oklahoma into a "Nanny State." And there definitely are, um, you know, groups that are concerned that, uh, you know . . . who feel that children should be taken care of by the mother in the home and, you know, who have a view of what child rearing in society ought to look like that's very different from current reality, and it makes them non-responsive to an early childhood agenda. So definitely state leaders face that as an obstacle.

In the case of Oklahoma, Hibbard described a situation where there was a policy against which to push back. Advocates must be prepared for conservative opposition if and when child care moves onto the public agenda. Lack of current opposition in the face of few policy proposals with traction cannot be taken as a sign that conservatives will remain silent.

Phyllis Schlafly of the Eagle Forum provided a telling critique, though not representative of all other conservative positions on child care: "We oppose any type of legislation that—for example the National Education Association calls for mandatory kindergarten and really they want mandatory free care, so-called early childhood education which is not education at all, it is just babysitting. And mostly we do not think the government should be providing babysitters for other people's children."

From earlier battles and the rhetoric around work and family, we can expect opposition for any national child care movement in several key areas. These include concerns about outsourcing child care, especially when it is not simply a work support, concerns about the regulation of child care (particularly of religion-based child care), and concerns from business groups and others about increasing government expenditures. The expansion of government regulation of child care services and the expanded funding that would be necessary to support either a national or state-based universal child care system in the United States would clearly be very expensive and, likely, many of the same groups that oppose government spending on health care for ideological reasons would, if faced with a viable policy, oppose national and/or universal state-funded child care. Though the focus on education has potentially swayed some of the electorate, some social conservatives still suggest that parents should be at home caring for their children.

The Current State of the Movement

Several groups are seeking to change the conversation regarding work and family. Pew and the National Women's Law Center have worked to reframe polls so that rather than asking what parents think about nonparental care, they ask, "Given that x percent of women are working outside of the home, how do you believe that care should be provided?" (Nancy Kolbin). Polling can influence how political issues are framed, and advocates use polls as political tools (Kinder & Nelson, 2005). In fact, a major component of Pew's ten-year pre-K campaign was to "assist state campaigns in using effective communication tools to get data in front of decision makers" (Watson, 2010, p. 5). Framing and media coverage play a large role in the development and provision of early childhood education.

Steffany Stern of the National Partnership explained, "[L]ots of policies are designed only to target low-income families. Child care costs are a huge hit on middle class families." Though many of the advocacy group leaders with whom we spoke seemed to recognize this fact, they felt that the middle class could handle their child care challenges better and that their children were at less risk of harm and therefore, as noted elsewhere in this chapter, focused their legislative advocacy on policies primarily designed to expand the funding of services for the poor. Others, however, are beginning to question the limited legislative focus on the low-income families. In addition to the National Partnership for Women and Families, the foundation-funded Birth to Five Policy Alliance,[5] and grassroots organizations such as Momsrising have begun to seek ways to influence cultural beliefs about what resources communities need to provide to care for children. For example, Momsrising has used several innovative strategies to not only influence legislators but also place stories about care for children in the media. One example was a large paper doll chain with stories from 120 mothers that was delivered by preschoolers to the Washington State governor. Sarah Francis of Momsrising described a campaign where advocates from forty-seven states bring pacifiers with the message that "we will not be pacified" to their senators in Washington, D.C., to support the passage of health care policy that will help children.

There are many different constituencies that are concerned with child care, and they have not yet set a unitary agenda. This is not surprising as they all come from different organizations with different goals and objectives. However, most of the people who were interviewed for this study acknowledged that one major problem is a fundamental lack of resources and a lack of consensus over which issues to prioritize. Many advocates in our study believed the Obama administration is more receptive to early care than any other recent administration (though notably these interviews occurred at the beginning of his administration, and it is not clear if this belief has persisted). According to Nancy Kolbin of the Center for Children's Initiatives, "[A]s a country, the administration is now more attuned to understanding the importance of the early years—we do not have a system or a commitment; some people are eligible sometimes." Dana Friedman, the president of the Early Years Institute, explained that "we know how to provide for kids but no one has the resources to do it." Last, almost all of the people with whom we spoke noted that one of the major problems with the way in which public child care is currently allocated is that there are multiple funding streams, and this creates multiple opposing interests between advocates. Joe Thiessen of Voices for America's children reflected, "One thing we do not know how to do is set an agenda. We send a message that we have not prioritized." Helen Blank emphasized that there are "different programs and providers. We do not pay enough for any of the existing programs." Also, "different people have different needs and some do not want to use center [-based care]." Yasmina Vinci, the executive director of Head Start, noted that "everything has its own constituency." As noted in Chapter 3, many of these constituencies hark back to the nineteenth century and early twentieth century when U.S. child care programs began. They are based in part of the class divisions in the development of programs (e.g., educationally based or "care" based) and also stem from the division of Head Start from more custodial care supported by CCDF funding (Rose, 1999).

Most, if not all, advocates for children recognize some of the major limitations of the existing early care and education system that most families of young children face. "We need more of a public outcry. There have been no rallies in recent years. People are so busy just getting by that no one is really interested or able to get involved" (Catherine Graham Hildum). Other advocates, who requested that they not be quoted, noted that a large-scale movement approach had been tried in the past and had not worked. They claimed that the electorate would not support the development of universal policies, and there is simply no public will for such policies. Furthermore, national or state-based child care policy is not currently a union priority. Though the union advocates with whom we spoke recognize the significance of unmet child care needs, at the time of the interviews it had fallen behind health care and the right to organize (Donna Dolan; Sara Lee Todd; Becky Levin). Unions are often important political allies because they are membership organizations that have financial resources and members who vote. This helps feed the lack of political will to address U.S. child care deficits.

Many groups have coalesced around "quality care." Though advocacy groups tend to disagree about the details of what quality care entails, few people question that children in nonparental care should be safe. However, Danielle Ewen is skeptical that we could actually coalesce around national quality care standards given that we do not have national quality standards for K–12 education, even though we have near universal support for public education in the United States. Proponents of quality standards saw them as one of the only politically viable focuses. In many ways, this is a low-cost intervention that would be largely unfunded. Requiring state standards does not necessarily translate into funding the cost of child care, education for early childhood teachers or staff, or the development of additional programs. As noted earlier, the Obama administration seems to be supporting the development of state-based quality rating standards, which may have more success than developing national standards through the portion of CCDBG and Race to the Top funds directed to this purpose.

Conclusion

Though advocates seem to believe that there has been a change in public perception of child care and little opposition to child care centers or government's role in helping poor children access quality care, they remain split in terms of where they believe child care advocacy efforts should focus. Should we try to improve existing programs that primarily benefit the poor? Should we focus on providing information regarding quality programming? Some believe that the first focus should be on services primarily for the poor. Others focus more heavily on the need to promote educational services for three- and four-year-olds. Though some recognize that we need more universal solutions, they believe that we do not have strategies to garner support for these positions. Policy feedback helps to explain why they are constrained by the frames that provide them with their current funding and political salience.

The child care advocacy coalition, if in fact there is a real coalition, has a fragmented focus. The one area where advocates have been unified is in terms of support for poverty-based programs. As a result of the current framing of child care as well as the history and culture of child care policy in the United States, advocates are unlikely to bring about radical change. Though there is no fundamental opposition to the expansion of child care policies in the United States, conservative groups tend to oppose government intervention in social policy, and child care policy falls within that realm. It seems likely that they have not expended much energy fighting against the expansion of child care policy since there has been little effort to formulate universal or more expansive child care policies in the United States.

8

Child Care as a Social Movement

In this chapter, we examine child care as a social movement by looking at the interplay of organizations involved with child care advocacy. In the previous chapter, we provided a more in-depth examination of how different organizational strategies and goals have shaped the conceptualization of child care as a problem and how it has been framed in the political arena. This chapter uses insights from social movement theory as a lens through which to examine the strategic choices of child care advocates. According to Snow, Soule, and Kriesi (2004), social movements are characterized by their actions toward a common agenda or goals, by their outsider political status, and by oppositional or confrontational tactics. As the field of social movement studies has matured and grown, our understanding of what constitutes a social movement has changed, particularly as we have a better understanding of how social movement actors have intersected with changing political and social environments and the multiplicity of targets for change (Levitsky & Banaszak-Holl, 2010). The social movement literature provides a number of insights into what makes a successful movement; some of the key features include the ability to find common ground regarding the definition of, and the appropriate government response to, the problem and the existence of political opportunity (Imig, 2006).

Some scholars have examined how social movement actors can work to create change from within structures of power, when oppositional tactics are not feasible given the political and social climate (Spalter-Roth

& Schreiber, 1995). This not only expands the definition of social movements to include work within existing structures to advance policy issues that challenge mainstream politics, but also alerts us to the risks that such tactics engender. These risks include the alienation of the social movement base who may not wish to work within existing power structures and the danger of member co-optation (Nathanson, 2010; Spalter-Roth & Schreiber, 1995). Such an expanded definition allows us to consider the field of organizations that work toward a more comprehensive child care policy as a social movement. At least since the 1980s, child care advocacy can be characterized largely by insider tactics in which advocates have worked closely with the political establishment and intellectual elites rather than building movements or confrontational tactics. The advantage of using a social movement lens to explore the work of child care policy advocacy organizations is that it allows us to examine the impact of these organizations on the strategies and outcomes of *other* organizations and actors within the field of child care advocacy and how these interactions have helped to shape the parameters of advocacy efforts (Armstrong, 2002).

Social movement theory also directs us to examine the intersection of political and social constraints and opportunities that affect these strategic decisions and outcomes. In Chapter 7, we identified four different policy frames. Despite differences in frames and strategy among the organizations, most identified with a broad vision that would include government support for safe, developmentally appropriate, quality care for young children.

Three main areas emerged as central to respondents' assessment of why a broad-based movement calling for government intervention to address child care does not exist, despite the documented existence of a public child care crisis (Tilly, 2004). First, public perceptions regarding the need for child care support and regulation have changed over time, and there is disagreement about the level of widespread public support for government intervention. Second, advocates have employed different framings of the problems in caring for children that call for different policy responses. Last, these efforts have tended to focus either on early childhood education or means-tested provision of care to low-income working parents with little overlap. These factors combine to thwart broad-based work toward universal child care, despite the ongoing struggles of families with child care needs and the belief on the part of many advocates that such struggles are, in fact, connected and worthy of public attention and resources.

Many of our respondents recognized that U.S. families struggle to find the most appropriate care settings for their children. While most had a chosen focus, they were generally concerned with the combination of child safety, quality of care, and whether children receive age-appropriate stimulation and learning to ensure healthy development. Denise Dowell of the Civil Service Employee's Association (CSEA), a New York affiliate of the American Federation of State, County, and Municipal Employees (AFSCME), viewed the problem through the eyes of a mother and her union that represents both consumers and providers of child care: "The problem is that there is not enough public support for early learning and care. It costs more for parents to send their kids to quality child care programs than it does to send them to community college."

Our respondents characterized the United States child care sector as piecemeal, with no one program meeting all types of needs for everyone. They cited Germany, Europe, federal employee benefits, and the U.S. military, all of which provide more comprehensive care in terms of coverage in a more universal rather than means-tested framework, as prototypes for what *could be*. Although most did not advocate for universal responses to child care concerns, with the exception of prekindergarten initiatives, this was largely due to perceptions of limited resources and political strategy rather than philosophical beliefs about what is needed.

Respondents overwhelmingly believed that opposition to child care in its various forms had grown less vehement and ideological than it was in the past. While several respondents cited gains since the 1970s and encouraging signs from the current administration, most advocates also saw the narrow and competing frameworks, such as early childhood education versus affordable child care, as a product of earlier advocacy and strategic policy work. Their perceptions reflect what is discussed in the social movement framing literature as a strategy that can both advance political causes and simultaneously hamstring nascent movements by limiting the way we identify problems and characterize beneficiaries of ameliorative policies (see Loseke, 1992, on the battered women's movement and Katz, 1989, on early the history of welfare).

Caring for Children as a Common Struggle

The advocates, funders, and researchers in our study believed that most families experience child care struggles of one sort or another, and at least half of them mentioned their own child care struggles or the struggles of people they know. Despite their recognition of the problems of caring for children as nearly universal, most agreed that child care needs have not been framed as a universal problem. Instead, child care advocacy efforts have largely been split along class lines, even while early education and development with a focus on children ages three to five have been more successfully framed as a universal need. Many of the respondents compared the piecemeal or patchwork system of child care fixes to more comprehensive systems in other countries. Becky Levin, lobbyist for AFSCME, noted, "When you look at other countries and how they set up education systems, child care is part of the public system. We've never had that. Even the pieces that we do have are piecemeal. They're only offered to people based on incomes below a certain level. There's never been a perception that everybody needs this; that all families could benefit from this; that all kids could benefit from this. It's just been very splintered from our concept of public education." The splintering itself is viewed as both a result and a cause of the insufficient child care policy solutions.

Our respondents viewed low-income families, in particular, as placed in untenable positions regarding their child care, often struggling to survive in low-wage jobs with little control over hours, sick leave, leave for family emergencies, and job mobility. Their difficulties are compounded by the well-documented lack of affordable, safe, accessible, and educationally appropriate child care (including after-school care for older children) arrangements. For reasons of dire need amid perceived resource limitations, as well as for advocacy strategy, many of the respondents focused on care for young children of low-income families. Adele Robinson, associate executive director of the National Association for the Education of Young Children (NAEYC), put the choices starkly:

> What we have found is that everybody understands that a lot of people need child care, whether it's that they are forced to go back to work for their families' budgets or they want to go back to work. The idea of universal support for child care is a little different. I would say that we are cognizant that the cost of universal child care, starting with babies, regardless of your income, probably makes it a nonstarter conversation. So, like, should Bill Gates get a voucher for his kid? However, we would say that a goal is universally-available free preschool. We would say threes and fours. We don't think the public is ready for this other conversation. We can't even get the threes, let alone the fours, funded.

However, child care is a much more slippery slope, with most U.S. families falling somewhere in between Bill Gates and the low-income families that are currently eligible for assistance. Becky Levin of AFSCME compared the conversation to public education for children in grades kindergarten through twelve, where no one would even consider asking whether or not it should be universal, regardless of need. The comparison of these positions underscores the importance of framing, and how this shapes the images that will resonate with policymakers and the public. Some organizations ally themselves with related issues that have successfully captured public support. This has been the tactic of early education activists who have drawn inspiration from the K–12 successes. These advocates actively promote the public's association of early education with school-age programs, which have long been accepted as permanent institutions worthy of support.

Lack of Political Will?

A number of respondents noted that attention to the needs of families, especially families with young children, has progressed significantly since the inception of advocacy campaigns of the 1970s. Helen Blank, director of leadership and public policy at the Women's Law Center, is considered by many to have the most comprehensive historical perspective on child care among our advocate respondents and informants. Blank remembered the earlier years of the movement as characterized by more grassroots agitation and confrontational political tactics. She noted that things have progressed from when people "walked around the Senate Office Buildings with baby carriages when we were trying to pass the child care bill," referring to a strategy of Phyllis Schlafly, who brought a baby carriage to the Senate to suggest that children would be harmed by the universal child care bill that Nixon ultimately vetoed. "[Nixon's] veto message was that [the bill that would put Head Start into child care] will 'Sovietize' the American family. And so it wasn't the time; we didn't have e-mail, we didn't have fax, but people on the right wing just bombarded their members of Congress with phone calls every time you raised child care up until the 80s, and you couldn't move it. It got stuck—it's a small fringe issue." Blank believes that since the 1980s, there has been progress in the way that Congress and the public have viewed government's role in helping families care for children, noting that "we got the child care bill signed under George Bush the first." This may be in part, as the quote above suggests, due to better means of organizing and reaching out. The advent of the Internet, blogs, and other social media, which helped to bring about organizations such as Momsrising, has made it possible for greater numbers of people to get their message out whether or not they can literally go to the streets. It may be that the issue was framed as that of less eligibility. The government was really helping only the very poor, and doing so only to make it possible for low-income mothers to work so as to cut the welfare rolls.

The majority of our respondents also noted greater receptivity to women working outside the home, especially low-income and middle-income women. As the statistics we cited earlier in this book demonstrate, there has been a dramatic increase in mothers of young children working outside the home for longer hours out of choice or necessity. This has served to remove the stigma of mothers' employment outside the home. Mothers' paid employment is now more likely to be viewed as a norm and thus considered a regular part of the political and economic landscape rather than an aberration. Denise Dowell of CSEA, who, when interviewed, had been working in the field of child care advocacy for nearly thirty years, noted what she called "the changing socioeconomic political climate."

> When I started doing this, people were still at odds about whether women should work, let alone kids should be in child care. And so much has changed. I think nowadays it's just commonly accepted and if there are two parents in a family—and many families don't have two parents—they are working and have to work to afford the basics. I think there are also these huge changes that have taken place in terms of the number of hours that people work. Many more families have to juggle nontraditional hour jobs. So there really is this kind of crisis and I think on some level that the case for parents and families having access and being able to afford quality early learning and care is—there's more of an understanding and an acceptance; it's more relevant.

Because of the greater acceptance and acknowledgment of women's paid employment, advocates no longer have to start advocating for child care policies by trying to persuade policymakers and potential supporters and opponents that women, many of whom are mothers, do and will continue to be employed outside the home.

Changing attitudes about mothers' employment in the paid labor force and the relationship between child care and child development may have made opposition to child care support less explicit or ideological than it once was. Adele Robinson of the NAEYC, however, explained that lack of opposition does not necessarily mean support. While it may be currently unpopular to oppose programs that benefit families and children, there is also very little political will to *actively support* such programs. She noted the difference between lip service and real support that would, in fact, make a difference. "I mean my goal is for every policymaker and governor to say, 'I'm looking at this budget. What does it do for kids and families?' I think how we get there, and you can't just do a straight percentage, because we're embedded in things like Medicaid and TANF that aren't just children. But to me it's sort of like when the slogan 'Who's for kids and who's just kidding' was with the tobacco campaign—we don't have that yet. We haven't figured that out yet." Nancy Kolbin, executive director of the Center for Children's Initiatives, voiced similar sentiments in her discussion of the FMLA: "We sort of give some lip service to family leave, but we don't really make it possible for most families, because we don't pay for it." She believes that if these policies were really designed to help families, they would be more widely available and would have been designed so that it would be more viable for eligible employees to take advantage of them. The way that they are set up reveals a lack of solid understanding of the needs and support for families and children. Such policies show that while there may not be outright hostility to the needs of families with young children, support is anemic at best and often based on a limited understanding of the dilemmas that families *actually* face.

Another change that was noted by some respondents is a better understanding of childhood development and the importance, backed by research, of getting a good start in life as a reason for broader potential public support for affordable quality child care. Though there were some data to support the need for quality, affordable care in the 1970s, in the past forty years there has been substantial new research that has corroborated the findings of earlier studies, some of which we have cited earlier. As we described in Chapter 6, economists have been able to use complex modeling to prove that the cost of quality child care provides a long-term economic/benefit to society. In addition, neuroscientists have been able to demonstrate the influence of a child's care experience on the brain (Kirp, 2007; Schonkoff & Phillips, 2000). This has fed the debate over whether programs should be universal or targeted.

Many advocates believe that the U.S. public is still ambivalent about what is the optimal way of caring for young children, which hinders broad-based child care advocacy. Kolbin saw the lack of real support as a lack of commitment to the needs of families:

> We don't have a commitment to supporting families of young children. And so some families are eligible some of the times for some things depending on where they're looking; we're very judgmental about child care and it's almost gotten a bad rep. We get into the battles of should parents be home or should they be at work. I think that, we—because of the ways that we've structured funding—how parents even know what's available, what they're eligible for; it's just not a system of supports designed to really support what families need. And it's not any one thing that families need at any point in time.

Whatever their focus or position, nearly all of our respondents agreed that current U.S. child care policy is woefully out of step with the needs of families. For Robinson, Kolbin, and other respondents who noted the lack of overt opposition to women's paid employment, this may be a start. However, it is clearly not sufficient. For the more pessimistic advocates, the real test of support is whether or not policies are actually created and adequately financed. It may be impossible to determine whether the incremental rate of change in child care policy is due to apathy or the prioritization of other justifiably important concerns (such as health care or the Great Recession). They may also be the result or powerful opposition that uses tactics that are less visible to the public, as our discussion of campaign finance suggests. Social movement theory underscores the importance of considering the entire social movement field in creating resonant frames to champion a cause. This broader social movement field includes organization that may work in opposition to advocates. It also includes those who are not yet committed but may be swayed in support of comprehensive child care (Evans, 1997).

Strategies and Considerations in Constructing
Child Care as a Salient Political Issue

Most political advocates are strategists. This means that they have to make practical decisions in order to advance agendas that often fall short of their more utopian visions and long-term goals. Our respondents often felt forced to make difficult choices in their advocacy efforts, and provided a number of different reasons for their strategic assessments. A number of our respondents pointed to the size and scope of child care concerns as overwhelming, making prioritization a necessity. The diversity of concerns wrapped up within child care, from affordability to quality to accessibility to educational components, was viewed as problematic. Child care debates are also complicated by the fact that child care was viewed by many advocates as part of the fiercely protected private sphere, in terms of both the providers who are private rather than government entities and the fact that in the United States raising children is considered to be a deeply personal matter. Danielle Ewen gives a sense of the complexity and expense of child care that make it a difficult political issue to frame:

> I think it's hard for us to think about [child care] as a state responsibility. I think it's also the notion that child care is a private business, and how do you intervene in a private business that is all about interacting with babies? You know, it's not about customer service writ large, or building a building and making sure you follow a bunch of codes. It's telling somebody they have to pick up a baby and talk to it every day. That's much more difficult to think about. It's also enormously expensive to do, right? And that's scary. I mean the health care debate is the biggest thing we've done in a really long time. But we did the child care groups that I talked about before, spent two years writing down a

vision for change in child care. And we costed it out and it came to $183 billion over five years. That's a lot of money. It's not a lot of money in the current environment of universal health care which is just under $1 trillion, but it's a lot of money. And given that the current investment is $5 billion for the subsidy program and $7 billion for Head Start, we're pretty far away from $183 billion. So the growth, the huge need to really fill the gaps is daunting.

The picture that Ewen paints adds to the complexity and the enormous cost of a broad-based child care policy response. The difficulty of funding child care at an adequate level deters many advocates from working toward universal child care; they are discouraged by the perceived infeasibility and so will often prefer to take on smaller chunks of the problem where they perceive a greater likelihood of success. While all respondents believed that strategic advocacy was necessary, there was disagreement about whether existing strategies rooted in historic and current assessments of the child care and early education advocacy organizations had benefited the movement.

Organizational strategies are influenced and sometimes constrained by the issue frames that they have created, funding streams, and existing ties with political allies inside and outside of government (e.g., policy feedback). The largest concern centered around whether the separation of related concerns, specifically education and child care, which was often negatively characterized as "babysitting," had been a good or a bad strategy for U.S. families. Lauren Hogan, policy director for the National Black Child Development Institute (NBCDI), used the term "early care and education" "because I think the dual purpose of child care is . . . a work support, it is a place where children are cared for while their parents are working, and it is also a place where children are learning and being prepared for school. And both of those things are incredibly important." She, like many others with whom we spoke, does not use the term "child care," which she said "has the potential to force people into seeing it as a place to just leave your kids during the day."

One respondent who focused on child care providers and standards, when asked to identify her opponents, jokingly referred to the "early education" folks. While this respondent spoke humorously, other respondents also saw the separation as particularly detrimental either to a broad-based child care movement or as competition for child care that was focused more on the needs of working parents rather than on education of children. In order to unite middle- and upper-income families with lower-income parents, they must perceive a common interest that is harder to develop when those with low incomes are recipients of poverty-based programs that are largely irrelevant to those in the middle class. Forming alliances is made harder with the division between work-related child care advocates and those who focus on early education. Negative connotations regarding custodial child care initiatives make it strategically beneficial for advocacy organizations focusing on early childhood to distance themselves from groups that might otherwise be logical allies.

Competing priorities among organizations, between advocates and funders, and between elite and grassroots activists have been noted in the social movement literature (Brulle & Jenkins, 2005; Hoffman, 2003). Child care organizations show similar struggles. While Hogan worried about earlier priorities eclipsing future possibilities, some of our respondents viewed prioritizing and separation of child care components as a necessary and successful tactic. Libby Doggett, deputy director of the Pew Charitable Trust's Center on the States, was one proponent of what Catherine Graham Hildum, consultant to a philanthropic consortium, the First Five Years Fund, referred to as a "laser-beam" effect. While Doggett and others believed that "visioning" needs to be expansive, it was her hope that organizations working toward child care options would continue to mount narrowly focused advocacy campaigns:

> Other funders realize that a focused approach is best, and that they would then say, you know, "help us fund a pre-K campaign" instead of a birth to five campaign. You may not know, but I'm actually married to a legislator . . . and I see his eyes glaze over when people come up and say, "You

know, we need to do this and this and this this year" in the environment
or in education or in health. And it's just so much easier if you have one or
two things—you can be very, very clear about what those are. And I'd like
to see that continue to happen. Yeah, I'm happy if a state will just say, or
advocates will say: "You know, what we want to do is we want to get health
care for each child or we want to get full-day kindergarten, or we want
to get a [quality rating] system that's well-funded that really will raise the
quality for, you know, 20 percent of our infants and toddlers." But I think
we have to have those clear goals, but not a whole slew of them. We have a
slew on the visioning, but for a legislative agenda it has to be very limited.

Doggett's experiences led her to believe that advocates can capture only
a limited amount of legislative and public attention and therefore only
narrowly focused and specific requests stand a chance in the competitive
policy arena.

On the other hand, strategic concerns also led to difficult decisions
around whether and when to eschew the concerns of specific constituencies for the broader good, which could leave some dissension. Lauren Hogan of NBCDI and Erika Beltran, a senior policy analyst at the
National Council of La Raza, which represents the interests of Latino
constituents, both said that the interests of their constituents were often
overlooked or not prioritized. These include racial and cultural com-
petency as part of any standards and concern about whether child care
mandates might narrow types of child care options available to the disproportionately low-income families among their constituent populations. For example, Beltran noted the difficulties her organization faced
when working with advocates who might ask her to forgo interests that
were of particular importance to her for a more general good, even if
this might ultimately mitigate the value of the very policy for which they
had sought to advocate. "[In the California campaign for universal pre-
school] our advocates and our focus was really looking at making sure
that bilingual services would be provided as part of that universal preschool approach. And . . . people perceived it as being off message. And

therefore people were more hesitant to partner with our affiliates or to really see them as a partner. I think there was a lot of tension. They would tell us 'could you please hold off on that? Can we not have that conversation right now? That is not important right now.'" This same tension also occurs for La Raza at the national level, where Beltran noted "it is always kind of a struggle or kind of a tension to remind people that yes there is a broader message, but the details are just as important as that broader message we are promoting." When such sacrifices accumulate they can be frustrating, especially if concerns of the same groups continue to be excluded from what is considered to be a "larger good."

Busy legislators and an inattentive public are not the only stakeholders whom child care advocates consider in their strategic equations. Danielle Ewen was one of the many respondents who spoke of the important and often unrecognized role of the funding community as a limiting factor in the creation of a broad-based child care movement: "We have to be careful what we do with the money, and certain funders have priorities. So the famous one obviously in early childhood is that for the last five years, Pew has been funding this major pre-K initiative to push for universal pre-K for four-year-olds. So if you want their money, you have to agree that that's your agenda. . . . I'm trying to get quality care for children birth through school entry and beyond, actually. So while I think pre-K is an important part of building this position, my priority is not their priority so I don't have Pew funding, for example." When funders, such as Doggett's organization, believe in a laser-beam strategy or have a particular priority out of a substantive vision, this will shape the advocacy field.

As in campaign financing, funding can skew the advocacy field in ways that may not align with the visions or needs of a broader public or advocacy organizations (Brulle & Jenkins, 2005; Covington, 2001). While some advocates viewed this situation with concern, others pointed to the important role of funding in raising awareness and providing a coherent and persistent public message. Eric Karolak, executive director of the Early Care and Education Consortium, saw private foundations as potential leaders of the child care movement:

I think it's really important to tune into the role of foundations. Thought leaders, you might call them. They have smart people and they have money. And so what priority they place on child care as opposed to something else, makes an enormous difference because they fund folks to do; they have such derivative impact; they fund folks to do stuff. When the Casey Foundation . . . for example, say [that] a key priority is third grade reading scores . . . key metrics, right? Well that has an implication then for how we think about everything, including what the purpose, goal behind child care would be. Or how to design something, right? So foundations are thought leaders.

Advocacy organizations with a broader or even slightly different vision might shape their agenda in order to garner support or forego support and find themselves unable to fund their efforts when funders are not behind their vision. This is particularly true when funders themselves are focused on a particular aspect of child care or education and want to use their grant-making capacity to steer and shape the agenda. While some child care advocacy organizations see such targeted funding streams as limiting, others see a big role for funders to play in organizing concerted efforts that lead to successful and more coordinated campaigns.

Encouraging Signs?

Yasmina Vinci, the executive director of Head Start, noted more cohesion between advocacy groups than there had been in the past. She suggested that perhaps because of the hopefulness that many felt around the current administration's sentiments toward child care, there was less of a need to fight over scarce resources. Other advocates remained skeptical about the prospect of more comprehensive and inclusive child care policy. Although everyone has been a child, not everyone has children over their life course. Some who have had children but are no longer in the business of child rearing may no longer connect to the need for child care. Adele Robinson of NAEYC pointed out that even basic needs that everyone would see as universal, such as health care or food security, do not always fare well on the policy agenda. For her, this does not auger well for child care policy:

> People can't say, "oh, of course everybody uses child care." . . . [E]ven [in] those areas are some of the most fundamental basics that everybody can understand: everybody's going to be sick someday in their life and everybody understands what it would mean to miss many meals—people don't yet have that universal feeling around early childhood. I think we're getting better at explaining that even if you don't benefit, why you should support it. Sort of like only 25 percent of the taxpayers have a child birth [age]—K through twelve. Well, actually, under twenty-five I think. So, there are a lot of people who don't have children who don't go through the public schools and they're like, "why should I have to pay taxes?" But that's not a growing enough voice for policymakers to feel differently about it . . . health care and hunger are still being debated in terms of spending? It's amazing, you know?

Despite the difficulties they have faced, nearly all of our respondents noted some successes over time. About half of them offered what some called "encouraging signs" in the current political landscape and most recently from the Obama administration. Catherine Graham Hildum believed that there is more openness to child care than in the past as more women have entered the workforce by choice or need: "The one example I'm thinking of is former [Republican] Senator Ted Stevens [of Alaska] introduced two bills on paid family leave in the 110th Congress. Like-what? But he really came at it from his daughter's perspective." Hildum's organization is self-described as bipartisan, although she noted it is often perceived as liberal. She and the organization's constituent members, who were relatively new to child care advocacy at the federal level at the time of the interviews, believed that child care could cut across political parties in its appeal to widespread need and assistance to a sympathetic constituency. This was also one of the tactics espoused by Momsrising, a grassroots organization that represents the perspectives of mothers across a range of concerns, including child care. Sarah Francis said that Momsrising, focusing primarily at the local level but also working at the national level, "collect[s] stories from members as a part of campaign because legislators do not recognize care [problems] families face—can't afford or cannot find and if they could, they could not afford it." Like Hildum, Francis believes that legislators are more likely to be moved to act on child care if they are able to conceive of the problems and associate faces and stories with the policy that otherwise may seem remote from their own experience.

Dana Friedman, president of the Early Years Institute, was similarly encouraged by signs of a more comprehensive vision at the federal level of what it takes to support children and families. She noted, "The Early Childhood Advisory Committee was mandated by Obama as part of the Head Start legislation. He said, 'I want every state to have an Early Childhood Advisory Committee that's really trying to build and bring together mental health, health, welfare, child care, et cetera under one umbrella.'" Many advocates do not believe that piecemeal solutions can adequately address the needs of most families. Though they may be necessary for strategic reasons, they are inadequate in terms of both scope and sustainability of gains over time.

Libby Doggett described the Pew Foundation's attempts to bridge some of the gaps that have reinforced the negative consequences of strategic bifurcation of early education and care.

[I]t was very deliberate to actually frame this as an education initiative rather than a child care initiative. And even though you're using the word "caring," I think there is a dichotomy in this field between education and care, and you hear, you know, early education care, early care and education. Then if the child care field, uh, sees that someone's talking about "learning," they think they're left out. I think there's still problems there. What I also learned more recently is—there's a long standing kind of animosity between the early education field—broadly, your caring field—and

the K through twelve field—the education field. And we've tried to actually—at Pew and at Pre-K Now—before coming to Pew, tried to be the
bridge between those two groups.

According to Nancy Kolbin of the Center for Children's Initiatives,
comprehensive framing that targets a broader array of child care needs
for a larger cross-section of the U.S. population not only is helpful for
families, but should be framed as a societal investment in the future: "I
think now we have an administration that's much more attuned to understanding the importance of the early years and investments and looking
at this as a system." There has also been renewed public attention to
work-life strains and efforts to reshape discourse around family concerns.
Journalist and political activist Maria Shriver, in collaboration with the
Center for American Progress,[1] issued "The Shriver Report: A Woman's
Nation Changes Everything" reporting on the status of women in the
United States. The widely covered Shriver Report explored work-life balance concerns facing families now that fully half or more of the U.S. labor
force is made up of women. This report combined the insights of leading
academics, journalists, researchers, and policy advocates with comments
from the American public to describe changes to U.S. families and workplaces and the way they interact. It noted the work-life strains that are
felt in the United States for both men and women as a result of women's
large-scale entry into the workforce and the need to increase flexibility
in the workplace to accommodate family responsibility (Shriver & Center for American Progress, 2009). Some people have advocated for the
inclusion of child care as part of the broader care movement that recognizes unpaid and paid care provided to others across population groups
such as the elderly, children, and those with short- or long-term illnesses
(Duffy, 2010).

As we have seen in the prior chapters, the hope for inroads to more
comprehensive child care policy has been borne out to some extent in the
form of increasing funding for low-income child care and quality-rating
systems. Some policymakers have publicly taken up the cause. Nancy

Pelosi (D-CA), a rare congressional advocate for child care, noted that "at the top of her to-do list, she says, will be 'doing for child care what we did for health-care reform'—pushing comprehensive change." Pelosi admits that she is stumped by the lack of progress on child care in the political arena: "One of the great pieces of unfinished business is high-quality child care; I wonder why we just can't do that" (Henneberger, 2011). Anemic support for child care at a time when need continues to increase may be largely due to the economic downturn, which worsened considerably after our interviews. "It is a challenging and ironic time," Helen Blank said, explaining that programs are being asked to increase quality but not given the resources with which to do it. At the same time, "things are moving backward in terms of access." There are fewer resources overall, and therefore fewer people are eligible for assistance. As a result, many communities are having trouble sustaining child care. In addition, there are an increasing number of low-wage jobs with inconsistent hours and nontraditional work schedules, which means that there is an expanding need for nontraditional hours of care.

Many protective U.S. social policies grew out of need that arose in challenging times. Blank pointed out that the history of child care is rife with examples of times that were not right for prioritizing child care, noting that "there is always some reason not to fund child care." This begs the question of what it takes to prioritize child care, as there will always be hurdles, even if the substance and shape of these obstacles change over time. Lack of broad-based social mobilization may also mean that the child care movement may not be poised to take advantage of the more acute need arising from the current economic downturn.

What Do Past Strategic Decisions and Current Assessments Mean for a Concerted Child Care Effort?

One question we may ask, given the different policy priorities of the respondents, is whether a child care movement exists. At what point are advocacy organizations' goals so divergent as to raise the question,

"Is there is a common vision?" We believe that it is fruitful to view the child care advocacy organizations as a potential movement for several reasons. Many of them do see themselves as connected, if not in their overall vision, then in the impact that the work of one group has on the others (negative and positive). Most respondents believed that if we were to solve the problem of caring for children through comprehensive strategies that cut across not only socioeconomic strata but also the age of the child, forms of caring, and types of parental employment, the agendas of all groups would be met. This is, in fact, the case in the examples provided by respondents of their more utopian visions that included other countries and benefits systems designed for U.S. federal government employees and military personnel. The existence of alternative, inclusive conceptions of child care is another reason to envision the existence of a movement with such a broad agenda.

Benford (1993, p. 679) identified "frame resonance" as a particularly thorny problem for social movements. Child care advocacy organizations may engage in conflict around what they perceive as the framing that will most likely resonate with the public and policymakers, and they may disagree over when a particular framing, despite its resonance, compromises movement integrity and goals. Certain framings will also privilege some groups over others, and can cause some groups to distance themselves from the movement or from other movement organizations. Movement organizations engaged in mainstream policy advocacy for the provision of care for children seem to be divided less by their tools or forms of activism, and more on what issues should be prioritized for both strategic and philosophical reasons. Where they differed markedly is on the framing of the problem to prioritize educational content or caretaking, particularly for children from low-income families, resulting in a division of constituencies and supporters. Similar to what Levitsky (2005) found in her study of LGBT social movement organizations (SMOs) in Chicago, while there was widespread respect for the work of a broad array of SMOs, the SMOs that represented less popular positions often felt sidelined or marginalized.

For example, the derogatory views of child care programs as "babysit-ting" that was mainly for low-income families were seen as separate from early education programs. This reinforced distinctions between the needs of low-income parents and the concerns of *all* U.S. families. While many of the organizations agree on the need to be strategic, it is clear that some prefer to separate goals while others believe in a more unified vision seeking more comprehensive care for a broader range of constituents, including providers and consumers of child care across income. As our respondents note, funding may also provide an obsta-cle to creating a common agenda. Child care funding efforts seem to have some of the pitfalls noted with other progressive funding streams, including fragmentation and short-term foundation funding as well as lack of a unified agenda, as evidenced by the laser-beam strategy approach noted by some (Miller-Cribbs, Cagle, Natale, & Cummings, 2010). According to Covington (2001), the majority of funding for chil-dren's issues tends to be channeled to interventions and programming rather than constituency building and advocacy.

Myra Marx Ferree (2003) points out that although the strategic con-cerns of frame resonance can be a powerful pull for many advocates who choose to adopt dominant narratives for tactical reasons, these strategy concerns do not *have to* dominate advocates' efforts. In an examina-tion of abortion rights activists in Germany and the United States, Feree showed how efforts in both countries were influenced by pivotal court decisions that set the framing for the debate. Despite a trend to frame the issues in accordance with perceived political opportunity, there were still "radical" advocates in both countries who continued to resist politically expedient framing in favor of what they saw as a more idealistic narra-tive. It is clear that advocates must make these choices.

The price of bending to frame resonance is not always clear, even in hindsight, nor is its relationship toward continued radical advocacy, which seeks fundamental changes that are not always acceptable to policymakers or the general public. Mainstream advocacy that does not challenge dominant framing can also have powerful implications.

Advocates often have to make objectively difficult choices. However, in some instances, a focus on political expediency can be viewed as self-serving. One's perspective on the framing choices made in light of perceived political constraints and opportunities is also likely influenced by whether one's interests have been "sacrificed" for a larger "good" through the use of expedient framing, as advocates representing minority child care interests in our study perceive to be the case. It is also influenced by whether one is a part of a group whose needs have been met through strategic framing, as some of the early education advocates have been viewed by those more interested in universal child care policies.

While this is a common problem that has appeared throughout history (Should the women's movement ally themselves with lesbian women? Should mother's pensions be for all or only "deserving" widows?), what we find most striking about child care is that it affects so many families (see Shriver & Center for American Progress, 2009). Everyone is, at one time, a child and thus a dependent. We know that growing numbers of U.S. women are in the workforce. We know that there is simply not enough quality child care, at the right hours, and that even families who can afford child care struggle to meet child care needs. Child care is a concern that cuts across race, gender, political orientation, and socio-economic status. It appears that some child care advocacy organizations, particularly those that are most marginalized, are chafing against the once-strategic decisions and seeking reconsideration. It remains to be seen, however, whether encouraging signs of a more unified vision are sufficiently compelling for a large enough sector of the advocacy groups to risk losing the benefits of a focused approach. It is also not clear whether the relatively privileged organizations that represent more popular constituents using highly resonant frames, such as the need for early education, will be willing to abdicate some of their strategic privilege to join themselves with more marginalized organizations, such as those that focus on the care needs of young children (ages zero to three) and their families. Organizations that have made important strides for their constituents may be understandably reluctant to jeopardize hard-won gains, particularly in a precarious fiscal climate.

Nearly all respondents are committed to the goal of keeping children safe while their parents work and promoting early childhood. There was philosophical agreement on these points across the board, including among some unlikely champions who may otherwise be considered conservative in their outlook. Although our advocates noted that there are some vocal opponents who were not willing to engage in dialogue around the topics of concern to early childhood advocates, these were largely considered "fringe." Opposition to child care and early education is "soft opposition." Some of the respondents indicated that while there was little philosophical opposition to supporting families and children, there was also little active support. It might be harder to galvanize movement support when there are no good targets to challenge.

This second type of opposition comes both from within the movement of advocates and from outside. Strategizing to set priorities has, in the field of advocacy around child care policies, turned some potential allies into competitors, even though they are not opponents. While they do not campaign in active opposition, and will also support the idea of a broader agenda, many are critical of activists whom they see as asking for too many things at once or, alternatively, who aim for support of one program instead of another. Advocates are competing over small slices of the policy and funding pie rather than seeking to reframe the public debate to garner support for a larger pie. As we have shown, gains to some organizations may come at the expense of other organizations. Expanding the frame may appear to be a strategic mistake for child care advocacy organizations that currently enjoy a privileged or favored status relative to other child care advocacy organizations. Revised agendas can also endanger alliances that all organizations, regardless of their relative status or popularity, have made with particular constituencies, such as advocates for low-income families or business alliances. It appears that the child care advocacy organizations are at a possible crossroads, where there are newly existent political opportunities that may create fertile ground for a more broad-based movement; however, this is coming at a time when the U.S. economy is weak and new social programs are suspect.

Paul Sabatier and Hank Jenkins-Smith's work in the early 1990s set up a framework for understanding advocacy coalitions (Sabatier & Jenkins-Smith, 1993). They and others since have used this framework to identify how "people mobilize, maintain, and act in advocacy coalitions" (Weible et al., 2011). Their policy framework includes social and cultural values, the basic attributes of the problem being identified, and external events such as changes in socioeconomic conditions, changes in public opinion, and changes in government or other policy subsystems. Long-term coalition structures include the degree of consensus regarding needed policy change, openness of the political system, and overlapping societal "cleavages." Child care advocacy efforts have been plagued by difficulties on nearly all of these fronts, which might explain the lack of coalescence needed to mobilize a broad-based social movement. All of these factors influence the extent to which advocacy coalitions are able to affect government authorities and ultimately cause policy change (Weible et al., 2011).

Child care advocacy groups are trying to respond to perceived political shifts and public resonance around child care. The Institute for Women's Policy Research recently reported that "likely voters overwhelmingly support paid leave for family care and child birth, quality and affordable child care, paid sick days, a right to request a flexible schedule, a right to refuse overtime, and a higher minimum wage" (Dobuzinskis, 2010, p. 1). Prentice (2009) indicates that business interest in the economic importance of child care is also an indication of a broader constituency. At the same time, she notes that business alliances might shift the kind and scope of child care policies for which the constituency will likely advocate. A recent report funded by the Annie E. Casey Foundation written by two prominent policy advocates calls for an examination of the problem of child care across socioeconomic strata to both highlight and advocate for comprehensive policies (Williams & Boushey, 2010). These are indications of potential alliances and the search for a common definition and framing of the problem—all of which are necessary to the formation of a broad-based social movement, even as they may not be sufficient.

One of the most important challenges that seemed to come out of our data is the apparent contradiction between what seems to be a ubiquitous need and the insufficient public demand for government intervention to meet this need (as differentiated from stories of hardship and triumph). History shows us that grassroots activism has been a crucial component for the adoption of policies to benefit children and families; a review of the recent policy landscape shows us that this has been one of the biggest challenges to contemporary efforts (Imig, 2001). This missing component to much of today's efforts is what we recognize as a *movement*. Many people complain; many people have child care problems. Many organizations have been educating, researching, advocating, and lobbying for years. However, child care still seems to be stuck in a place where it is a not considered by enough people to be a social problem worthy of public investment and government intervention. In 2001, an edited volume by the Urban Institute tackled the limited demand for U.S. public policy to address the needs of children and families more broadly. Several authors in this volume cite organizational disconnects from grassroots and local constituencies, as well as the political process, as hurdles to mobilizing around the needs of children and families. De Vita, Mosher-Williams, and Stengel (2001) examined child advocacy organizations and found that although many exist, they are not spread evenly geographically, with more per capita organizations in the Northeast than in the South, for example. Many more of the organizations focus on direct service rather than advocacy. While these provide very important resources to children, families, and community, they do little to foster a broader public movement or to shine a light, let alone address, systemic problems that U.S. families face such as declining resources in cities, workplace policies, and wages. Last, many of these organizations are small and do not have the deep pockets necessary for large-scale advocacy efforts even at the state level. Those organizations that do engage in advocacy, like other public interest groups, are increasingly professional rather than membership or constituency based. According to Skocpol and Dickert (2001), "In the past, the needs of children or families were most visibly and consistently addressed by women's voluntary membership associations. White and African-American women addressed children's upbringing and the needs of families through church-connected groups, the female auxiliaries of unions and fraternal brotherhoods, and a wide variety of moral-reform crusades" (p. 141). With the increased participation of women in the paid workforce, these groups have shrunk in both size and their ability to mobilize.

Philanthropic funding patterns and practices have also separated organizations and their activities from broad-based constituencies. One study of child-directed philanthropic funding found that funding sources often operate from the top down and tend not to be redistributional or focused on public policy activities. The bulk of funding goes toward basic and applied research. Existing funding largely ignores structural issues. Moreover, there has been little funding to build local constituent support around family and child policy (Covington, 2001). Philanthropic organizations often mistrust the general public and grassroots activities.

In a 2002 article in the *American Prospect* in which Robert Kuttner observed a right-wing conservative philanthropy conference, he cites a liberal funder who attended the meeting and "observed that liberal funders would never speak a language of movement building. 'We promote policies piecemeal,' . . . but we don't think of it as building a progressive movement" (Kuttner, 2002, p. 3). He noted that "mainstream foundations have a tradition of emphasizing research and reform. Often, the social change goals are impeccably liberal—empower the poor, clean up the environment, improve the welfare of children—but the political dimension leaves many senior foundation executives uneasy" (Kuttner, 2002, p. 3). According to Kuttner, the idea behind this "harkens back to the Progressive Era conceit that social problems have technical solutions" (Kuttner, 2002, p. 3).

A study of the influence of evangelical Christianity and the influence of conservative philanthropy confirms that liberal funders are spending money on trying to find technical solutions rather than building a movement or advancing their political agenda (Russell, 2005). In the United States, child care advocates have historically been liberals who have put forth positions that are largely cost-benefit-related rather than value-based. In fact, Rose (2010) suggests that the rationale for developing universal pre-K should rest on more than the results of research from experimental programs, because large-scale programs may be unable to replicate these results. Inflated promises of the 1960s that education programs, including Head Start, could inoculate children against the problems associated with poverty led to significant backlash. According to Rose (2010), pre-K programs must be added in concert with other antipoverty and family support programs such as early childhood programs, public health, and nutrition programs as well as paid leave for parents. There is a "need to conceive of different early education programs as parts of a whole rather than as separate items vying for the same scarce resources" (p. 228).

For example, the Birth to Five Policy Alliance, a group supported by many of the major donors who support organizations to improve the options for children in the United States, including more expansive, high-quality child care. The group "invests in three strategies: strategic and broad-based leadership to build new champions for early childhood policy" by investing "in activities to inform policy and budget debates and decisions" "state-based advocacy, and knowledge development and dissemination including research and policy analysis" (http://birthto-fivepolicy.org/AboutUs/tabid/59/Default.aspx). This is consistent with the way in which liberal funders have traditionally operated. They have focused on research dissemination and policy analysis, believing that arguing the logic of expanding or developing new programs from economic perspectives is more persuasive than focusing on movement building. In contrast, conservative funders have been more flexible with their resources, often supporting organizations without requiring that they apply for funding on a regular basis. The requirement that groups apply for funding on a short-term basis, which is the norm for liberal organizational funders, and show short-term successes limits their ability to focus on longer-term social-movement-building solutions. Philanthropic child care funding streams have also focused largely on local interventions rather than political advocacy or movement building (Covington, 2001). Conservative, antigovernment groups have spent large amounts of money to support candidates who have helped create an ethos that government spending is harmful. The development of a high-quality system of early child care and education may require a change in cultural beliefs about the appropriate role of government in the United States.

Echoing Pew's "laser-beam approach," the small proportion of philanthropic funding in the area of children and families that does go toward advocacy is often for work on a single issue and employs a single strategy. According to Covington, this may weaken advocacy efforts overall and constrain advocates' efforts to mobilize: "[I]t is not hard to draw at least some tentative conclusions about how foundations reinforce, if not create, some of the acknowledged weaknesses or limitations of the children's movement. What are those criticisms? They include the failure to develop a politically mobilized constituency for children, the lack of an overarching children's policy agenda, and relatively weak or unsophisticated efforts to target legislative leaders in the policy change process" (Covington, 2001, p. 61). All of the strategies that our respondents outlined have advantages; they also come with a price. To what extent is this the right time to revisit these choices to begin to garner more broad-based and politically effective support for child care and other child- and family-friendly policies (Imig, 2006)?

We have indicated here that the inability of social movements to coalesce around broad-based child care demands has a self-perpetuating effect. The lack of political receptivity and political opportunity has reinforced splits among organizations in the field of child care policy. In order to achieve a more universal policy, there may need to be a broader social movement in support of a more expansive role for government into which child care may fall. Furthermore, existing groups must remain open to working with less established groups that may not wish to make short-term political gains at the expense of the inability to focus on longer-term goals.

Conclusion

In this chapter, we have presented the viewpoints and strategies of representatives of a diverse group of organizations that advocate for child care. All are members of larger coalitions and often collaborate with other groups in their advocacy efforts. The lack of coalescence seems more nuanced than is generally portrayed, and upon reflecting on impediments, advocates portray less of an "us versus them" perspective than might be suggested by the widespread need for child care and the emergence of potentially more inclusive policy frameworks. Examining child care policy through a social movement lens highlights some of the organizational, contextual, and strategic factors that contribute to how U.S. child care policy has moved forward in a way that is slow, fragmented, and fails to meet the needs of many.

Our data provide a lens on the perspectives of advocates on the child care advocacy movement at what some might view as a crossroads. The ability of this movement to make major progress relies not only on how advocates position themselves but also on the larger sociopolitical context in which they are advocating. The current economic crisis could be seen as a window of opportunity, or could continue to be seen as a reason to limit spending on programs such as those that support child care. Economic stimulus programs could be designed to educate and employ people as child care workers. Child care workers need adequate training as well as living wages. Not everyone can provide quality care for children. Financial benefits could be provided to parents to care for their own children in such a way that women in relationships who chose not to work are not unduly burdened if they become single after having invested years caring for children. This would effectively reduce the workforce, thus lowering unemployment. These benefits could then be used by families who spend money on their children, thus stimulating the economy.

If We Have a Major Social Problem, Why Is There No Movement for Change?

U.S. child care policy must be understood in terms of the larger political and social context that influences beliefs about the proper role of government and the responsibilities of family and community in raising children. Public policy regarding child care has not defined it as a universal need since the 1970s. Policies have framed child care primarily as a poverty-based concern. This is both a cause and a symptom of the lack of more universal public policies. Though the early education movement has been more universally targeted, it often considers educational needs to the exclusion of the needs of parents to ensure care for their children. We do not fault the pre-K movement for focusing on the educational components. Indeed, their success may be a result of their dedicated focus on education that has led to their impressive accomplishments and even greater recent promise. Given the existing political, social, and financial constraints, the tactics and strategies used by the pre-K movement have proven remarkably successful. However, the problem definition and causal stories of child care as *either* a custodial *or* an educational concern have limited potential policy solutions that address the overwhelming needs of all U.S. families for developmentally appropriate, quality care that *also* functions as a work support. Policy feedback has reinforced the fragmentation of interest among advocates.

Attempts to provide care for young children in the United States have been fraught with tensions. The concern for child safety and early development is often deemed to be at odds with a reticence toward state interference in the domain of family (Durst, 2005). Policy feedback has led to potential allies competing for meager resources. Social control agendas that limit care to those considered "deserving" and make assistance contingent on conformity with class-based family ideals have also been at odds with the economic realities of many low-income families, whether during the day nursery movement of the late eighteenth and early nineteenth centuries or in the debates over 1996 welfare reform legislation (Durst, 2005; Gilbert, 1998). These tensions lead to contested understandings of what support should be provided for which children, and how the provision of support for children should be framed and structured. In the absence of a clear policy, the free market has been left to determine how child care (and other caretaking) can and will occur in the United States (Eichner, 2012).

Based on our review of legislative testimony in three different decades and our interviews with child care advocates, we identified a division of interests among advocates fed by political, social, and economic constraints. Some membership-based groups, such as women's organizations, ethnic and religious groups, and unions, identified the needs of children based on the impact that child care has on parents in the workforce. Other leadership-oriented groups (many of which are funded by foundations) spoke for children's interests since children themselves are not a constituency with economic resources or voting power. Some groups focused primarily on early childhood education, whereas other groups focused more heavily on the custodial and work support aspects. Still others prioritized the needs of low-income women and families for substantive or strategic reasons. Policies focused on improving the quality of care do not provide funding and, in the case of the Quality Rating and Improvement System (QRIS), provide information that is helpful only to those who can afford to make choices regarding their children's care. Other groups, such as National Council of La Raza and the National Black Child Development Institute, view child care through the lens of ethnic or racial discrimination and disparities.

Advocates of expanded child care resources not only face political and cultural forces that call for government downsizing, but also must develop strategies to deal with access to limited resources and multiple competing frames that can cause tensions and competition within existing alliances. These factors often put advocates on the defensive, trying not to jeopardize existing funding streams and government programs. All of these factors work against the creation of new problem framing and new policies. At least in part because of the existing debates over the allocation of resources, debates over the development of universal or universal-like programs for children, outside of pre-K, are nonexistent. Most advocates we spoke to were aware of the constraints they faced and worried about their long-term impact. Susan Hibbard was among the more skeptical, noting that "current job[s] and current funding helps perpetuate them as advocates for no change." For obvious reasons, people do not want to undermine their own jobs or agencies or the hard-fought gains they have made for their children and families thus far. They do not easily embrace changes that may be outside of, or in conflict with, their existing organizational mission or framing strategies. Though there could conceivably be a social movement to establish greater access to quality care for all children, in recent history advocacy groups have continued to define the needs of children and the needs of their parents in largely unrelated ways. This makes sense given the larger political context in the United States in which children are likely to be seen as more worthy than their families.

Existing government policies also shape how advocates lobby for education and care services for young children (Karch, 2010). Many of the advocates who were interviewed for this study suggested that existing government funding patterns lead to a multiplicity of interests, which sometimes compete. For example, Head Start provides education to low-income children to help them start school on an equal footing with their middle-class peers and promote better long-term outcomes. Head Start lobbies to continue and increase its own funding. Though it is not child care, some Head Start programs effectively function as high-quality care.[1] The Child

Care and Development Block Grant (CCDBG), on the other hand, funds a variety of child care programs that, depending on the state, may include school- and home-based care as well as family, friend, and neighbor care, with priority for services to low-income and special needs children. Temporary Assistance for Needy Families (TANF) also allows states to spend a percentage of their federal money on child care, and TANF money, combined with CCDBG dollars, flow to the Child Care Development Fund (Schott, 2009). These overlaps mean that different constituencies often vie for the same funds. Indeed, our advocates described competition for resources among would-be allies, a phenomenon noted by other scholars such as Andrew Karch (2010), who found that state-level preschool programs have been seen as a threat to Head Start beneficiaries.

In addition to the challenges faced by existing constituencies fighting over limited resources, broad-based beliefs about child care and the role of government have also constrained the work of U.S. child care advocates. Despite growing awareness of the need for government involvement in the provision of care for children (Institute for Women's Policy Research, 2010), neither the message that child care is "important for gender equality, [nor that] child care [i]s 'good for children,' resonate well with extant norms" (White, 2009, p. 399). Norms that perpetuate the centrality of male breadwinners and noninterventionist government, and stigmatize outsourced child care as inferior to maternal care, continue to limit government participation in United States child care policy. There is virtually no serious public discussion about the value of bearing and raising children for the broader society nor the common interest that these tasks be done well. As noted throughout this book, the narrowing of child care legislation to reflect poverty-based concerns or special needs mirrors the current political climate that involves a retrenchment of federal government involvement with citizens and their communities. This has been accompanied by a backlash against taxation. Like many others, we believe that the push against what is often derogatorily called "big government" has been affected by the powerful conservative influences through campaign financing, issue ads, and political priming.

Building and Sustaining a Movement

As we have noted throughout the book, several factors conspire against such a broad-based movement. First, the United States is not a politically engaged country. For those who might support government involvement in child care policy, there is often a disconnect between their concern and their political participation (Imig, 2006). Other related factors limiting the potential for change include a political system built upon votes that are heavily influenced by advertising. Recent campaign finance policies and Supreme Court decisions have potentially amplified this problem. Advertising costs money, an asset that children do not have, and this weakens the potential to change policies that affect them. There is currently no consensus that caring for children is, in fact, a societal interest rather than an individual family need. The electorate is disproportionately composed of "an aging, white middle class that has less regular contact with children and is increasingly unlikely to feel connected to problems afflicting families with children and families of color" (Imig, 2006, p. 25). Unless and until we change the way child care is perceived by the majority of the electorate, little is likely to change.

The strategies and accomplishments of individual advocacy organizations and sectors always take place within a particular political landscape (Meyer & Imig, 1993). Most of the advocates we interviewed are keenly aware of the impact of the work of advocacy organizations (including their own) on others, as well as the benefits and risks of certain strategies, including framing strategies. Many had a long-term or utopian vision, even as they made much narrower strategic decisions. However, some also claim that the time is right to revisit some long-held strategic decisions and to rethink about what they might now be able to achieve. Any movement for child care should consider the role that women play in leadership positions, both at the government level and with unions and philanthropic organizations. As McDonagh (2009) found, countries that have greater female representation in government are more likely to have better policies for families.

A more populist mobilization that encompasses people from different socioeconomic classes and racial and ethnic backgrounds is likely required for fundamental transformation of U.S. child care policy. Here we describe some of the steps that we believe are necessary to build the movement. They include leveraging facts to increase public awareness of the problem, allowing for comparisons across jurisdictions; garnering moral outrage for the state of U.S. child care; and crafting a vision for universal child care. This vision can be drawn based on existing model programs. The potential role of government must also be reconsidered to allow for the development of a new broad-based social problem.

Leveraging the Facts

One tactic that is increasingly used by children's advocates at the state and national levels is watchdog and comparison campaigns. Throughout this book, we have drawn heavily from reports and policy briefs prepared by advocacy institutions such as the Institute for Women's Policy Research, the National Women's Law Center, the Center for American Progress, and the Center for Law and Social Policy. These are important resources for those studying and making policy about child care in the United States. They have also served a crucial function in highlighting progress and where we fall short. Efforts of other groups that specifically focus on children have also tracked child care policy.

The Annie E. Casey Foundation, "a national and state-by-state effort to track the well-being of children in the United States," has published KIDS COUNT since 1990 (Annie E. Casey Foundation, 2013). This annual report highlights how U.S. policies, including child care and education, have failed our children. The Children's Defense Fund has begun tracking provision of full-day kindergarten, using the slogan "Full-Day K," with its own logo (Children's Defense Fund, 2013), an interactive map, and state-specific fact sheets. This is part of an advocacy tool to activate statewide campaigns and to provide local groups with expanded informational resources. In 2013, they published state-by-state comparisons which they intend to update tracking whether programs are mandatory, full day, or half day, and the extent of state financial support. QRIS has been using similar publications to trace implementation. The "Cradle to Prison Pipeline® State Factsheets," published in 2009, include three markers: poverty, health care, and early childhood education (Children's Defense Fund, 2009). The Urban Institute's Annual "Kids' Share" tracks past and future federal and state trends spending on children both in absolute terms and as a portion of the budget (e.g., Isaacs et al., 2013). The Urban Institute views this as a gauge of how government prioritizes children (Urban Institute, 2013).

Under the leadership of Robert Fellmeth, the Children's Advocacy Institute (CAI), an academic center on child rights at the USD School of Law, began issuing publications in 1998 examining budget and legislative activities impacting children, called the California Children's Report Card. One of the ten priority items listed in the Report Card's "Children's Agenda" is ensuring access to appropriate and affordable care and education from birth through twelfth grade. Other states produce similar reports.

In collaboration with other advocacy work, public report cards and policy briefs may serve a number of important advocacy functions. They set out clear priority areas that are disseminated widely. This creates a public record that can be used to hold state and local government accountable. When reports are produced over multiple years, they allow advocates to track progress and, when progress is slow or there is a regression, to mark this publicly as a means to galvanize citizens. The data provided in these reports are used widely by researchers and advocates for educational, organizing, and advocacy purposes. The reports can also help states or localities compare themselves. They can have a shaming role, creating incentives not to be at the bottom of the list. In addition, they can provide models for state agencies or advocates that want to improve child care policy and services.

Children's reports may also serve as a rallying point for coalition building since they are usually framed in terms of society's responsibility for children. One problem with current formats is that not all reports include measures of early education or child care. Advocates for child care and early education should work to make sure that their interests are represented. Also, many of these reports explicitly highlight concerns of low-income families, so they may not always push toward universal programs or fuel cross-class coalitions. The California Children's Report Card provides an excellent model that includes a wide range of policies important to children (education, child care, family-friendly workplaces), and while it highlights the needs of low-income families, it addresses the concerns of all children regardless of socioeconomic status.

"Who's for Kids and Who's Just Kidding": Placing Child Care Front and Center

Report cards and policy briefs are important tools in the fight for better child care policy. While knowledge itself does not lead to change, it can be leveraged to advocate for change. This is the goal of most of the organizations producing the reports. As mentioned above, reports and report cards can become a resource for developing a vision of universal care. In order to gain political support for broader-based policies, the needs of children must first be embraced as a moral value or a public good.

Advocates and advocacy groups are currently working hard to place the care for young children on the national agenda. The issue has not yet garnered widespread outrage, although the popular media portray it as a prevalent concern for individual families across income brackets. Though fewer women remain home during the day to care for young children than did fifty or even ten years ago, neither federal nor state governments help provide adequate options to ensure that children are safe and stimulated during working hours. Though universal pre-K has gained some momentum, as discussed earlier, there have been no efforts to develop universal policies to address care for children aged zero to three or to address the care needs for children when they are not receiving educational services. As noted throughout this book, policies relating to care for children have been largely framed along class lines, such as subsidies for low-income families (which fall short of actual need) and minimal tax benefits for the middle class. Though many of the leaders of the groups with whom we spoke work for organizations that have supported tax benefits for child care, none seemed to think that tax benefits could adequately address the child care needs that parents in the United States face given the limited sums of money that they usually entail and the fact that they are usually nonrefundable and do not benefit low-income families.

Advocates and interested citizens can work to create a window of opportunity and to take advantage of those that already exist. Media coverage that documents the death of children in inadequate unsafe child care can galvanize public outrage. One such example is Jonathan Cohn's (2013) graphically titled *New Republic* exposé. "The Hell of American Daycare" weaves the heart-wrenching story of Kenya Mire, whose daughter died in a home day care fire, through data and descriptions of other systems of child care such as provided by the U.S. military and the French government. Widespread economic hardship has historically created fruitful windows of opportunity for enacting policies to benefit vulnerable populations. Financial insecurity may lead to a fractured electorate that can create opportunities for marginalized voices to become more powerful. We agree with Adele Robinson of the National Association for the Education of Young Children, among others, who indicated the need for a public rallying cry such as that used against tobacco companies who were accused of targeting children in their campaigns. She suggested the slogan "who's for kids and who's just kidding," which stakes out a moral claim that goes beyond the details and may be more likely to engage a broader base of citizens. As we have described earlier in the book, arguments around morality and fairness helped to win the day for California's paid leave policy.

If the broader social and political context is changed in the United States, then any broad movement for children and their care would have to be framed as a public value. In examining U.S. social policy, it seems that we, as a society, do not value children and families. Whether this is because children do not vote, or because women are woefully underrepresented in the political arena, or because we see family as an off-limits domain, this needs to change. The opposition could simultaneously be framed as antichildren and antiwomen or, even, to tap into conservative rhetoric, as antifamily. Precisely such framing was used, by conservative and liberal proponents alike, in testimony supporting the Act for Better Child Care Services, the Comprehensive Child Development Act, and the Family and Medical Leave Act. Child care provides a clear benefit to society; the absence of accessible, affordable, and safe child care harms us all.

Providing Visions of Child Care Solutions That Work

If the current age of austerity gives way to a more expansive vision of what government can do in the United States, it will be incumbent on advocates to frame child care policy in a more universal way and craft concrete proposals that respond to such frames. Advocacy groups have already outlined several policies to address current needs. They include paid parental leave as well as increased funding for existing programs to provide greater access for low-income families to high-quality care. For higher-income families, there has been a focus on developing a quality rating system to help ensure that parents have access to better information when they make child care choices. In our culture, where many people may have a preference toward parental care for ages zero to three (even if it is not a viable option for most), it is important to develop a system that does not require children to be placed in institutional care settings but rather one that provides a multiplicity of care options.

Based on our data and review of the legislative record, research, and literature, we provide a number of ideas for a more universal child care policy. Any successful U.S. proposal would have to incorporate many different ideas and allow families flexibility to determine the type of care most appropriate for them. It is likely that any program would need to contain universal out-of-home care options as well as tax supports for parents who wish to keep their children in their homes and not work.

Existing child care policies that generally limit funding to low-income children are grossly underfunded and are often on the chopping block when government spending is reduced. If these programs were more universal and provided quality services like Medicare and Social Security, they would be able to gain the support of the middle class and be less vulnerable to funding cuts. This, however, requires the development of comprehensive programs that meet the needs of middle-class citizens and addresses their particular concerns, including, but not limited to, quality standards. Tax benefits could also be provided to companies who provide flexible working conditions for families to enable parents to work part-time or share jobs or other flexible arrangements that are necessary for parents with young children.

If mothers must (or choose to) return to work when their children are twelve to twenty-two weeks old, there should be publicly supported care options available for their children. Women who return to work after the birth of a new child are less likely to experience either short- or long-term financial hardships. That does not mean that all women should return to work or that policy should be used to encourage women to return to work. It does, however, mean that women who seek to avoid economic hardships must have options for providing safe, developmentally appropriate care for their children. These should include reasonable tax subsidies or tax rebates for parents who choose to care for their own children at home or for those who choose to provide in-home care for their child (in either their home or that of the care provider). Though it is imaginable that the tax code could be used as a way to supplement the cost of care, at present it provides only minimal assistance.

Suggestions for reforming the tax code range from those that attempt to alter existing social structures on which work (McCaffery, 1996) and family are built to those that suggest providing increased tax credits for child care within our existing tax system. Along these lines, Alstott (2004) suggested developing a universal $5,000 grant per child, mirroring policies that exist in Western Europe, to help defray the costs of child care. These funds could be used either to supplement the cost of child care or to defray the costs incurred by parents who choose to care for their own children and leave the paid labor force to do so.

Dowd (1997) cautions that policies that target parents, such as tax policies, are limited by their very nature and, as such, cannot deal with many of the needs of children. "In our focus on adults' equality, we have lost sight not only of children's economic needs but also of their other dependency needs, for psychological, social and cultural care. I worry about our inability to deal with dependency, to acknowledge children's needs, or to care for their care givers" (Dowd, 1997, p. 601). Though changes to the tax structure alone cannot address all of the child care limitations we face in this country, providing support to families can improve the circumstances in which children are raised.

U.S. child care policy changes should also include increasing available high-quality child care settings in which care is provided on a sliding scale basis. Ideally, these centers would provide care for both traditional and nontraditional hours so that parents who do shift work could avail themselves of such care. These programs must support children until they are able to attend either full-day preschool or kindergarten. At that time, parents must be provided either with the option of full-day high-quality early education/child care settings for their children or some tax benefits to defray the costs that they incur should they choose not to select public options and wish to send their children to another program, stay home with their children, or make other child care decisions.

In order to develop public care settings, there will need to be an initial investment in infrastructure as well as publicly financed support for early childhood education. It is possible that some of the infrastructure development could occur as public-private partnerships. Current and future child care workers must be provided with educational opportunities to ensure that they learn to react to children in a developmentally appropriate manner and provide high-quality care. In an age of high unemployment, another draw of providing training and education to child care workers is that it could promote job creation. In addition, child care providers must be paid enough so that the people who choose to do the work are both skilled and choosing this work as a result of their interest rather than their inability to get other more highly skilled work. Higher pay also leads to lower turnover of employees, which improves the quality of care that children receive in these settings.

A hopeful perspective for those seeking broad-based change that takes advantage of U.S. federalism is that local or state changes can serve as models or test cases for policies that, if successful, can later be adopted at the national level. State-level change can prompt change at the federal level, as in the case with the living wage campaigns at the state level that prompted a rise in the minimum wage in twenty-four states and the District of Columbia prior to the federal rise in the minimum wage (Holland, 2007). Health care changes that took root at the state level eventually influenced national health care reform (Benz & Gray, 2011). In the area of child care, trends in pre-K education show that the growing role of the federal government was preceded by years of state-level action, in some states even during a recessionary economy that is generally hostile to program creation or expansion (Bushouse, McGhee, & Imig, n.d.). Unless more state efforts prompt changes at the federal level, however, it is unlikely that individual states will be able to create and maintain comprehensive and universal child care support systems.

State-level experimentation has already begun. In order to develop a comprehensive child care policy, several pieces of existing child care policy could be expanded. For example, California has both temporary disability and paid parental leave. Foundations could be encouraged to support more expansive programming in states that have already laid the groundwork such as California with paid leave or Oklahoma and Illinois, which have universal pre-K programs. If one state were able to demonstrate benefits of a universal plan, others may be convinced to follow, and, at the very least, there would be more data to show the utility of universal care. This could be used to demonstrate the viability of such a plan in the U.S. context. Foundations could help develop universal child care policies in California to help fill the gap between the first weeks of birth and the availability of pre-K or kindergarten. California is being suggested as a model since it is one of few states that have paid leave and there has been a foundation presence there seeking to increase the availability of universal pre-K. Other states such as Oklahoma, which has universal pre-K, could also be encouraged, again with foundation support, to provide care support for families from the cradle to first grade.

A national system could emulate the state-level models that provide both disability leave for mothers giving birth and comprehensive paid leave for mothers who give birth and for both mothers and fathers who adopt children.[2] Research suggests that neither policy would financially burden employers, and both have demonstrated individual and broader public health benefits. However, given the current political climate, any leave model is likely to last, at most, twenty to twenty-two weeks (eight to ten weeks of paid disability and twelve weeks paid leave). At this time, all parents must be provided with subsidies that enable them either to stay home or to access quality care for their children (as they choose). Similar local experiments in pre-K education and child care subsidies or services such as the existing U.S. military model can also expand our public imagination and lay the groundwork for scaled-up nationwide or state-level policies.

Reframing the Role of Government

Changing broader conceptions of the proper role of government more generally, particularly in the area of social supports and regulation, is crucial to changing what we expect of government in crafting and implementing child care policy. In the past forty years, women have entered the workforce in greater numbers. In contrast, women have not entered the political arena in the United States at the same rate. Some, such as McDonagh (2009), speculate that there is a connection between poor social welfare policy in the United States and women's political leadership. Public policy has not kept up with the changing role of women in the family. Perhaps this should come as no surprise given that, at the same time women entered the workforce en masse, there was also a

movement to reduce the role of government. Since the Reagan administration, both major U.S. political parties have been focused on reducing
government spending rather than improving government services. Even
the recent health care law largely relies on privatization of the insurance
and hospital industries. Advocates must first work to change the public perceptions of the potentially helpful role that government can play.
There are some recent indications of populist pushback against government retrenchment. It behooves child care advocates, whose interests are
tied to conceptions of the proper role of government, to support and tap
into these mobilizations (Imig, 2006).

Several things could help to reframe the role of government, thereby
laying the groundwork for the possibility of developing a more universal
child care (or possibly broader family care) policy in the United States.
First, money is needed to invest on movement building. Foundation
funding could be used to support movement building and a greater role
for populism in the United States. However, expecting foundations to
fund populism is potentially fraught. Money from foundations generally
comes from the very rich, who are usually invested in the existing social
structure. Still, there may be exceptions, such as the Soros Foundation.
Two other possible sources of funding are direct citizen donations and
unions. If people who want to change the impact of citizen participation
in government, they could stop giving money to 503(b) charitable organizations and give money to organizations that are engaged in political
organizing and movement building. The Tea Party movement provides
an example of the potentially transformative role of strategic funding in
creating and sustaining a broad-based movement. Progressive supporters
of child care policies could do well in emulating this model by channeling
funds not only into demonstration projects and elite think tanks, but also
into movement building and advocacy, areas that have heretofore gone
woefully unsupported.

Absent (or alongside) funding, there are signs that citizen activism is
on the rise. In Europe, for example, there have been some recent challenges to the government austerity that have not relied on the deep

pockets of philanthropists. Citizen activism has played a large role in changing the ruling parties in France, where citizens have resisted efforts at austerity. In Iceland, citizens voted on a referendum opposing government austerity measures, choosing instead to let the government default on its loans to foreign banks. Over time, if grassroots economic reform movements like the Occupy Wall Street movement in the United States lead to an increase in civic engagement (this remains to be seen), the political climate might be more receptive to advocacy for universal access to quality child care. Without a loud cry seeking this change, it is unlikely to happen (Piven & Cloward, 1973). Social change involving the possible role(s) of government in the United States must occur at a level that is broader than simply a vision for child care policy. This is a necessary but not sufficient condition to change U.S. child care policy.

Obama's 2012 campaign advertisements included references to the important role that government plays in the United States for middle- and lower-income women and their families. Once there is a public recognition of the value of government, U.S. child care needs must be identified as a broad-based social issue. Advocates have tried to do this for many years, but as noted above, given the political climate they have not had the opportunity to be successful. Many school districts and some states have made efforts to universalize early education beginning at age three. Despite the voluminous research regarding the value and necessity of child care for so many, it is still considered an individual rather than a social problem by a vocal majority of the population.

As long as government is seen as "the problem" and public spending is therefore seen as the root of all evil, a vision for universal child care seems unlikely. Broad citizen movements that include the use of social media such as Occupy Wall Street that challenge the current behavior of the U.S. government may provide an avenue for reframing government's role. The heightened discussion of "precarity," which describes the vulnerability of an increasing segment of the public in a market predominated by the interests of business seeking to avoid regulation, has been felt by many who would not consider themselves poor (Schram,

2012). Nearly all parents, regardless of income, experience vulnerability in their role as caretakers. Defining the need for child care within a broader causal story of vulnerability might help frame a more adequate and universal policy solution.

Signs of Hope

Advocates are already working together in many ways. For example, many of the advocates from groups that were interviewed for this book work together and meet on regular basis. There is an annual conference of child care advocates. In late July and early August 2013, the National Women's Law Center and the Grow America Stronger campaign began an effort to unify state and local early education and care advocates to begin a national plan for advocacy. This included a phone call with presidential representatives as well as the distribution of advocacy toolkits and plans for collaborative actions. A part of this effort included an action during Senate budget hearings in September 2013 that was sponsored by the Women's Law Center, Momsrising, and the Strong Start for Children's Campaign. The action involved playing a game of Chutes and Ladders, which has early learning themes, on the grounds of the capital and then delivering to senators storybooks that depicted early childhood services that assist families and children. At the same time, the groups sent emails to members asking them to call their senators to request that they support early learning initiatives (Blank, 2013; Grow America Stronger, 2013).

The National Domestic Workers Alliance has begun the Caring Across Generations campaign, whose primary goal is to address the needs of in-home care providers for the aged and disabled but includes home child care providers, particularly those who work in others' homes. The aim is to provide home caregivers with adequate pay, benefits and a decent work environment. These advocates have built relationships with traditional unions such as the American Federation of State, County, and Municipal Employees and the Service Employees International Union SEIU as well as organizations such as the Institute for Women's Policy

Research, Family Values @ Work, 9 to 5, the YWCA, and the Alliance of Retired Americans.

One of their first steps is to get people and perhaps the nation as a whole to speak publicly about care giving. If this goal is met, ultimately it could help child care workers who work in institutional or group settings. Improving child care workers' standard of living and rights may make child care jobs more appealing to skilled care providers. Training and education could also be provided to unskilled child care workers, thus making them more qualified (Flanders, 2012; Poo, 2013). The Caring Across Generations Campaign has used their network of alliances to advocate on behalf of the Domestic Workers Bill of Rights in New York, which now provides in-home workers with the right to overtime pay, three days of paid leave, and protection from harassment and discrimination in the workplace. This bill includes both home health care workers and nannies (Flanders, 2012). We believe that the extension of worker rights policies to other states is one piece of the puzzle that is necessary in order to improve access to quality child caring.

Existing cross-coalitional efforts are positive. They indicate that child care workers and care recipients and their families may be able to work together to successfully lobby for change in child care that benefits children, families, and child care workers. As noted above, this will improve the quality of care for all children. Parents, grandparents, employers of people who have young children, and care providers must all work together to lobby for change that will improve care and education for children in the United States, ensure greater worker reliability and longevity, and improve the status of women with young children in the workforce. Until government involvement is seen as a viable means to address social problems, this cannot happen. The participation of citizens in movements such as Occupy Wall Street, which see a positive role for government, is encouraging. This may be the beginning of a new populist movement that reframes the role of government and may help to pave the way for more expansive family care policy in the United States. As the electorate ages, more people, both men and women, will have experienced the problems currently associated with child care giving in the United States. This, too, may help advocates garner support for change.

Without a broad-based social movement relying on a greater populism, solutions will continue to be piecemeal and largely inadequate for large swaths of the population. Advocates will likely continue to fight to ensure the existence of current funding and programs. Existing actors should try to expand on the universal pre-K movement, which has garnered some support from the Obama administration, so, at the very least, every four-year-old and potentially every three-year-old whose parents wish to participate gets access to some early educational services. Advocates may also wish to continue to frame early education and care as significant for future workforce development (as they now do) in order to seek support from more conservative constituents including business groups. As noted above, states and localities, with potential help from foundations, should to be seen as venues for experimentation with the hope that successful programs may someday, when there is a stronger movement, be replicated on a broader scale. Recent media coverage and reports have become more critical of the many ways that U.S. child care policy fails children and families. This perhaps signals a readiness to move from commiseration to indignation that targets systems, programs, and workplaces rather than individual solutions.

If we are considering major changes to the way in which child care is viewed in the public arena as a public good rather than a private need, these alliances are fraught. Business owners are generally concerned with their bottom lines and not the welfare of the public. Most do not believe that it is in their best interest to support government regulation of business. They would prefer not to pay their workers a minimum wage or overtime. In a capitalist society, government regulations are needed to regulate and control businesses to support the greater public welfare (Eisner, 2010). As a result, working with business groups may require too much compromise. However, given the current political climate, where there is no clearly convincing moral message and limited public outrage, it may be necessary (as many advocacy groups have decided) to frame child care as a work support or as a necessary support to help educate future workers. This will mean that changes to policies will continue to be minimal and likely involve, at most, increased funding to already established policies so that they can better meet the needs of low-income parents. While that is necessary, it is far from sufficient.

Beginning during the Progressive Era, those promoting change often focused on creating information and distributing information with the hope that, if people had a better knowledge base, they would be more likely to support progressive policies. Unfortunately, this has not been true. There is a plethora of information telling us that the situation for children, particularly low-income children, in the United States is abysmal. Yet, current public policy in the United States is insufficient to address these needs. Like the conservatives, who have built an antitax antigovernment "populist" movement, those who disagree and wish to challenge these conservative beliefs need to focus on movement building in support of greater government-based social welfare for citizens. Universal child care will likely happen only within this government lens. We need a moral message not only about the role of government but also about society's responsibility for raising children. Without such a movement, the rich will continue to get richer and more low-income children and families will suffer. Child care is just one piece of a larger puzzle in which working- and middle-class Americans are losing out on the American dream.

At present, in lieu of alternatives, using state-based programs as models is one potential strategy. However, there are many existing models of programs, some in the United States, that work better than the largely market-based model we are currently using. Ultimately, we do not need more information or more models and we do not need minor changes to existing policies. We need a revolution.

AFTERWORD

To us, as mothers of young children, the problems outlined here are not only theoretically compelling but also personally and professionally obvious. Prior to examining child care policy, Elizabeth looked at the implementation of special education policy in American public schools, particularly related to mental illness and student discipline. Corey has examined child welfare policy and housing, which was largely a proxy for poverty, and truancy. In both fields, we have recognized the extreme challenges faced by families (and more particularly, mothers). We have also been struck by how much more circumscribed the choices are for low-income families and how much more serious are the consequences of failure. In order to situate our scholarly work and call for action, in this afterword we share our personal reflections on why and how this book is important.

Elizabeth

Six years ago, when I had my first child, I began to wonder why the challenges of providing quality care for my infant daughter still existed. I wanted to send her someplace clean with licensed, credentialed staff where she would be well cared for and loved. When my daughter was a month or two old, I spent days searching for quality infant child care in the New York City area where I could send my daughter once I returned to work, which I had no choice but to do when she was three months old. There were very, very few. Only one was located within a reasonable distance from my home. It had a long waiting list and I was told that because I did not receive public assistance, my daughter would not likely be admitted there. Most of the child care centers in the area provided care only for children either eighteen months or two years old and older. I hired a nanny and, then, placed my daughter in a home day care when she was about one and a half years old. I was lucky that, with some strain, I could afford that option, but I recognized that for many women such expensive care options were not feasible. Then, when she was two, I began researching preschools. There were few full-day preschools within a reasonable distance from my home and I found myself applying for preschool a full year before my daughter could attend. I applied to five schools and was wait-listed at three. I panicked. What would I do if my daughter did not get into any preschool? Who would care for her during the day? How could I afford to pay a child care provider a living wage and provide early enrichment activities (part-day preschool) that I believed she would need? What did other parents do? Most cannot afford a home-based babysitter, particularly if they want to pay their employee a livable wage. I met many mothers in the neighborhood who had ceased working because they could not afford child care. In some ways, these were the lucky people since their families were able to survive on one income. Many parents, whose children are in preschool (including me), struggle to provide care when their children are sick, when they have school holidays, and when the child's day is over at noon or at three o'clock. Again, I recognize that I have much more flexibility than most parents, and, still, my husband and I struggle.

Forty years ago, my mother worked full-time, as did most of her friends. I went to preschool and had a nanny. My mother's income was not necessary for my family to remain in the middle class, and she could therefore afford to pay for someone to care for my brother and me. She worked because she wanted to. I work both because I want to and because my family could not afford our modest three-bedroom apartment in Brooklyn without my income. Middle-class women entered the workforce in large numbers in the 1970s. Many women worked before the 1970s, including my grandmothers, but most mothers of young children had not worked or had relatives who had watched their children while they did. In 1971, Nixon vetoed a major legislative initiative to provide universal preschool. It had bipartisan support. This issue largely dropped off the national agenda. Since the 1970s, the problems families face in ensuring quality care for their children have become only greater as the expectation and need for women to work has increased and there have been no commensurate public policies to ensure the existence of broad-based quality care for children. Though much of the rest of the industrialized world has already tackled these issues, the United States has not. What happened? Recently, I have seen some signs that things may be changing. The struggle that all families are facing seems to be more frequently reported in the media than when we began this project. I am hopeful this means things will change and that other parents will not have to face the same sorts of struggles that I faced.

Corey

I am sitting on a Philadelphia commuter train on my own way home from work, where my youngest is with our full-time babysitter, an au pair on a special visa who is living in our home. Although my husband and I juggled a combination of part-time students and day care centers with my older children while I was in graduate school, now my two-hour commute to work twice a week requires child care at "odd" hours, sometimes starting at 6:15 in the morning, which is not available anywhere in my neighborhood. Even with child care, the cost of "vacation programs" and alternative hours for three children makes this the most affordable option, and we are privileged to be able to afford it and to have a room in our house (when the kids are doubled up) to allow us to be a "host family." My laptop is open and I am working on a paper that Elizabeth and I are presenting on child care policy, taking advantage of the last twenty minutes of potential work time (i.e., child care). While I can often shut out conversation around me, I hear that the woman next to me is on her cell phone, scrambling to figure out what to do with her son. From what I hear she has arranged for an after-school program for him during the afternoon until she gets home, but it turns out that there is no transportation from school to the program, which is not on-site. She is trying to phone her husband or figure something out. The woman is clearly frustrated, confused, and worried.

As I listened to her there were a number of thoughts running through my head. First was the worry that is so easy to identify with. As a full-time working mother to three children, then ages five, ten, and thirteen, the stress emanating from my fellow traveler was nothing I haven't felt before. I wondered how old her child was and whether the school would keep him there (and, if so, they would no doubt chastise her roundly). Or would the relief come just in time in the form of a relative, neighbor, or schoolmate's parent? What would happen if her son went home by mistake and ended up at an empty house with a locked door? This not only ups my own stress level, as I pick up my phone to dial home, but makes me want to reach out to her, although I would not dare distract her from her search-and-rescue mission.

The second set of feelings comes from the researcher part of me. This confirms what we are writing about! I should tape-record the conversation. Indeed not long after I recounted this to Elizabeth, it made me cook up a new research component to our project—I could travel the commuter rails with a tape recorder and ask parents to tell me their worst child care nightmare story in two-minute increments. I have no doubt that every parent on this train—or at least all of the women—would be concerned about only which story to pick rather than having none to tell. Then the activist in me got angry. This is a ubiquitous, if not universal, problem. Why don't I turn to my neighbor and others in this very car and tell them that they should be demanding better child care or better workplaces or better supports for families? Why are we so complacent?

APPENDIX 1

A Brief Note on Research Methods

The majority of interviews that provide the basis for this analysis were conducted by Elizabeth from September 14, 2009, to December 10, 2009, and Corey conducted three interviews in 2011 to follow up with leads that emerged as we were analyzing the data. Snowball sampling was used to identify experts on child care and early education policy (Johnson & Reynolds, 2008). We wanted to speak with leaders in the child and women's advocacy movements and asked our participants to direct us to other leaders, thus identifying a purposive sample, which uses a limited number of focused participants rather than a representative sample (Johnson & Reynolds, 2008). Meghan Duffy et al. (2010) note that it is important to understand the social change efforts of elite led organizations, because "in recent decades, much social and political change has resulted from the efforts of elite actors" (p. 51).

Most interviews, conducted in person or over the phone, lasted between a half hour and an hour. We targeted lobbyists, and snowball sampling was used to identify respondents who were experts on child care and early education policy and could shed light on the research questions (Johnson & Reynolds, 2008; Patton, 2002) (see Appendix 4 for a list of organizational participants). We asked key informants at organizations and in academia for referrals to organizations, lobbyists, or unions that would be able to provide us with an in-depth assessment of child care and early education policy efforts across different interest domains as well as a historical perspective. Based on a review of people who have testified in Congress on behalf of child care issues over the past five years, we identified and spoke with leaders from educationally focused advocacy organizations, broader child advocacy organizations, foundations, research and advocacy organizations with an interest in child care, and early education policy and women's rights organizations (see Appendix 3 for a list of study respondents). Some of our respondents had worked at more than one organization over the course of their career, which broadened their perspective. We cannot say that this sample of progressive child care advocacy elites is representative. However, it includes enough of the major players in the child advocacy arena to provide a broad range of perspectives on the obstacles they face. The common themes that emerged among respondents and the fact that we were often referred to people we ourselves had identified confirmed our choice of organizations and activists. We attempted to reach out to those who would likely oppose child care expansion, including the U.S. Chamber of Commerce, the National Small Business Association, Americans for Tax Reform, and groups such as the American Enterprise Institute, the Christian Coalition, and Concerned Women for America. All groups either declined to make someone available to speak with us or did not respond to our attempts to contact them. As indicated in the text, the only advocate overtly opposed to child care who provided us with an interview was Phyllis Schlafly of the Eagle Forum.

We used a semistructured interview guide, which is provided in Appendix 2 (Rubin & Rubin, 2005). We audio-recorded the interviews and transcribed them verbatim. Because of their public roles, these leaders were not offered anonymity or confidentiality, and we provide their names and affiliations when citing them.

We coded the sample interviews and analyzed the data using qualitative descriptive methods (Sandelowski, 2000). In coding the data, we used sensitizing concepts (Blumer, 1954; Padgett, 2008) derived from the social movement and framing literatures, including the perceived impact that organizations have on each other in defining problems and strategies and the way that policy advocates understood political constraints and opportunities to affect their agendas and tactics.

*Interview Guide for Interest Groups and
Organizations Including Unions*

These are topic areas to be explored with respondents. The interviewer will allow the respondents to set the timing and order of the discussion. The interviewer will ask respondents to clarify with examples, asking for in-depth descriptions where possible.

The interviewer with thank the respondent for agreeing to meet with her. She will review the interview format. If the respondent consents, she will proceed with the interview. If the interviewer is unfamiliar with the organization, she may begin with a general question about the organization.

1. Could you tell me a little bit about the mission and goals of your organization.
2. How does your organization define child care? How does this fit within the organizations' mission/goals?
3. What problems do you see that U.S. families face regarding care for children? Does your organization define these as individual problems or national, state, or local social problems?
   a. If national/state/local, how do you think they should be addressed?
4. What does your organization do to try to affect change in this area? Fight against such policies?
   a. How has your organization tried to get these issues placed on or kept off of the national legislative agenda or the agenda of states?
5. What strategies do you use? What issues does your organization face with respect to your funders and your ability to advocate these positions? How do you manage them? (probe for donation information/

connection to politicians)

   a. From where do you receive your funding?

6. Do you think that we should have national quality standards for the care of preschool children? For infants? To whom should these standards apply?

7. What is your organization's position on universal child care?

   a. For left organizations: A previous interviewee stated that the term "universal child care" was not politically viable and therefore had not been used in many years? Do you agree and, if so, why do you think this is the case?

8. What position does your organization take (if any) on policies to affect change in the workplace to promote parenting (e.g., FMLA)? Specifically probe for paid leave.

9. What position does your organization take on promoting tax benefits to parents?

10. With whom do you work (your biggest allies) to promote these policies/prevent them from being expanded? Probe for organizations, state and federal representatives.

11. What impediments if any has your organization faced in advocating for your position on these issues or your ability to advocate for them?

12. Who do you see as your major adversaries? Probe for organizations/agencies, state and federal representatives.

APPENDIX 3

Study Respondents by Organization and Role

Name	Role	Organization	Focus[a]
Erika Beltran	Senior policy analyst, Education and Children's Policy Project	National Council of La Raza	"NCLR . . . works to improve opportunities for Hispanic Americans [through] applied research, policy analysis, and advocacy, providing a Latino perspective in five key areas—assets/investments, civil rights/immigration, education, employment and economic status, and health [and] provides capacity-building assistance to . . . state and local level [affiliates] to advance opportunities for individuals and families."
Helen Blank	Director, Leadership and Public Policy	National Women's Law Center	Policy research, analysis, and advocacy organization focused on women's issues
Libby Doggett	Deputy director, Pew Center on the States	Pew Charitable Trusts	Nonprofit that funds efforts aimed at "improving public policy, informing the public, and stimulating civic life"
Donna Dolan	District One staff representative, director of work/family issues, chair of NY State	Communication Workers of America	Communications and media workers union
Denise Dowell	Director, Early Care and Learning Program	Voice of Organized Independent Childcare Educators (VOICE)/Civil Services Employees Union (CSEA)	"[A] union made up of and working for family childcare providers from across New York State, organizing for power to take on challenges facing us and the children and families we serve"
Danielle Ewen	Director, Child Care and Early Education	Center for Law and Social Policy	Policy research, analysis, and advocacy organization working to benefit low-income people

Name	Role	Organization	Focus[a]
Sarah Francis	Campaign director on Child Care and Early Education	Momsrising.org	"a network of people just like you, united by the goal of building a more family-friendly America"; core issues include "maternity/paternity leave," "open flexible work," and "sick days, paid"
Dana Friedman	President	The Early Years Institute	Nonprofit that seeks to "create . . . early learning support, services and systems" in Long Island (NY)
Ellen Galinsky	Cofounder and president	Family and Work Institute	Nonprofit research organization that "studies the changing workforce, family and community"
Susan Hibbard	Consultant	Build Initiative	Early Childhood Funders Collaborative (ECFC) project is designed to help "states construct a coordinated system of programs, policies and services" for young children
Catherine Graham Hildum	Policy expert	First Five Years Fund	Collaboration of family foundations advocating for children to be considered more in federal policy and funding decisions
Lauren Hogan	Policy director	National Black Child Development Institute	"to improve and advance the lives of Black children and their families, through advocacy and education"
Eric Karolak	Executive director	Early Care and Education Consortium	Nonprofit alliance of early learning program providers
Nancy Kolbin[b]	Executive director	Center for Children's Initiatives (formerly Child Care, Inc.)	Information, referral, assistance, development, and advocacy organization in the New York City area
Becky Levin	Lobbyist	AFSCME	Public employee and health care workers union
Linda Meric	Executive director	9 to 5: National Association of Working Women	National membership organization whose advocacy efforts are "dedicated to putting working women's issues on the public agenda"
Adele Robinson	Associate executive director	NAEYC	Association of early childhood professionals
Phyllis Schlafly	President	Eagle Forum	Conservative interest group
Steffany Stern	Policy analyst, Work and Family Programs	National Partnership for Women and Families	Advocacy organization for "policies that help women and men meet the dual demands of work and family"
Joe Thiessen	Vice president, Policy and Government Affairs	Voices for America's Children	Network of multi-issue child advocacy organizations

Name	Role	Organization	Focus[a]
Sara Lee Todd	Senior legislative advocate	SEIU	Union for workers in health care, public services, and property services
Yasmina Vinci	Executive director	National Head Start Association	Nonprofit membership organization that provides resources and advocates for policies that will strengthen the delivery of Head Start programs
John Wilcox	Deputy director	Corporate Voices for Working Families	"National business membership organization representing the private sector on public and corporate policy issues involving working families"

a. Descriptions are drawn from the agency websites.

b. The name and mission of the organization have changed since our interview; the role of our respondent did not change. The information provided here is the current organization's name and mission.

APPENDIX 4

Conservative Organization Websites Reviewed

Americans for Tax Reform

The Christian Coalition

Concerned Women for America

Eagle Forum

The Family Research Council

Focus on the Family

Heritage Foundation

International Women's Forum

National Small Business Association

The Tea Party Movement

U.S. Chamber of Commerce

Note: Though websites for all of these groups were reviewed, several are not cited in the book as these groups do not seem to take an overt position about child care policy.

NOTES

NOTES TO CHAPTER 2

1. Aid to Families with Dependent Children had been changed earlier from Aid to Dependent Children. This first change to include "families" recognized that the children who were being assisted were connected to the parents or guardians who cared for them.

2. One of the most influential cases on the expansion of federal power was *Wickard v. Filburn* in 1942. In this case, the Supreme Court upheld the Agricultural Adjustment Act, which was passed to stabilize the price of wheat during the Depression. It limited individual farmers' rights to grow wheat on their land. Filburn had sought to grow excess wheat for use on his own farm. However, the Supreme Court held that he was in violation of the law that, the Court noted, was passed to protect interstate commerce. This is important because it demonstrates the Supreme Court's use of the interstate commerce clause to expand far beyond what is traditionally considered commerce. In the United States, child care is a form of commerce. Agencies that provide child care are businesses and therefore can be regulated as a participants in commerce. They also allow commerce to take place. As a general rule, however, they take place in a single state and are not interstate.

3. The Family and Medical Leave Act and accompanying state paid leave programs address only the first few weeks of a newborn's life.

4. Throughout much of its early history, women and nonwhites (and, in many states, those who did not own land) were not counted as full citizens and government rights were not articulated or formulated with their participation in mind.

NOTE TO CHAPTER 3

1. Reich testified in the Senate as secretary-designate as his confirmation hearing was later that same day. He was the first to provide testimony on the Senate bill and left immediately thereafter to attend his confirmation hearing.

NOTE TO CHAPTER 4

1. Though neither was identified as a core issue by NOW, the NOW website did include a discussion of HR 2392 (2007), a bill proposing a comprehensive family care policy, including both national support for child care and paid family leave and a link to the bill's contents on the website of the Library of Congress.

NOTES TO CHAPTER 5

1. As we discussed in Chapter 3, the Child Care Development Fund is funded through a combination of Child Care Development Block Grant and Social Security Act sources.
2. These cases are based on the Family and Medical Leave Act (FMLA) as well as other state and federal statutes.
3. It is important to note that the data on leave-needers include all employees surveyed, not just those eligible for FMLA.
4. Percentages sum to greater than 100 percent because the survey permits multiple answers to this question.
5. 26 Me. Rev. Stat. Ann. § 843 (3)(A) and (C).
6. Minn. Stat. § 181.940 (Subd. 3).
7. Or. Rev. Stat. § 659A.153 (1).
8. 23 Vt. Stat. Ann. § 471(3) and (4).
9. D.C. Code § 32-516(2).
10. FMLA benefits are provided to employees who work in organizations that employ at least fifteen employees in Maine, ten in Vermont, twenty-one in Minnesota, and twenty-five in Oregon, and benefits are provided to all employees in Hawaii and the District of Columbia.
11. 23 Vt. Stat. Ann. § 471(3) and (4).
12. Minn. Stat. § 181.940 (Subd. 3).
13. Conn. Gen. Stat. § 5-248a (a).
14. D.C. Code § 32-502(a).
15. Or. Rev. Stat. § 659.470-494.
16. Cal. Unemp. Ins. Code. §§ 3301–3306.
17. Washington Family Leave Insurance Act of 2007.
18. New Jersey Temporary Disability Benefits Law (2008), Pub. L. No. 1948 c110 (43: 21–26).
19. Rev. Code Wash. § 49.78.005 (2009); Rev. Code Wash. § 49.12.270 (2009); Washington Family Leave Insurance Act of 2007 (retrieved from http://apps.leg.wa.gov/RCW/default.aspx?cite=49.78).
20. Cal. Unemp. Ins. Code. §§ 3301–3306.

NOTES TO CHAPTER 6

1. Morgan notes that despite efforts to the contrary, the achievement of a fully egalitarian "dual earner/dual caregiver" model remains elusive due to political structures and contexts that stymie the comprehensive change necessary to create such a model (Morgan, 2008).
2. Crèches are child care centers that are run by the municipal council or a voluntary-sector organization, by parents, or in a registered child minder's home (Embassy of France, n.d.).
3. In Canada, many people are entitled to paid maternity leave through private employment insurance policies (Canadian Worker Rights, n.d.).

NOTES TO CHAPTER 7

1. More detail on the study, our interview guide, and a table of respondents are provided in Appendices 1, 2, and 3, respectively.

2. Although they were begun at the state level, they ultimately became Aid to Dependent Children (ADC), then Aid to Families with Dependent Children (AFDC), the program that preceded TANF, which we have discussed at length earlier.

3. Funds for the program have fluctuated, with the first year allocation, FY2011, at $497 million, FY2012 at $133 million, and FY2013 again raised to $300 million, still below 2011 allocations (U.S. Department of Education, 2013b). These grants were awarded to states competing for funds under the Race to the Top—Early Learning Challenge Initiative (U.S. Department of Education, 2013a)

4. The difference between universal and targeted programs is that universal programs are available to all whereas targeted programs are available to only a subset of the overall population. In the United States, targeted programs generally target the needs of those living in poverty and are means tested (Jansson, 2009).

5. The Birth to Five Policy Alliance is funded by the Buffett Early Childhood Fund, the W. K. Kellogg Foundation, the Bill & Melinda Gates Foundation, the J. B. and M. K. Pritzker Family Foundation, the George Kaiser Family Foundation, and the Irving Harris Foundation.

NOTE TO CHAPTER 8

1. The Center for American Progress defines itself as an "independent political and educational institute dedicated to improving the lives of Americans through progressive ideas and action" (Center for American Progress, n.d.).

NOTES TO CHAPTER 9

1. Because Head Start is locally run, there are great discrepancies between programs (Rose, 2010).

2. In this statement, we do not intend to endorse the model of childbirth as a disability. However, when women have children they often need time to physically recuperate, and these existing laws are one way that women have been able to physically recuperate and spend time with their newborns without being forced into a situation where they have no income, and this is the existing legal rubric for current antidiscrimination policy. Since women are in a better situation in places with disability policies that include childbirth, we are suggesting that these policies could be expanded to states where they do not exist. Ultimately, however, changing our conception of childbearing and child rearing as regular, ongoing events in the life course of many Americans would likely obviate the need for casting childbirth as disability.

REFERENCES

Abbott v. Burke, 119 N.J. 287, 575 A.2d 359 (1990).

Abramowitz, A. I. (1991). Incumbency, campaign spending, and the decline of competition in U.S. House elections. *Journal of Politics, 53*, 34–56.

Act for Better Child Care Services of 1987, S1885, S. Hrg. 100-882, 100th Cong. (1987).

Adema, W. (2012). Setting the scene: The mix of family policy objectives and packages across the OECD. *Children and Youth Services Review, 34*(3), 487–498.

Administration for Children and Families. (2008). *2008 CCDF state expenditure data.* Retrieved from www.acf.hhs.gov/programs/occ/resource/expenditures-2008-25k-2013-09-10.

———.(2011). *2010 CCDF expenditure data.* Retrieved from http://www.acf.hhs.gov/programs/occ/resource/expenditures-2010.

———.(2013). *QRIS elements.* Retrieved from http://childcare.gov/sites/default/files/254_1302_qris_elements.pdf.

———.(n.d.). *Fundamentals of CCDF administration.* Retrieved from the Office of Child Care: https://ccdf-fundamentals.icfwebservices.com/.

AFL-CIO. (2006). *Asking a working woman: Survey report.* Retrieved from http://www.ibew.org/IBEW/departments/HumanServices/2006%20Ask%20A%20Working%20Woman%20Survey%20Results.pdf.

———.(2013). *Rhode Island legislature passes paid family leave bill.* Retrieved from http://www.aflcio.org/Blog/In-The-States/Rhode-Island-Legislature-Passes-Paid-Family-Leave-Bill.

Albiston, C. R. (2008). Bargaining in the shadow of social institutions: Competing discourses and social change in workplace mobilization of civil rights. *Law and Society Review, 39*(1), 11–50.

Allen, C. (2013, April 11). 23: Pre-K education. *USA Today.* Retrieved from http://www.usatoday.com/story/news/politics/2013/02/28/obama-pre-k-state-of-the-union/1935699/.

Alstott, A. L. (2004). *No exit: What parents owe their children and what society owes parents.* New York: Oxford University Press.

American Bar Association. (1990). Report of the child care credit task force. *Tax Notes, 46*, 331.

American Enterprise Institute. (2007). *New study by AEI scholar Douglas J. Besharov reveals the true cost of government-sponsored early childhood education and care.*

Retrieved from http://www.aei.org/press/society-and-culture/poverty/new-study-by-aei-scholar-douglas-j-besharov-reveals-the-true-cost-of-government-spon-sored-early-childhood-education-and-care/

American Federation of Teachers. (n.d.). *Key issues.* Retrieved from http://www.aft.org/issues/index.cfm#reform.

Americans for Tax Reform. (n.d.). *About Americans for Tax Reform.* Retrieved from http://atr.org/about.

Annie E. Casey Foundation. (2013). *Kids count: Data book: State trends in child well-being.* Retrieved from http://datacenter.kidscount.org/files/2013KIDSCOUNTDataBook.pdf.

Appelbaum, E., & Milkman, R. (2011). *Leaves that pay: Employer and worker experi-ences with paid family leave in California.* Washington, DC: Center for Economic and Policy Research. Retrieved from http://www.cepr.net/index.php/publications/reports/leaves-that-pay.

Armstrong, E. A. (2002). *Forging gay identities: Organizing sexuality in San Francisco, 1950–1994.* Chicago: University of Chicago Press.

Associated Press. (2013, May 29). Mothers now top earners in 4 of 10 households. *New York Times.* http://www.nytimes.com/aponline/2013/05/29/business/ap-ap-us-breadwinner-moms.html?_r=0.

Avellar, S., & Smock, P. (2003). Has the price of motherhood declined over time? A cross cohort comparison of the motherhood wage penalty. *Journal of Marriage and Family, 65*(3), 597–607.

Barnett, W. S. (1996). *Lives in the balance: Age 27 benefit cost analysis of the High Scope Perry Preschool Program.* Ypsilanti, MI: High Scope Education Research Foundation.

Barnett, W. S., & Ackerman, D. J. (2006). Costs, benefits, and long-term effects of early care and education programs: Recommendations and cautions for community developers. *Community Development Society, 37*(2), 86–100. Retrieved from http://search.ebscohost.com/login.aspx?direct=true&db=sih&AN=21560459&site=eh ost-live.

Barnett, W. S., Brown, K., & Shore, R. (2004). *The universal vs. targeted debate: Should the United States have preschool for all?* New Brunswick, NJ: National Institute for Early Education Research.

Barnett, S., & Carolan, M. (2013). *Trends in state funded preschool programs: Survey findings from 2001–2002 to 2011–2012.* Center on Enhancing Early Learning Out-comes, National Institute for Early Education Research, Rutgers, State University of New Jersey. Retrieved from http://nieer.org/sites/nieer/files/Trends%20in%20 State%20Funded%20Preschool%20Programs_0.pdf.

Barnett, S., Carolan, M., Fitzgerald, J., & Squires, J. H. (2012). *The state of preschool 2012.* Retrieved from the National Institute for Early Education Research: http://nieer.org/publications/state-preschool-2012.

Baum, C. (2006). The effects of government mandated family leave on employer family leave policies. *Contemporary Economic Policy, 24*(3), 432–445.

Becker, M. (2011). *Union muscle eclipsed by high-profile conservative groups during the 2010 election*. Washington, DC: Center for Responsive Politics. Retrieved from http://www.opensecrets.org/news/2011/03/union-muscle-eclipsed-by-conservative-groups.html#.

Belfield, C. R., Nores, M., Barnett, W. S., & Schweinhart, L. J. (2006). The High/Scope Perry Preschool Program: Cost-benefit analysis using data from the age-40 follow-up. *Journal of Human Resources, 41*(1), 162–190.

Benford, R. D. (1993). Frame disputes within the nuclear disarmament movement. *Social Forces, 71*(3), 677–701.

Benz, J., & Gray, V. (2011). *The influence of state policy experience on national policy support*. Paper presented at the Annual Conference of State Politics and Policy Section, Dartmouth College, Hanover, NH.

Berry, J. M. (1997). *The interest group society* (3rd ed.). New York: Longman.

Berry, J. M., & Wilcos, C. (2008). *Interest group theory* (5th ed.). New York: Longman.

Berry, M. F. (1993). *The politics of parenthood*. New York: Penguin.

Besharov, D. (1994, December 11). Trapped in the daycare maze. *Washington Post*. Retrieved from AEI: http://www.aei.org/article/18938.

Besharov, D., Morrow, J. S., & Fengyan Shi, A. (2006). *Child care data in the survey of income program and participation: Inaccuracies and corrections*. Retrieved from the American Enterprise Institute for Public Policy: http://www.aei.org/papers/education/child-care-data-in-the-survey-of-income-and-program-participation-sipp/.

Besharov, D., Myers, J., & Morrow, J. (2007). *Cost per child for early childhood education and care*. Retrieved from University of Maryland and the American Enterprise, Welfare Reform Academy: http://www.welfareacademy.org/pubs/childcare_edu/costperchild.pdf.

Bianchi, S. M., Robinson, J. P., & Milkie, M. A. (2006). *Changing rhythms of American family life*. New York: Russell Sage Foundation.

Birth and Adoption Unemployment Compensation Rule, 20 C.F.R. 604 (1999).

Bjerre-Poulsen, N. (2002). *Right face: Organizing the American conservative movement 1945–65*. Copenhagen: Museum Tusculanum Press.

Blank, H. (2013, September 18). *Chutes and ladders?* [Newsletter]. Washington, DC: Women's Law Center.

Blau, D. (2001). *The child care problem*. New York: Russell Sage Foundation.

Blow, C. M. (2011, August 5). The decade of lost children. *New York Times*, p. A15. Retrieved from http://www.nytimes.com/2011/08/06/opinion/the-decade-of-lost-children.html.

Blumer, H. (1954). What is wrong with social theory. *American Sociological Review, 18*, 3–10.

———.(1971). Social problems as collective behavior. *Social Problems, 18*(3), 298–306.

Bosso, C. J. (1994). The contextual bases of problem definition. In D. A. Rochefort & R. W. Cobb (Eds.), *The politics of problem definition* (pp. 182–202). Lawrence: University Press of Kansas.

Bostrom, M. (2002). *The whole child—Parents and policy: A meta analysis of opinion data concerning school readiness, early childhood and related issues.* Retrieved from the Frameworks Institute: http://www.frameworksinstitute.org/assets/files/ECD/the_whole_child.pdf.

Boushey, H. (2007). *Perspectives on work/family balance and the federal equal employment opportunity laws.* Testimony to the Equal Employment Opportunity Commission. Retrieved from http://www.cepr.net/index.php/perspectives-on-workfamily-balance-testimony-to-the-eeoc/.

———.(2009). Family friendly for all families. In Maria Shriver & the Center for American Progress (Eds.), *Shriver report: A woman's nation.* Retrieved from http://www.americanprogress.org/issues/2009/10/pdf/awn/a_womans_nation.pdf.

Boushey, H., & Wright, J. (2004). *Working mothers and child care.* Washington, DC: Economic Policy Institute.

Bowman, B. T., Donovan, M. S., & Burns, M. S. (Eds.). (2000). *Eager to learn: Educating our preschoolers.* Washington, DC: National Academies Press.

Boyd, J., Barnett, W. S., Bodrov, E., Leong, D. J., Gomby, D., Robin, K. B., & Hustedt, J. T. (2005). *Promoting children's social and emotional development through preschool.* New Brunswick, NJ: National Institute for Early Education Research. Retrieved from http://nieer.org/resources/policyreports/report7.pdf.

British Government. (2013). *Guide: Paternity pay and leave.* Retrieved from https://www.gov.uk/paternity-pay-leave/pay.

Brooks, F. P. (2005). New turf for organizing: Family child care providers. *Labor Studies Journal, 29*(4), 45–64.

Brulle, R. J., & Jenkins, J. C. (2005). Foundations and the environmental movement: Priorities, strategies, and impact. In D. Faber & D. McCarthy (Eds.), *Foundations for social change: Critical perspectives on philanthropy and popular movements* (pp. 151–173). Lanham, MD: Rowman & Littlefield.

Budig, M. J., & England, P. (2001). The wage penalty for motherhood. *American Sociological Review, 66*(2), 204–225.

Budig, M., Misra, J., & Böckmann, I. (2012). The motherhood wage penalty in cross-national perspective: The importance of work-family policies and cultural attitudes? *Social Politics, 19*(2), 163–193.

Buehler, S. (1998). Child care tax credits, the child tax credit, and the Taxpayer Relief Act of 1997: Congress' missed opportunity to provide parents needed relief from the astronomical costs of child care. *Hastings Women's Law Journal, 9*, 189.

Burchinal, M. (1999). Child care experiences and developmental outcomes. *Annals of the American Academy of Political and Social Sciences, 563*, 73–97.

Burke, M. E. (2003). *Family Medical Leave Act.* Alexandria, VA: Society of Human Resource Managers. Retrieved from http://www.protectfamilyleave.org/research/2003_SHRM_FMLA_Survey.pdf.

Burstein, P., & Hirsch, C. E. (2007). Interest organizations, information, and policy innovation in the U.S. Congress. *Sociological Forum, 22*(2), 174–199.

Bushouse, B., McGhee, R., & Imig, D. (n.d.). *Not the usual suspects: The politics of pre-kindergarten during the recession.* Unpublished manuscript.

Business and Legal Resources. (2011). *Benchmark benefit survey series: Family leave practices.* Brentwood, TN: Author.

California Department of General Services. (2000, July). *Family and Medical Leave Act and California Family Rights Act, policy and procedures.* Retrieved from http://www.documents.dgs.ca.gov/ohr/Supervisor/DGSFMLAPolicyProcedures.pdf.

California Head Start Association. (2011). *Head Start program history timeline.* Retrieved from http://caheadstart.org/HeadStartHistory.pdf.

Calvert, C. T. (2010). *Family responsibilities discrimination: 2012 litigation update.* San Francisco: Center for WorkLife Law.

Canadian Worker Rights. (n.d.). *Taking time off: Maternity.* Retrieved from http://www.workrights.ca/content.php?doc=81.

Cantor, D., Waldfogel, J., Kerwin, J., Wright, M. M., Levin, J., Rauch, T., Hagerty, J., & Kudela, M. S. (2001). *Balancing the needs of families and employers: Family and medical leave surveys. 2000 update.* Rockville, MD: Westat.

Capizzino, J., & Main, R. (2005). *Many young children spend long hours in child care.* Retrieved from the Urban Institute: http://www.urban.org/publications/311154.html#n1.

Carmody, D. (1970, March 21). General strike by U.S. women urged to mark 19th Amendment; Militant leader sees 50th anniversary of voting rights, Aug. 26, as time for instant sexual revolution. *New York Times*, p. A20.

Center for American Progress. (n.d.). *About the Center for American Progress.* Retrieved from http://www.americanprogress.org/about/mission/.

Center for the Child Care Workforce. (n.d.). *About us.* Retrieved from http://www.ccw.org/index.php?option=com_content&task=view&id=13&Itemid=42.

Center for Responsive Politics. (2013a). *Super PACS.* Retrieved from http://www.opensecrets.org/pacs/superpacs.php.

———.(2013b). *Top PACS.* Retrieved from http://www.opensecrets.org/pacs/toppacs.php?Type=C&cycle=2012.

———.(n.d.-a). *Top spenders 2011.* Retrieved from http://www.opensecrets.org/lobby/top.php?indexType=s&showYear=2011.

———.(n.d.-b). *Top spenders 2012.* Retrieved from http://www.opensecrets.org/lobby/top.php?indexType=s&showYear=2012.

Chaudry, A. (2004). *Putting children first: How low-wage working mothers manage child care.* New York: Russell Sage Foundation.

Child Care Aware of America. (2012). *Parents and the high cost of child care.* Washington, DC: Author. Retrieved from http://www.naccrra.org/sites/default/files/default_site_pages/2012/cost_report_2012_final_081012_0.pdf.

Child Care and Development Block Grant Act of 1990, as amended. Pub. L. No. 101-508, 42 U.S.C. 9858 (1990). Retrieved from https://www.cfda.gov/?s=program&mode=form&tab=step1&id=ed161a0641a9a2e1e33505571634778f.

Child Welfare League of America. (2004). *National fact sheet: Children 2004: Visions, action, results.* Retrieved from http://www.cwla.org/advocacy/nationalfactsheet04.htm.

Children's Defense Fund. (2009, March 31). *Cradle to prison pipeline state fact sheets.* Retrieved from http://www.childrensdefense.org/child-research-data-publications/ data/state-data-repository/cradle-to-prison-pipeline-state-factsheets.html.

———.(n.d.). *Policy priorities: Full day kindergarten.* Retrieved from http://www. childrensdefense.org/policy-priorities/early-childhood-education-care/full-day-kindergarten.html.

Chira, S. (2013, June 30). To have (it all) and have not. *Sunday Times Review.* Retrieved from http://www.nytimes.com/2012/07/01/sunday-review/working-mothers-at-the-top.html?pagewanted=all&_r=0.

Chong, D. (1996). Creating common frames and references on political issues. In D. Mertz, P. Sniderman, & R. Brody (Eds.), *Political persuasion and attitude* (pp. 195–224). Ann Arbor: University of Michigan Press.

Ciazza, A. (2007). *I knew I could do this work. Seven strategies that promote women's activism and leadership in unions.* Washington, DC: Institute for Women's Policy Research. Retrieved from http://www.iwpr.org/initiatives/women-in-unions.

Citizens United v. Federal Election Commission, 130 S.Ct. 876 (2010).

Clearinghouse on International Developments. (2009). *The Clearinghouse on International Developments in Child, Youth and Family Policies at Columbia University.* New York: Columbia University. Retrieved from http://www.childpolicyintl.org.

Clemetson, L. (2006, February 9). Work vs. family, complicated by race. *New York Times.* Retrieved from http://www.nytimes.com/2006/02/09/fashion/ thursdaystyles/09MOMS.html?pagewanted=all&_r=0.

Coates, D. (1998). Additional incumbent spending really can harm (at least some) incumbents: An analysis of vote share maximization. *Public Choice, 95*(1–2), 63–87.

Cobb, R., & Elder, D. (1971). The politics of agenda-building: An alternative perspective for modern democratic theory. *Journal of Politics, 33*(4), 892–891.

———.(1983). *Participation in American politics: The dynamics of agenda building.* Baltimore, MD: Johns Hopkins University Press.

Cohen, S. S. (2001). *Championing child care.* New York: Columbia University Press.

Cohn, J. (2013, April 15). The hell of American day: An investigation into the barely regulated, unsafe business of looking after our children. *New Republic.* Retrieved from http://www.newrepublic.com/article/112892/hell-american-day-care.

Coiner, C., & George, D. H. (Eds.). (1998). *The family track: Keeping your faculties while you mentor, nurture, teach and serve.* Champaign: University of Illinois Press.

Committee for Economic Development. (2002). *Preschool for all: Investing in a productive and just society.* New York: Author.

———.(2006). *The economic promise of investing in high-quality preschool: Using early education to improve economic growth and the fiscal sustainability of states and the nation.* New York: Author. Retrieved from http://search.ebscohost.com/login.aspx? direct=true&db=eric&AN=ED502290&site=ehost-live.

Comprehensive Child Development Act of 1971: Joint Hearings before the Subcommittee on Employment, Manpower, and Poverty and the Subcommittee on Children and Youth of the Committee on Labor and Public Welfare, U.S. Senate, 92nd Cong. (1971). Washington, DC: Government Printing Office.

Confessore, N. (2011, August 28). Lines blur between candidates and PACs with unlimited cash. *New York Times*, p. A1.

Connelly, J. (2013, January 23). Will state's Family Leave Act get axed? *Seattlepi. org*. Retrieved from http://blog.seattlepi.com/seattlepolitics/2013/01/23/will-states-family-leave-act-get-axed/.

Consolidated Appropriations Act 2012, Pub. L. No. 112-74. Retrieved from http://www.gpo.gov/fdsys/pkg/PLAW-112publ74/pdf/PLAW-112publ74.pdf.

Consumer Health Products Association. (n.d.). *Healthcare flexible spending accounts facts and figures*. Retrieved from http://www.chpa-info.org/printer.aspx?id=110.

Conway, D. A., Ahern, D. W., & Steuernagel, G. A. (1995). *Women and public policy*. Washington, DC: CQ Press.

Cove, M. (2012). *I love Mondays: And other confessions from devoted working moms*. Emeryville, CA: Seal Press.

Covington, S. (2001). In the midst of plenty: Foundation funding of child advocacy organizations in the 1990s. In C. J. De Vita & R. Mosher-Williams (Eds.), *Who speaks for America's children? The role of child advocates in public policy* (pp. 39–80). Washington, DC: Urban Institute Press.

Criscione, V. (2011, March 18). Paternity rights and wrongs. *Guardian*. Retrieved from http://www.guardian.co.uk/money/2011/mar/19/parental-rights-norway-reduce-inequality.

Crittenden, A. (2002). *The price of motherhood: Why the most important job in the world is still the least valued*. New York: Henry Holt.

Crouse, J. (2004). *Feminism and the Family*. Remarks at the World Conference of Families, Mexico City, Mexico. Retrieved from http://www.worldcongress.org/wcf3_spkrs/wcf3_crouse.htm.

C-SPAN. (2012, September 27). *Child care issues and the presidential election*. Retrieved from http://www.c-spanvideo.org/program/308421-1.

Currie, J. (2001). *A fresh start for Head Start*. Retrieved from Brookings Institution: http://www.brookings.edu/papers/2001/03education_currie.aspx.

Dahl, R. A. (1998). *On democracy*. New Haven, CT: Yale University Press.

Davidson, J. (2010, December 7). Child-care subsidy spotty for federal employees. *Washington Post*, p. B3. Retrieved from http://proquest.umi.com/pqdweb?did=2205802501&Fmt=7&clientId=13234&RQT=309&VName=PQD.

DeNavas-Walt, C., Proctor, B. D., & Smith, J. C. (2010). *Income, poverty and health insurance in the United States: 2009*. Retrieved from U.S. Census Bureau, U.S. Department of Commerce: http://www.census.gov/prod/2010pubs/p60-238.pdf.

De Vita, C. J., Mosher-Williams, R., & Stengel, N. A. J. (2001). Nonprofit organizations engaged in child advocacy. In C. J. De Vita & R. Mosher-Williams (Eds.), *Who *speaks for America's children? The role of child advocates in public policy* (pp. 3–38). Washington, DC: Urban Institute Press.

DeWitt, L. (1999). *The 1937 Supreme Court rulings on the Social Security Act*. Retrieved from http://www.ssa.gov/history/court.html.

Dinner, D. (2010). The universal childcare debate: rights mobilization, social policy, and the dynamics of feminist activism, 1966–1974. *Law and History Review, 28,* 577–628.

Dobuzinskis, C. (2010). *Majority of voters support workplace flexibility, mob quality, and family support policies*. Washington, DC: Institute for Women's Policy Research.

Dobuzinskis, C., & Mpare, M. (2012, November 5). *Four key policy priorities for women missing from election debate*. Washington, DC: Institute for Women's Policy Research. Retrieved from http://www.iwpr.org/blog/2012/11/05/five-key-policy-priorities-for-women-missing-from-election-debate/.

Dorfman, L., & Lingas, E. O. (2003). *Making the case for paid family leave: How California's landmark law was framed in the news* (Issue 14). Berkeley, CA: Berkeley Media Studies Group.

Douthat, R., & Salam, R. (2008). *Grand new party: How Republicans can win the working class and save the American dream*. New York: Double Day Press.

Dowd, N. (1997). Taxing women: Thoughts on a gendered economy: Symposium: A look at equality: Women's, men's and children's equalities: some reflections and uncertainties. *Southern California Review of Law and Women's Studies, 6,* 287–289.

———.(2004). Symposium: Women's work is never done: Employment, family and activism: Bringing the margin to the center: Comprehensive strategies for work/family policies. *University of Cincinnati Law Review, 73,* 433–455.

Dowell, D. (2003). *Regional sectoral strategies to improve low wage jobs: A case study in child care—The Philadelphia experience* (Unpublished doctoral dissertation). Bryn Mawr College, Graduate School of Social Work and Social Research, Bryn Mawr, PA.

Druckman, J. (2001). On the limits of framing effects: who can frame. *Journal of Politics, 63*(4), 1041–1066.

———.(2004). Priming the vote: Campaign effects in the US Senate election. *Political Psychology, 25,* 577–590.

Druckman, J., & Nelson, K. (2003). Framing and deliberation: How citizens conversations limit elite influence. *American Journal of Political Science, 47*(4), 729–745.

Drummond, M., & Seid, R. (2001). *Caring for infants and toddlers: Issues and ideas. The future of children*. Los Altos, CA: David and Lucille Packard Foundation.

Duffy, M. (2010). "We are the union": Care work, unions, and social movements. *Humanity and Society, 34*(2), 125–140.

Duffy, M. M., Binder, A. J., & Skrentny, J. D. (2010). Elite status and social change: Using field analysis to explain policy formation and implementation. *Social Problems, 57*(1), 49–73.

Duncan, G. J., Ludwig, J., & Magnuson, K. A. (2007). Reducing poverty through preschool interventions. *Future of Children, 17*(2), 143–160. Retrieved from http://futureofchildren.org/futureofchildren/publications/docs/17_02_07.pdf.

Durkheim, E., & Sidel, R. (1998). *Keeping women and children last: America's war on the poor.* New York: Penguin.

Durst, A. (2005). Of women, by women, and for women: The day nursery movement in the progressive-era United States. *Journal of Social History, 39*(1), 141–159.

Dvorak, P. (2010, December 10). Cutting DC's child-care subsidy isn't the way to fix the city's budget. *Washington Post,* p. B1. Retrieved from http://www.washingtonpost.com/wp-dyn/content/article/2010/12/09/AR2010120906380.html.

Early Care and Education Consortium. (2009). *Child care and the economy.* Retrieved from http://www.ececonsortium.org/federal.php.

Edelman, M. (1988). *Constructing the political spectacle.* Chicago: University of Chicago Press.

Educare. (n.d.). *About us: What is Educare?* Retrieved from http://www.educare-schools.org/about/educare-Platform.php.

Eichner, M. (2010). *The supportive state: Families, government, and America's political ideals.* New York: Oxford University Press.

———.(2012). Rights and obligations in the contemporary family: Retheorizing individualism, families and the state: The family and the market. *Theoretical Inquiries in Law, 12,* 97–124.

Eidelson, J. (2012, July 23). Paid-sick-leave fight escalates in New York City, expands across the nation. *In These Times.* Retrieved from http://inthesetimes.com/working/entry/13560/paid-sick-leave_fight_escalates_in_new_york_city_expands_across_the_nation/.

Eisner, M. A. (2010). *The American political economy: Institutional evolution of market and state.* New York: Routledge.

Embassy of France. (n.d.). *Childcare.* Retrieved from http://www.ambafrance-us.org/spip.php?article555.

EMILY's List. (n.d.). *Our mission.* Retrieved from http://emilyslist.org/who/mission/.

Employment Act 2008, chapter 24. Retrieved from http://www.legislation.gov.uk/ukpga/2008/24/pdfs/ukpga_20080024_en.pdf.

Esping-Andersen, G. (1999). *Social foundations of postindustrial economies.* New York: Oxford University Press.

———.(2009). *The incomplete revolution: Adapting to women's new roles.* Malden, MA: Polity Press.

Esping-Andersen, G., Garfinkel, I., Han, W., Magnuson, K., Wagner, S., & Waldfogel, J. (2012). Child care and school performance in Denmark and the United States. *Children and Youth Services Review, 12*(3), 576–589.

Evans, J. J. (1997). Multi-organizational fields and social movement organization frame content: The religious pro-choice movement. *Sociological Inquiry, 67*(4), 451–469.

Fagnani, J. (2010). Childcare policies in France: The influence of organizational changes in the workplace. In S. B. Kamerman, S. Phipps, & A. Ben-Arieh (Eds.), *From child welfare to child well-being an international perspective on knowledge in the service of policy making* (pp. 385–402). New York: Springer.

———.(2012). Recent reforms in childcare and family policies in France and Germany: What was at stake? *Children and Youth Services Review, 34*(3), 509–516.

Family and Medical Leave Act of 1993, Pub. L. No. 103-3 (1993).

Family Research Council. (n.d.). *Marriage and family: Parental rights.* Retrieved from http://www.frc.org/marriage-family#rights.

Farkas, S., Duffett, A., & Johnson, J. (2000). *Necessary compromises: How parents, employers and children's advocates view child care today.* Public Agenda. Retrieved from http://www.publicagenda.org/files/necessary_compromises.pdf.

Farnam, T. W., & Keslo, N. V. (2010). All interest groups and political parties active this year. *Washington Post.* Retrieved from http://www.washingtonpost.com/wp-srv/politics/campaign/2010/spending/committee_list.html.

Farrell, N. (2012). California's paid family leave is worth replicat-ing. *The Hill.* Retrieved from http://thehill.com/blogs/congress-blog/presidential-campaign/260739-californias-paid-family-leave-is-worth-replicating.

Federal Election Commission. (2011). *The biennial contribution limit.* Retrieved from http://www.fec.gov/pages/brochures/biennial.shtml.

Ferree, M. M. (2003). Resonance and radicalism: Feminist framing in the abortion debates of the United States and Germany. *American Journal of Sociology, 109*(2), 304–344.

Firestone, S. (1970). *The dialectic of sex: The case for feminist revolution.* New York: Morrow.

First Five Years Fund. (2013). *Take action now.* Retrieved from http://growamericas-tronger.org/wp-content/uploads/2013/07/Poll-Fact-Sheet.pdf.

Flakoll, C. (2009). *In other words: Preschool plans oversold, unproven and unrealistic.* Retrieved from http://www.cwfa.org/articledisplay.asp?id=18143&department=FIELD&categoryid=misc.

Flanders, L. (2012, April 11). Can "caring across generations" change the world. *Nation.* Retrieved from http://www.thenation.com/article/167354/can-caring-across-generations-change-world.

Focus on the Family. (2010). *What do you think of placing children in child-care centers so mothers can work?* Retrieved from http://family.custhelp.com/cgi-bin/family.cfg/php/enduser/std_adp.php?p_faqid=784&p_created=1043443394.

Folbre, N. (2008). *Valuing children: Rethinking the economics of the family.* Cambridge, MA: Harvard University Press.

Forum on Child and Family Statistics. (2011). *America's children: Key national indica-tors of well-being 2011.* Retrieved from http://www.childstats.gov/americaschildren/famsoc3.asp.

Friedan, B. (1966). *The National Organization for Women's 1966 statement of purpose.* Retrieved from NOW: http://www.now.org/history/purpos66.html.

Fuller, B., Loeb, S., Strath, A., & Carrol, B. A. (2004). State formation of the child care sector: Family demand and policy action. *Sociology of Education, 77*(4), 337–358.

Garofalo, P. (2011, February 16). *Republican officials cut Head Start funding, saying women should be married and home with kids.* Retrieved from Think Progress: http://thinkprogress.org/politics/2011/02/16/144869/gop-women-kids/?mobile=nc.

Gerber, E., & Lupia, A. (1999). Voter competence in direct legislation elections. In S. Elkin & K. Soltan (Eds.), *Citizens, competence and democratic institutions* (pp. 147–160). College Station: Pennsylvania State University Press.

Gerstel, N., & Clawson, D. (2001). Unions responses to family concerns. *Social Problems, 48*(2), 277–297.

Gilbert, N. (1998). From service to social control: Implications of welfare reform for professional practice in the United States. *European Journal of Social Work, 1*(1), 101–108.

———.(2008). *A mother's work: How feminism, the market and policy shape family life.* New Haven, CT: Yale University Press.

Gilens, M. (1996). "Race coding" and white opposition to welfare. *American Political Science Review, 90*(3), 593–604.

———.(1999). *Why Americans hate welfare.* Chicago: University of Chicago Press.

Glantz, S., Abramowitz, A., & Burkart, M. (1976). Election outcomes: Whose money matters? *Journal of Politics, 38,* 1033–1038.

Glynn, S. (2012, August 16). *Fact sheet: Child care: Families need more help to care for their children.* Washington, DC: Center for American Progress. Retrieved from http://www.americanprogress.org/issues/labor/news/2012/08/16/11978/fact-sheet-child-care/.

Goffman, E. (1974). *Frame analysis: An essay on the organization of experience.* Cambridge, MA: Harvard University Press.

Goldberg, G. S. (Ed.). (2009). *Poor women in rich nations: A study of the feminization of poverty.* New York: Oxford University Press.

Golden, C. (1990). *Understanding the gender gap: An economic history of American Women.* New York: Oxford University Press.

Goldstein, K., & Freedman, P. (2000). New evidence for new arguments: Money and advertising in the 1996 Senate elections. *Journal of Politics, 62*(4), 1087–1108.

Goodman, P. (2010, May 24). Cuts to child care subsidy thwart more job seekers. *New York Times,* p. A1.

———.(2012, April 6). Child care cuts leave working poor parents struggling. *Huffington Post.* Retrieved from http://www.huffingtonpost.com/2012/04/04/child-care-cuts-california_n_1402819.html.

Gottfried, P., & Fleming, P. (1988). *The conservative movement.* Boston: Twayne.

Government Accounting Office. (2002). *Child care: States have undertaken a variety of quality improvement initiatives, but more evaluations of effectiveness are needed.* Retrieved from http://www.gao.gov/new.items/d02897.pdf.

———.(2003). *Women's earnings: Work patterns partially explain differences between men's and women's earnings.* Retrieved from http://www.gao.gov/new.items/d0435.pdf.

———.(2010). *Child care: Multiple factors could have contributed to the recent decline in the number of children whose families receive subsidies.* Retrieved from http://www.gao.gov/new.items/d10344.pdf.

GPO Access. (2008). *Budget of the United States: Fiscal year 2008* [Data set]. Retrieved from Office of the President: http://www.gpoaccess.gov/usbudget/fy08/sheets/8_23.xls.

Graff, E. J. (2012). Why does The Atlantic hate women? Why men (oh, and women, too) still can't have it all. *American Prospect.* Retrieved from http://prospect.org/article/why-does-atlantic-hate-women.

Grant, J., Hoorens, S., Sivadasn, S., van het Loo, M., DaVanzo, J., Hale, L., Gibson, S., & Butz, W. (2004). *Low fertility and population ageing causes, consequences, and policy options: A report prepared for the European Commission.* Santa Monica, CA: RAND. Retrieved from http://www.rand.org/content/dam/rand/pubs/monographs/2004/RAND_MG206.pdf.

Greenhouse, S. (2009, May 16). Bill would guarantee up to 7 days paid sick leave. *New York Times,* p. A9.

———.(2011, January 21). Union membership in U.S. fell to a 70-year low last year. *New York Times.* Retrieved from http://www.nytimes.com/2011/01/22/business/22union.html.

Grodzins, M. (1999). The federal system. In S. Nivola & P. Rosenbloom (Eds.), *Classic readings in American politics* (pp. 52–67). New York: Wadsworth Press.

Grosswald, B. (2004). The effect of shift work on family satisfaction. *Families in Society: The Journal of Contemporary Social Services, 85*(3), 413–423.

Grow America Stronger. (2013). *Sample outreach discussion guide.* Retrieved from http://growamericastronger.org/wp-content/uploads/2013/07/Sample-state-team-outreach-discussion-guide.pdf.

Halfon, N., Russ, S., Oberklaid, F., Bertrand, J., & Eisenstadt, N. (2009). An international comparison of early childhood initiatives: From services to systems. *Journal of Developmental and Behavioral Pediatrics, 30*(5), 471–473.

Hamilton, J. (1999). Federalist No. 28: The same subject continued (The idea of restraining the legislative authority in regard to the common defense considered). In S. Nivola & P. Rosenbloom (Eds.), *Classic readings in American politics* (pp. 76–79). New York: Wadsworth Press.

Hamm, K. (2006). *More than meets the eye: Head Start programs, participants, families and staff in 2005* (Policy Brief 8). Washington, DC: Center for Law and Social Policy.

Hamm, K., Gault, B., & Jones-DeWeever, A. (2005). *In our own backyards: Local and state strategies to improve the quality of family child care.* Washington, DC: Institute for Women's Policy Research.

Harkin, T. (2012). *Under threat: Sequestration's impact on nondefense jobs and services.* Retrieved from http://harkin.senate.gov/documents/pdf/500ff3554f9ba.pdf.

Harrington, M. (1999). *Care and equality: Inventing a new family politics.* New York: Routledge.

Hartz, L. (1955). *The liberal tradition in America: An interpretation of American political thought.* New York: Harcourt, Brace and World.

————.(1999). The concept of a liberal society. In S. Nivola & P. Rosenbloom (Eds.), *Classic readings in American politics* (pp. 8–15). New York: Wadsworth Press.

Haxton, B. (2007). *A brief history of changes in the Head Start Program.* Retrieved from California Head Start Association: http://caheadstart.org/HeadStartHistory.pdf.

Heath, T. (2011, May 2). These "mompreneurs" do circles around the mommy track. *Washington Post*, p. A11. Retrieved from http://articles.washingtonpost.com/2011-05-01/business/35263989_1_mompreneurs-dance-classes-three-kids.

Heckman, J. J. (2008). Schools, skills and synapses. *Economic Inquiry, 46*(3), 289–324.

Heckman, J., Grunewald, R., & Reynolds, A. (2006). The dollars and cents of investing early: Cost-benefit analysis in early care and education. *Zero to Three, 26*(6), 10–17.

Heckman, J., & Masterov, D. (2007). The productivity argument for investing in young children. *Review of Agricultural Economics, 29*(3), 446–493.

Heckman, J. J., Stixrud, J., & Urzua, S. (2006). The effects of cognitive and noncognitive abilities on labor market outcomes and social behavior. *Journal of Labor Economics, 24*(3), 411–482.

Hegewisch, A., & Hara, Y. (2013, May). *Briefing paper: Maternity, paternity and adoption leave in the U.S. Institute for Women's Policy Research.* Retrieved from www.iwpr.org/publications/pubs/maternity-paternity-and-adoption-leave-in-the-united-states-1.

Henley, J. R., Shaefer, H. L., & Waxman, E. (2006). Nonstandard work schedules: Employer- and employee-driven flexibility in retail jobs. *Social Service Review, 80*(4), 609–634.

Henneberger, M. (2011, November 11). "Princess Nancy" Pelosi calls Cain "clueless"; vows to do more for child care. *Washington Post*. Retrieved from http://articles.washingtonpost.com/2011-11-17/lifestyle/35282356_1_child-care-care-for-low-income-parents-drew-hammill.

Hewlett, S. A., & West, C. (1998). *The war against parents.* Boston: Houghton Mifflin.

Heymann, S. J. (2000). *The widening gap: Why working families are in jeopardy and what can be done about it.* New York: Basic Books.

Heymann, S. J., Earle, A., & Hayes, J. (2007). *The work, family and equity index: How does the United States measure up?* Retrieved from The Project on Global Working Families, Institute for Health and Social Policy, McGill University: http://www.mcgill.ca/files/ihsp/WFEI2007.pdf.

Hirokazu, Y. (1995). Long-term effects of early childhood programs on social outcomes and delinquency. *Future Children, 5*, 51–75. Retrieved from http://www.princeton.edu/futureofchildren/publications/docs/05_03_02.pdf.

Hoefer, R. (2000). Human services interest groups in four states: Lessons from effective advocacy. *Journal of Community Practice, 7*(4), 77–94.

Hoffman, B. (2003). Health care reform and social movements in the United States. *American Journal of Public Health, 93*(1), 75–85.

Hoffman, E. (2010). *Head Start participants, programs, families, and staff in 2009.* Retrieved from the Center for Law and Social Policy: http://www.clasp.org/admin/site/publications/files/hs-preschool-pir-2009.pdf.

Hojnacki, M., Kimball, D., Baumgartner, F., Berry, J., & Leech, B. (2012). Studying organizational advocacy and influence: Reexamining interest group research. *Annual Review of Political Science, 15*, 379–399.

Holland, J. J. (2007, July 23). Federal minimum wage to rise by 70 cents. *USA Today.* Retrieved from http://www.usatoday.com/money/economy/2007-07-23-1912707305_x.htm.

Hollo, T. (2012). *Evaluating family and medical leave insurance for Washington state.* Retrieved from the Economic Opportunity Institute: http://www.eoionline.org/work_and_family/reports/EvaluatingFamilyandMedicalLeave-May12.pdf.

Hoplin, N., & Robinson, R. (2008). *Funding fathers: The unsung heroes of the conservative movement.* New York: Regency.

Hurwitz, J., & Peffley, M. (2005). Playing the race cared in the post-Willie Horton era: The impact of racially coded words on support for punitive crime policy. *Public Opinion Quarterly, 69*(1), 99–112.

Imig, D. (2001). Mobilizing parents and communities for children. In C. J. De Vita & R. Mosher-Williams (Eds.), *Who speaks for America's children? The role of child advocates in public policy* (pp. 191–207). Washington, DC: Urban Institute Press.

———.(2006). Building a social movement for America's children. *Journal of Children and Poverty, 12*(1), 21–37.

Imig, D., & Meyer, D. S. (2007, August). *The politics of universal pre-kindergarten.* Paper presented at the annual meeting of the American Political Science Association, Chicago.

Improving Head Start for School Readiness Act of 2007, HR 1429, 110th Congress (2008).

Institute for Women's Policy Research. (2007, August). *Maternity leave in the United States: Paid parental leave is still not standard, even among best U.S. employers.* Washington, DC: Author.

———.(2010, October 29). *Majority of voters support workplace flexibility, job quality, and family support policies.* Washington, DC: Author. Retrieved from http://www.iwpr.org/press-room/press-releases/majority-of-workers-support-workplace-flexibility-job-quality-and-family-support-policies.

Internal Revenue Service. (2011a). *Publication 503: Child and dependent care expenses.* Retrieved from http://www.irs.gov/pub/irs-pdf/p503.pdf.

———.(2011b). *Ten Facts about the child tax credit.* Retrieved from http://www.irs.gov/uac/Ten-Facts-about-the-Child-Tax-Credit.

———.(2013). *Topic 602—Child and dependent care credit.* Retrieved from http://www.irs.gov/taxtopics/tc602.html.

Isaacs, J., Edelstein, S., Hahn, H., Toran, K., & Stuerle, C. E. (2013). *Kids' share 2013: Federal expenditures on children in 2012 and future projections.* Washington, DC: Urban Institute. Retrieved from http://www.firstfocus.net/sites/default/files/KS2013.pdf.

Israel, J., & Mehta, A. (2010). *Who bank roles Congress? The big money behind top law makers.* Washington, DC: Center for Public Integrity. Retrieved from http://www.publicintegrity.org/articles/entry/2111/.

Jaffe, S. (2013, January 28). Trickle down feminism. *Dissent*. Retrieved from http://www.dissentmagazine.org/article/trickle-down-feminism.

Jansson, B. (2009). *The reluctant welfare state: Engaging history to advance social work practice in contemporary society* (6th ed.). Belmont, CA: Brooks-Cole.

Johnson, J. B., & Reynolds, H. T. (2008). *Political science research methods* (6th ed.). Washington, DC: CQ Press.

Jones, G. (2002, September. 23). Davis to sign bill allowing paid family leave benefits: Measure grants most workers time off to care for a new child or sick family members. Supporters see it as a model for the nation. *Los Angeles Times*. Retrieved from http://articles.latimes.com/2002/sep/23/local/me-family23.

Joo, M. (2008). The impact of availability and generosity of subsidized childcare on low-income mothers' work hour. *Journal of Policy Practice, 7*(4), 298–313.

Kahn, A., & Kamerman, S. (1991). *Child care, parental leave, and the under 3s: Policy innovation in Europe*. Westport, CT: Praeger.

Kamerman, S., & Kahn, A. (1976). *Child-care programs in nine countries: A report*. Washington, DC: U.S. Department of Health, Education, and Welfare, Office of Human Development/Office of Child Development, Research and Evaluation Division.

———.(1981). *Child care, family benefits and working parents: A study in comparative family policy analysis*. New York: Columbia University Press.

Karch, A. (2010). Policy feedback and preschool funding in the American States. *Policy Studies Review, 38*(2), 217–235.

Karin, M. (2009). Time off for military families: An emerging case study in a time of war . . . and the tipping point for future laws supporting work-life balance? *Rutgers Law Record, 33*, 46–64.

Katner, D. R. (2010). Delinquency and daycare. *Harvard Law & Policy Review, 4*, 49–72.

Katz, M. (1989). *The undeserving poor: From the war on poverty to the war on welfare*. New York: Pantheon.

———.(1996). *In the shadow of the poorhouse*. New York: Basic Books.

Kinder, D., & Nelson, T. (2005). Democratic debate and real opinion. In K. Callaghan & F. Schnell (Eds.), *Framing American politics* (pp. 103–122). Pittsburgh, PA: University of Pittsburgh Press.

Kirp, D. L. (2007). *The sandbox investment: The preschool movement and kids-first politics*. Cambridge, MA: Harvard University Press.

Klein, A. G. (1992). *The debate over child care: A sociohistorical analysis*. Albany: State University of New York Press.

Klerman, J. A., Daley, K., & Pozniak, A. (2013). *Family and Medical Leave Act in 2012: Technical report*. Prepared for the U.S. Department of Labor. Cambridge, MA: Abt Associates. Retrieved from http://www.dol.gov/asp/evaluation/fmla/FMLATechnicalReport.pdf.

Kornbluh, F. (2007). *The battle for welfare rights: Politics and poverty in modern America*. Philadelphia: University of Pennsylvania Press.Koven, S., & Michel, S. (2003). *Mothers of a new world: Maternalist politics and the origins of the welfare states*. New York: Routledge.

Krugman, P. (2011, February 20). Wisconsin power play. *New York Times*, p. A17. Retrieved from http://www.nytimes.com/2011/02/21/opinion/21krugman.html.

Kunin, M. (2012). *The new feminist agenda: Defining the next revolution for women, work, and family.* White River Junction, VT: Chelsea Green.

Kuttner, R. (2002, July 15). Philanthropy and movements. *American Prospect*, pp. 2–3.

LaCorte, R. (2013, January 24). Dueling bills introduced on paid family leave law. *Seattle Times.* Retrieved from http://seattletimes.com/html/localnews/2020208345_apwapaidfamilyleave4thldwritethru.html?syndication=rss.

Laughlin, L. (2010). Who's minding the kids? Child care arrangements: Summer 2005/summer 2006. *Current Population Reports.* Retrieved from the U.S. Census Bureau: http://www.census.gov/prod/2010pubs/p70-121.pdf.

———.(2011). Maternity leave and employment patterns of first-time mothers: 1961–2008. *Current Population Reports.* Retrieved from the U.S. Census Bureau: http://www.census.gov/prod/2011pubs/p70-128.pdf.

Lenhoff, D. (2004, October). *Family and medical leave in the United States: Historical and political reflections.* Paper presented at After Birth: Policies for Healthy Women, Families and Workplaces, Hubert H. Humphrey Institute of Public Affairs, School of Public Health, University of Minnesota. Retrieved from http://www.hhh.umn.edu/img/assets/6266/lenhoff.pdf.

Leonard, S. (2013, Winter). The new feminism. *Dissent.* Retrieved from http://www.dissentmagazine.org/article/introduction-new-feminism.

Lester, G. (2011). Can Joe the plumber support redistribution? Law, social preferences, and sustainable policy design. *Tax Law Review, 64,* 313–375.

Levitsky, S. R. (2005). *Niche activism: Negotiating organizational heterogeneity in contemporary American social movements.* Paper presented at the American Sociological Association annual meeting, Philadelphia.

Levitsky, S., & Banaszak-Holl, J. (2010). Social movements and the transformation of American health care. In J. Banaszak-Holl, S. R. Levitsky, & M. Zald (Eds.), *Social movements and the transformation of American health care* (pp. 3–22). New York: Oxford University Press.

Lindbloom, C., & Woodhouse, E. (1992). *The policy making process* (3rd ed.). Upper Saddle River, NJ: Prentice Hall.

Lipnic, V. A., & DeCamp, P. (2007). *Family and Medical Leave Act regulations: A report on the Department of Labor's request for information.* Washington, DC: U.S. Department of Labor. Retrieved from http://digitalcommons.ilr.cornell.edu/key_workplace/315/.

Lipton, E. (2011, February 22). Billionaire brothers' money plays role in Wisconsin budget dispute. *New York Times*, p. A16.

Lombardi, J. (2003). *Time to care: Redesigning child care to promote education, support families and build communities.* Philadelphia: Temple University Press.

Loseke, D. (1992). *Battered women and shelters: The social construction of wife abuse.* Albany: State University of New York Press.

Lovell, V., O'Neill, E., & Olsen, S. (2007). *Maternity leave in the United States: Paid parental leave is still not standard, even among the best U.S. employers* (IWPR #A131). Washington, DC: Institute for Women's Policy Research. Retrieved from http://www.iwpr.org/publications/pubs/maternity-leave-in-the-united-states-paid-parental-leave-is-still-not-standard-even-among-the-best-u.s.-employers.

Lovely, E. (2010, April 26). *Finding Hill day care not child's play.* Retrieved from Politico: http://www.politico.com/news/stories/0410/36321.html.

Lowrey, A. (2013, January 17). Difficult choices on debt if U.S. hits the ceiling. *New York Times*, p. A18. Retrieved from http://www.nytimes.com/2013/01/18/us/politics/hard-choices-on-debt-if-the-us-hits-the-ceiling.html.

Lukas, C. (2009). *Keep Uncle Sam away from toddlers: The case against government funding for preschool* (Policy brief). Retrieved from International Women's Forum: http://www.iwf.org/files/ccd51591aa7467a111d9f4437830ea9c.pdf.

Lynch, K. E., & McCallion, G. (2010). *The Child Care and Development Block Grant: Background and funding* (Congressional Research Service Report RL30785). Retrieved from http://www.policyarchive.org/handle/10207/bitstreams/19845.pdf.

Lynch, R. G. (2005). *Early childhood investment yields big payoff.* San Francisco: WestEd. Retrieved from http://www.wested.org/online_pubs/pp-05-02.pdf.

Macartney, S. (2011). *Child poverty in the United States 2009 and 2010: Selected race groups and Hispanic origin American community survey briefs.* Washington, DC: U.S. Department of Commerce.

Macartney, S., Bishaw, A., & Fontenot, K. (2013). *Poverty rates for selected detailed race and Hispanic groups by state and place: 2007–2011.* U.S. Census Bureau. Retrieved from http://www.census.gov/prod/2013pubs/acsbr11-17.pdf.

Macomber, J., Isaacs, J., Vericker, T., & Kent, A. (2010). *Public investment in children's early and elementary years (birth to age 11).* Washington, DC: Urban Institute and Brookings Institution. Retrieved from http://www.brookings.edu/~/media/research/files/reports/2010/4/15%20public%20investment%20isaacs/0415_pub-lic_investments.pdf.

Madison, J. (1999). Federalist No. 39: The conformity of the plan to Republican principles. In S. Nivola & P. Rosenbloom (Eds.), *Classic readings in American politics* (pp. 80–84). New York: Wadsworth Press.

Martin, S. B. (2009). FMLA protection recently expanded to military families: Qualifying exigency and servicemember family leave. *Compensation and Benefits Review*, 41, 43–51.

Maternity and Paternal Leave (Amendment) Regulations 2002, Pub. L. No. 2789 (2002). Retrieved from http://www.legislation.gov.uk/uksi/2002/2789/introduction/made.

Maternity and Paternity Leave Regulations 1999, Pub. L. No. 3312 (1999). Retrieved from http://www.legislation.gov.uk/uksi/1999/3312/regulation/10/made.

Matthews, H., & Schumacher, R. (2008). *Ensuring quality care for low income babies: Contracting directly with providers to expand and improve infant care.* Retrieved from the Center for Law and Social Policy: http://www.clasp.org/admin/site/publications/files/0422.pdf.

Mayer, G. (2011). *The Family and Medical Leave Act: Current legislative activity* (Congressional Review Service Report RL31760). Retrieved from http://assets.opencrs.com/rpts/RL31760_20110214.pdf.

McCaffery, E. J. (1996). Equality, of the right sort. *UCLA Women's Law Journal, 6*, 289–320.

McDonagh, E. (2009). *The motherless state: Women's political leadership and American democracy.* Chicago: University of Chicago Press.

McGuire, K. (2011, June 11). Grandparents come to rescue. *Baltimore Sun*, p. A8. Retrieved from http://proquest.umi.com/pqdweb?did=2372433211&Fmt=7&clientId=13234&RQT=309&VName=PQD.

McNeil, L. L. (1999). Assessing child care need under welfare reform. *Journal of Children and Poverty, 5*(1), 5–19.

Mead, L. (2011). Welfare politics in Congress. *Policy Studies: Political Science and Politics, 44*, 345–356.

Melmed, M. (2008, January 28). *Statement of Matthew Melmed, executive director of Zero to Three, to the Committee on Education and Labor, U.S. House of Representatives.* Retrieved from Zero to Three: http://www.zerotothree.org/site/DocServer/1-23-08_Investing_in_Early_Education_Testimony.pdf?docID=4841.

Mendelberg, T. (2001). *The race card: Campaign strategy, implicit messages, and the norm of equality.* Princeton, NJ: Princeton University Press.

Meyer, D., & Imig, D. (1993). Political opportunity and the rise and decline of interest group sectors. *Social Science Journal, 30*(3), 253–270.

Mezey, J., Greenberg, M., & Schumacher, R. (2002). *The vast majority of federally-eligible children did not receive child care assistance in FY 2000.* Retrieved from Center for Law and Social Policy: http://www.clasp.org/publications/1in7full.pdf.

Michel, S. (1999). *Children's interests/mothers' rights.* New Haven, CT: Yale University Press.

Milkman, R., & Appelbaum, E. (2004). *Paid family leave in California: New research findings* (Paper 02). Oakland: State of California Labor, University of California Institute for Labor and Employment.

Miller-Cribbs, J., Cagle, B. E., Natale, A. P., & Cummings, Z. (2010). Thinking about think tanks: strategies for progressive social work. *Journal of Policy Practice, 9*(3), 284–307.

Mills, C. W. (2000). *The sociological imagination.* New York: Oxford University Press.

Minsberg, T., & Williams, T. (2011, July 8). Shutdown in Minnesota ripples out to day care. *New York Times*, p. A13. Retrieved from http://www.nytimes.com/2011/07/09/us/politics/09minnesota.html.

Mishel, L., Bernstein, J., & Allegretto, S. (2005). *The State of Working America 2004–2005.* Ithaca, NY: Cornell University Press.

Misra, J., Budig, M., & Boeckmann, I. (2011). Work-family policies and the effects of children on women's employment hours and wages. *Community, Work & Family, 14*(2), 139–157.

Misra, J., Moller, S., Strader, E., & Wemlinger, E. (2012). Family policies, employment and poverty among partnered and single mothers. *Research in Social Stratification & Mobility, 30*(1), 113–128.

Mistry, R., Stevens, G. D., Sareen, H., De Vogli, R., & Halfon, N. (2007). Parenting-related stressors and self-reported mental health of mothers with young children. *American Journal of Public Health, 97*(7), 1261–1268. doi:10.2105/AJPH.2006.088161.

Mitchell, A. (2012). *Financial incentives in Quality Rating and Improvement Systems: Approaches and effects.* QRIS National Learning Network. Retrieved from http://www.qrisnetwork.org/sites/all/files/resources/gscobb/2012-05-24%2015:13/Approaches%20to%20Financial%20Incentives%20in%20QRIS.pdf.

Mitchell, A., Stoney, L., & Dichter, H. (2001). *Financing child care in the United States: An expanded catalog of current strategies* (2001 ed.). Philadelphia: Ewing Marion Kauffman Foundation. Retrieved from http://sites.kauffman.org/pdf/childcare2001.pdf.

Morgan, K. (2006). *Working mothers and the welfare state.* Stanford, CA: Stanford University Press.

———.(2008). The political path to a dual earner/dual career society: Pitfalls and possibilities. *Politics & Society, 36*(3), 406–420.

———.(2009). Caring time policies in Western Europe: Trends and implications. *Comparative European Politics, 7*(1), 37–55.

Morgan, K. J., & Zippel, K. (2003). Paid to care: The origins and effects of care leave policies in Western Europe. *Social Politics, 10*(1), 49–85.

Mulligan, G. M., Brimhall, D., & West, J. (2005). *Child care and early education arrangements of infants, toddlers, and preschoolers: 2001* (NCES 2006-039). Washington, DC: U.S. Department of Education, National Center for Education Statistics.

Nathan, R. P. (2008). Updating theories of American federalism. In T. Conlan & P. Possner (Eds.), *Intergovernmental management for the twenty first century* (pp. 3–17). Washington, DC: Brookings Institution.

Nathanson, C. A. (2010). The limitations of social movements as catalysts for change. In J. Banaszak-Holl, S. R. Levitsky, & M. Zald (Eds.), *Social movements and the transformation of American health care* (pp. 23–38). New York: Oxford University Press.

National Archives and Records Administration, Office of the Federal Register. (1998). *Public papers of the presidents of the United States, William J. Clinton, 1996, book 2, July 1 to December 31, 1996.* Washington, DC: Author.

National Association of Child Care Resource and Referral Agencies. (2006a). *Child care in America.* Washington, DC: Author.

———.(2006b). *We can do better: NACCRRA's ranking of state child care center standards and oversight.* Retrieved from http://www.naccrra.org/publications/naccrra-publications/we-can-do-better.

———.(2006c). *What do parents think about child care?* Retrieved from http://issuu.com/naccrra/docs/what-do-parents-think-about-child-care.

———.(2008a). *Child care in America: State facts sheets.* Retrieved from http://www.naccrra.org/policy/docs/childcareinamericafactsheet.pdf.

———.(2008b). *Leaving children to chance: NACCRRA's ranking of state standards and oversight of small child family child care homes.* Retrieved from http://www.naccrra.org/publications/naccrra-publications/leaving-children-to-chance.

———.(2008c). *Parent perceptions of child care in the United States.* Retrieved from http://www.naccrra.org/publications/naccrra-publications/publications/NAC-009%20Parents%20Perception%20Report-r3.pdf.

———.(2011). *Child care in America: 2011 state facts sheets.* Retrieved from http://www.naccrra.org/sites/default/files/default_site_pages/2011/childcareinamericafacts_full_report-2011.pdf.

———.(2012). *Parents and the cost of child care: 2012 update.* Retrieved from http://www.naccrra.org/sites/default/files/default_site_pages/2012/cost_report_2012_final_081012_0.pdf.

National Child Care Information and Technical Assistance Center. (2009). *NCCIC: QRIS definition and statewide system.* Retrieved from http://www.dataqualitycampaign.org/files/4_NCCIC_QRIS.pdf.

National Center for Responsive Politics. (n.d.). *Women's issues.* Retrieved from http://www.opensecrets.org/industries/indus.php?ind=Q08.

National Conference of State Legislators. (2008). *State family and medical leave laws.* Retrieved from http://www.ncsl.org/Portals/1/Documents/employ/StateFamilyand-MedicalLeaveLaws.pdf.

National Infant and Toddler Child Care Initiative and Zero to Three. (2008). *Designing quality rating systems inclusive of infants and toddlers.* Retrieved from http://main.zerotothree.org/site/DocServer/QRS_Design_Elements_for_Infants_and_Toddlers.pdf?docID=6150.

National Institute of Child Health and Human Development. (2006). *The NICD study of early child care and youth development: Findings for children up to 4 1/2 years.* Retrieved from U.S. Department of Health and Human Services, National Institute of Health: https://www.nichd.nih.gov/publications/pubs/documents/seccyd_06.pdf.

National Organization for Women. (1966). *The National Organization for Women's 1966 statement of purpose.* Retrieved from http://now.org/history/purpos66.html.

National Partnership for Women and Families. (2012). *Voters support paid leave legislation in Obama's second term, opinion piece states.* Retrieved from http://npwf.convio.net/site/News2?abbr=daily2_&page=NewsArticle&id=36893.

National Women's Law Center. (2012). *Tax credits outreach.* Retrieved from http://www.nwlc.org/tax-credits-outreach.

New York State Council on Children and Families. (n.d.). *Quality stars New York.* Retrieved from Council on Children and Families: http://earlychildhood.org/QSNY/index.cfm.

Newall, M. (2013, February 28). Parents sue in boy's day-care drowning death. *Philadelphia Inquirer.*

Nivola, P., & Rosenbloom, D. H. (Eds.). (1999). *Classic readings in American politics* (3rd ed.). New York: St. Martin's/Worth.

Nixon, R. (1971). 92nd Cong., S2007.

NPR. (2013, February 14). *Georgia to show off preschool successes.* Retrieved from http://www.npr.org/2013/02/14/171975380/georgia-to-show-off-preschool-successes.

Obama, B. (2013, February 12). *State of the Union Address.* Retrieved from http://www. nytimes.com/2013/02/13/us/politics/obamas-2013-state-of-the-union-address. html?pagewanted=all&_r=0.

Oden, S., Schweinhart, L., Weikart, D., Marcus, S., & Xie, Y. (2000). *Into adulthood: A study of the effects of Head Start.* Clinton, MI: High Scope Press.

Office of Child Care. (2011). *Administration on Child Care and Development Fund (CCDF) state spending under the fiscal year 2011 appropriation as of 9/30/2011.* Retrieved from http://www.acf.hhs.gov/sites/default/files/occ/final_fy11_over-view_9_30_11_508_compliant.pdf.

Office of Economic Development. (2010). *PF4.2 quality of childcare and early education services.* Retrieved from http://www.oecd.org/els/soc/37864559.pdf.

———.(2011). *PF3.2 enrollment in child care and preschools.* Paris: Author.

———.(2012). *PF10: Public spending on childcare and early education.* Retrieved from http://www.oecd.org/els/family/PF3.1%20Public%20spending%20on%20child-care%20and%20early%20education%20-%20290713.pdf.

Open Secrets. (n.d.). *EMILY's List.* Retrieved from http://www.opensecrets.org/orgs/summary.php?id=d000000113.

Opinion Research Corporation International. (1999). *Fight crime: Invest in kid: Back to school poll.* Washington, DC: Author.

Organisation for Economic Co-operation and Development. (2006). *Starting strong II: Early childhood education and care. Country profile: Sweden.* Retrieved from http:// www.oecd.org/document/56/0,3746,en_2649_39263231_37416703_1_1_1,00.html.

———.(2011). *Doing better for families: France.* Retrieved from http://www.oecd.org/els/familiesandchildren/47700963.pdf.

Padgett, D. K. (2008). *Qualitative methods in social work research* (2nd ed.). Thousand Oaks, CA: Sage.

Palin, S. (2008). *Acceptance speech.* Retrieved from http://www.youtube.com/watch?v=NUzVLRWWqqI.

Palley, E. (2010). Who cares for children? Why are we where we are with American child care policy? *Children and Youth Services Review, 32*(2), 155–163.

———.(2012). Expected struggles: U.S. child care policy. *Children and Youth Services Review, 34*(4), 628–638.

Palley, E., & Shdaimah, C. (2011). Child care policy: A need for greater advocacy. *Children and Youth Services Review, 33*(7), 1159–1165.

Parker, L. O. (2005). *I'm every woman: Remixed stories of marriage, motherhood, and work.* New York: HarperCollins.

Patton, M. Q. (2002). *Qualitative research and evaluation methods* (3rd ed.). Thousand Oaks, CA: Sage.

Pearce, D. (1978). The feminization of poverty: Women, work, and welfare. *Urban and Social Change Review, 11,* 28–36.

Personal Responsibility and Work Opportunity Reconciliation Act of 1996, Pub. L. No. 104-193, 104th Cong. (1996).

Peterson, B (Director). (2012, November 29). Working moms decide: Work or kids [Television series episode]. In *Katie*. Retrieved from http://bcove.me/ahpnigcu.

Pew Center on the States. (2009). *Votes count: Legislative action on pre-K: Fiscal year 2010*. Retrieved from http://www.pewtrusts.org/our_work_report_detail. aspx?id=55555.

———.(2011). *Transforming public education: Pathway to a pre-K through 12 future*. Retrieved from http://www.pewtrusts.org/uploadedFiles/wwwpewtrustsorg/ Reports/Pre-k_education/pathway-pre-k-12-future.pdf.

Pew Research Center for People and the Press. (1999). *Survey results: Retro politics*. Retrieved from http://www.people-press.org/1999/11/11/retro-politics/.

Phillips, D., & Zigler, E. (1987). The checkered history of federal child care regulation. *Review of Research in Education*, *14*, 3–41.

Phillips-Fein, K. (2009). *Invisible hands: The making of the conservative movement from the New Deal to Reagan*. New York: Norton.

Pierson, P. (1993). When effect becomes cause: Policy feedback and political change. *World Politics*, *45*(4), 595–628.

Piven, F. F., & Cloward, R. (1973). *Regulating the poor: The functions of public welfare*. New York: Vintage.

———.(1978). *Poor people's movements: Why they succeed, how they fail*. New York: Vintage.

Ploug, N. (2012). The Nordic child care regime—History, development and challenges. *Children and Youth Services Review*, *34*(3), 517–522.

Pomper, K., Blank, H., Campbell, N. D., & Schulman, K. (2004). *Be all that you can be: Lessons from the military for improving our nation's child care system*. Washington, DC: National Women's Law Center. Retrieved from http://www.nwlc.org/sites/ default/files/pdfs/BeAllThatWeCanBe_2004FollowUp.pdf.

Poo, A. (2013, April 22). Building a caring economy. *The Huffington Post*. Retrieved from http://www.huffingtonpost.com/aijen-poo/care-economy_b_3118846.html.

Pregnancy Discrimination Act of 1978, Pub. L. No. 95-555, 92 Stat. 2076, 29 C.F.R. Part 1604 (1978).

Prentice, S. (2009). High stakes: The "investable" child and the economic reframing of childcare. *Signs: Journal of Women in Culture and Society*, *34*(3), 687–710.

Quart, A. (2013, August 17). Crushed by the cost of child care. *New York Times*. Retrieved from http://opinionator.blogs.nytimes.com/2013/08/17/ crushed-by-the-cost-of-child-care/?_r=0.

A real, unnecessary crisis for families. (2011, May 3). *New York Times*, p. A22. Retrieved from http://www.nytimes.com/2011/05/03/opinion/03tue4.html.

Resmovitz, J. (2012, November 19). No Child Left Behind reauthorization debate likely to continue in Obama second term. *Huffington Post*. Retrieved from http://www.huff-ingtonpost.com/2012/11/19/no-child-left-behind-reauthorization_n_2161498.html.

Rigby, E. (2007). Same policy area, different politics: How characteristics of policy tools alter the determinants of early education policy. *Policy Studies Journal*, *35*, 653–670.

Robin, C. (2011). *The reactionary mind: Conservatism from Edmund Burke to Sarah Palin*. New York: Oxford University Press.

Robison, J. (2002). *Should mothers work?* Princeton, NJ: Gallup.

Rochefort, D. A., & Cobb, R. W. (1994). Problem definition: An emerging perspective. In D. A. Rochefort & R. W. Cobb (Eds.), *The politics of problem definition* (pp. 1–31). Lawrence: University Press of Kansas.

Roll, S., & East, J. (2012). Child care as a work support: A socialist feminist policy analysis. *Affilia, 27*(4), 358–370.

Rolnick, A., & Grunewald, R. (2003, March). Early childhood development: economic development with a high public return. *Fedgazette*. Retrieved from http://www. minneapolisfed.org/publications_papers/pub_display.cfm?id=3832.

Romer, C. (2010). *Work-life balance and the economics of the workplace*. Washington, DC: Executive Office of the President's Council of Economic Advisors.

Rose, E. (1999). *A mother's job*. New York: Oxford University Press.

———.(2009). Poverty and parenting: Transforming early education's legacy in the 1960s. *History of Education Quarterly, 49*(2), 222–235.

———.(2010). *The promise of preschool: From Head Start to universal pre-kindergarten*. New York: Oxford University Press.

Rosen, R. (2007). The care crisis. *Nation, 284*(10), 11–16.

Rubin, H. J., & Rubin, I. (2005). *Qualitative interviewing: The art of hearing data*. Thousand Oaks, CA: Sage.

Russell, John. (2005). *Funding the culture wars: Philanthropy, culture and state*. Washington, DC: National Committee for Responsive Philanthropy.

———.(2011). *Double standard: Social policy in Europe and the United States* (2nd ed.). Lanham, MD: Rowman & Littlefield.

Sabatier, P., & Jenkins-Smith, H. (1993). *Policy change and learning: An advocacy coalition approach*. Boulder, CO: Westview.

Sandelowski, M. (2000). Whatever happened to qualitative description? *Research in Nursing and Health, 23*(4), 334–340.

Schattschneider, E. E. (1960). *The semisovereign people*. New York: Holt, Rinehart and Winston.

Schatz, E. (2009). *Political ethnography: What immersion contributes to the study of power*. Chicago: University of Chicago.

Schilder, D., Kimura, S., Elliott, K., & Curenton, S. (2011, January). *Policy brief—Perspectives on the impact of pre-K expansion*. Retrieved from NIEER: http://nieer.org/resources/policybriefs/22.pdf.

Schneider, A., & Sidney, M. (2009). What is next for policy design and social construction theory. *Policy Studies Journal, 37*, 103–119.

Schneider, S. K., & Ingram, H. (1993). Social construction of target populations. *American Political Science Review, 87*(2), 334–346.

Schneider, S. K., & Jacoby, W. (2005). Elite discourse and American public opinion: The case of welfare spending. *Political Research Quarterly, 58*(3), 367–379.

Schonkoff, J., & Bales, S. N. (2011). Science does not speak for itself: Translating child development research for the public and its policymakers. *Child Development, 82*(1), 17–32.

Schonkoff, J. P., & Phillips, D. (Eds.). (2000). *From neurons to neighborhoods: The science of early child development.* Washington, DC: National Academies Press.

Schott, L. (2009). *Policy basics: An introduction to TANF.* Retrieved from Center on Budget and Policy Priorities: http://www.cbpp.org/cms/?fa=view&id=936.

Schram, S. F. (2002). *Praxis for the poor: Piven and Cloward and the future of social science in social welfare.* New York: New York University Press.

———.(forthcoming). Occupy precarity: Coalitions, movements, and multivariate marginality post great recession. *Theory and Event.*

Sears, D. O., & Henry, P. J. (2003). The origins of symbolic racism. *Journal of Personality and Social Psychology, 85*(2), 259–275.

Sered, G. (1995). Day care and tax policy. *American Journal of Tax Policy, 12,* 159.

Shapiro, J., & Applegate, J. S. (2002). Child care as a relational context for early development: Research in neurobiology and emerging roles for social work. *Children and Adolescent Social Work Journal, 19*(2), 97–114.

Shdaimah, C. S., Bryant, V., Sander, R., & Cornelius, L. (2011). Knocking on the door: Juvenile and family courts as a forum for facilitating school attendance and decreasing truancy. *Juvenile and Family Court Journal, 62*(4), 1–18.

Shdaimah, C. S., & McCoyd, J. L. M. (2011). Social work sense and sensibility: Reclaiming an integrated perspective across historical splits. *Social Work Education, 30*(1), 22–35.

Shdaimah, C., & Palley, E. (2012). Baby steps or big steps? Elite advocate perspectives on U.S. child care advocacy. *Journal of Policy Practice, 11*(3), 158–177.

Shriver, M., & Center for American Progress. (2009). *The Shriver report: A woman's nation changes everything.* Retrieved from http://www.americanprogress.org/issues/2009/10/womans_nation.html.

Shulman, K., & Blank, H. (2007). *State child care assistance policies 2007: Some steps forward, more progress needed.* Washington, DC: National Women's Law Center. Retrieved from http://www.nwlc.org/sites/default/files/pdfs/StateChildCareAssistancePoliciesReport07Web.pdf.

———.(2011). *State child care assistance policies 2011: Reduced support for families in challenging times.* Washington, DC: National Women's Law Center. Retrieved from http://www.nwlc.org/sites/default/files/pdfs/state_child_care_assistance_policies_report2011_final.pdf.

———.(2012). *Downward slide: State child care assistance policies 2012.* Washington, DC: National Women's Law Center. Retrieved from http://www.nwlc.org/sites/default/files/pdfs/NWLC2012_StateChildCareAssistanceReport.pdf.

Shumacher, R., & Hoffman, E. (2008). *Charting progress for babies in child care. Building supply of quality care.* Center for Law and Social Policy and Zero to Three. Retrieved from http://www.clasp.org/babiesinchildcare/recommendations?id=0013.

Simkin, C. F. (1972). Child care and household expense tax deduction under the new Section 214: Is this really the reform we were waiting for? *Women's Rights Law Reporter*, *1*(3), 15–17.

Simon, H. A. (1982). *Models of bounded rationality: Empirically grounded economic reason*. Boston: Massachusetts Institute of Technology.

Skocpol, T. (1992). *Protecting soldiers and mothers: The political origins of social policy in the United States*. Cambridge, MA: Harvard University Press.

Skocpol, T., & Dickert, J. (2001). Speaking for families and children in a changing civic America. In C. J. De Vita & R. Mosher-Williams (Eds.), *Who speaks for America's children? The role of child advocates in public policy* (pp. 137–164). Washington, DC: Urban Institute Press.

Slaughter, A. (2012, July/August). Why women still can't have it all. *Atlantic*. Retrieved from http://www.theatlantic.com/magazine/archive/2012/07/why-women-still-can-8217-t-have-it-all/9020/.

Smith, J. A. (1991). *The idea brokers: Think tanks and the rise of the new policy elite*. New York: Free Press.

Smith, K., & Gozjolko, K. (2010). *Low income and impoverished families pay more disproportionately for childcare* (Policy Brief No. 16). Durham, NH: Carsey Institute. Retrieved from http://www.carseyinstitute.unh.edu/publications/PB_Smith_Low-Income-ChildCare.pdf.

Smith, L. K. (2012). *Statement to the Senate, Committee on Health, Education, Labor, and Pensions, Subcommittee on Children and Families. CCDBG reauthorization: Helping to meet the child care needs of American families, hearing, July 26, 2012*. Retrieved from U.S. Department of Health and Human Services: http://www.hhs.gov/asl/testify/2012/02/t20120726a.html.

Smith v. Commissioner, 40 B.T.A. 1038 (1939), aff'd, 113 F.2d 114 (2d Cir. 1940).

Snow, D. A., Soule, S. A., & Kriesi, H. (2004). Mapping the terrain. In D. Snow, S. Soule, & H. Kriesi (Eds.), *The Blackwell companion to social movements* (pp. 3–16). Malden, MA: Blackwell.

Snow, D. S., Rochford, E. B., Worden, S. K., & Benford, R. D. (1986). Frame alignment processes, micromobilization, and movement participation. *American Sociological Review*, *51*(4), 464–481.

Spain, D., & Bianchi, S. M. (1996). *Balancing act: Motherhood, marriage, and employment among American women*. New York: Russell Sage Foundation.

Spalter-Roth, R., & Schreiber, R. (1995). Outsider issues and insider tactics: Strategic tensions in the Women's Policy Network during the 1980s. In M. M. Ferree & P. Y. Martin (Eds.), *Feminist organizations: Harvest of the new women's movement* (pp. 105–127). Philadelphia: Temple University Press.

Steinfels, M. (1973). *Who's minding the children? The history and politics of day care in America*. New York: Simon & Schuster.

Stone, D. (1989). Causal stories and the formation of policy agendas. *Political Science Quarterly*, *104*(2), 281–300.

————.(1997). *Policy paradox: The art of political decision making.* New York: Norton.

Stratmann, T. (2009). How prices matter in politics: The returns to campaign advertising. *Public Choice, 140*(3–4), 357–377.

Styfco, S. (2006). A place for Head Start in the world of universal preschool. In E. Zigler, W. S. Gilliam, & S. M. Jones (Eds.), *A vision for universal preschool education* (pp. 216–240). New York: Cambridge University Press.

Sylvester, K. (2001). Caring for our youngest: Public attitudes in the United States. *Future of Children, 11*(1), 52–61.

Tavernise, S. (2011, December 14). Subsidies for child care keep dwindling when families need them most. *New York Times,* p. A24.

Taylor, K. (2012, March 4). Budget cuts may threaten city programs for children. *New York Times,* p. A15. Retrieved from http://www.nytimes.com/2012/03/05/nyregion/mayors-budget-cutbacks-may-threaten-city-programs-for-children.html?_r=1&emc=eta1.

————.(2013, May 9). City Council approves bill mandating sick-day pay. *New York Times.* Retrieved from http://www.nytimes.com/2013/05/09/nyregion/new-york-council-approves-paid-sick-leave-measure.html?_r=0.

Thurber, J., & Nelson, C. (2000). *Campaign warriors: The role of political consultants in elections.* Washington, DC: Brookings Institute.

Tilly, C. (2004). *Social movements, 1768–2004.* Boulder, CO: Paradigm.

Tout, K., Starr, R., Soli, M., Moddie, S., Kirby, G., & Boller, K. (2010). *Compendium of quality rating systems.* Washington, DC: Office of Planning, Research and Evaluation. Retrieved from http://archive.acf.hhs.gov/programs/opre/cc/childcare_quality/compendium_qrs/qrs_compendium_final.pdf.

Truman, D. (1964). *The governmental process.* New York: Knopf.

Tyre, P., Springen, K., & Juarez, V. (2006). Smart moms, hard choices. *Newsweek, 147*(10), 55–55. Retrieved from http://www.thedailybeast.com/newsweek/2006/03/06/smart-moms-hard-choices.html.

Umansky, L. (1996). *Motherhood reconceived: Feminism and the legacies of the sixties.* New York: New York University Press.

Urban Institute. (2013). *Kids' share: Analyzing federal expenditures on children.* Retrieved from http://www.urban.org/projects/kids_share.cfm.

U.S. Census Bureau. (2005). *Whose minding the children? Child care arrangements spring 2005..* Retrieved from http://www.census.gov/population/www/socdemo/child/ppl-2005.html.

————.(2011). *Child poverty in the United States 2009 and 2010: Selected race groups and Hispanic origin.* Retrieved from http://www.census.gov/prod/2011pubs/acsbr10-05.pdf.

U.S. Chamber of Commerce. (2003). *Paid family and medical leave.* Retrieved from http://www.uschamber.com/issues/index/labor/paidfmla.htm.

————.(2010). *U.S. Chamber policy priorities for 2010.* Retrieved from http://www.uschamber.com/issues/priorities.

———.(2013). *U.S. Chamber policy priorities for 2013*. Retrieved from http://www.uschamber.com/issues/priorities.

U.S. Department of Commerce. (2005). *We the people: Women and men in the United States: Census 2000 special reports*. Retrieved from http://www.census.gov/prod/2005pubs/censr-20.pdf.

U.S. Department of Education. (2013a). *Initiatives: Race to the Top—Early learning challenge*. Retrieved from http://www2.ed.gov/programs/racetothetop-earlylearningchallenge/funding.html.

———.(2013b). *Promise neighborhoods*. Retrieved from http://www2.ed.gov/programs/promiseneighborhoods.

U.S. Department of Health and Human Services. (2011). *About Head Start*. Retrieved from http://eclkc.ohs.acf.hhs.gov/hslc/About%20Head%20Start.

———.(2012). *FY 2012 Head Start funding increase*. Retrieved from http://eclkc.ohs.acf.hhs.gov/hslc/standards/PIs/2012/resour_pri_001_012612.html.

———.(2013). *Table 5 child care and development fund preliminary estimates of children in settings legally operating without regulation, average monthly percent served by relatives vs. non-relatives (FFY 2011)*. Washington, DC: Author. Retrieved from http://www.acf.hhs.gov/sites/default/files/occ/fy_2011_ccdf_data_tables_preliminary.pdf.

U.S. Department of Health and Human Services, Administration for Children and Families. (2013a). *Head Start program facts fiscal year 2012*. Retrieved from http://eclkc.ohs.acf.hhs.gov/hslc/mr/factsheets/2012-hs-program-factsheet.html.

———.(2013b). *History of Head Start*. Retrieved from http://eclkc.ohs.acf.hhs.gov/hslc/hs/about/history.

———.(n.d.). *Fiscal 2012 CCDF allocations (including realloted funds)*. Retrieved from http://www.acf.hhs.gov/sites/default/files/occ/final_allocations_2012.pdf.

U.S. Department of Labor. (2000). *Balancing the needs of families and employers*. Retrieved from http://www.dol.gov.edgekey.net/whd/fmla/toc.pdf.

———.(2010a). *Futurework: Trends and challenges for work in the 21st century*. Retrieved from http://www.dol.gov/oasam/programs/history/herman/reports/futurework/report.htm.

———.(2010b). *Table 6: Employment status of mothers with own children under 3 years old by single year of age of youngest child and marital status, 2008–09 annual averages*. Retrieved from http://www.bls.gov/news.release/famee.to6.htm.

———.(2011). *Quick stats on women workers, 2009*. Retrieved from http://www.bls.gov/spotlight/2011/women/.

———.(n.d.-a). *FY 2013 Congressional budget justification, employment and training administration, state paid leave fund*. Retrieved from http://www.dol.gov/dol/budget/2013/PDF/CBJ-2013-V1-10.pdf.

———.(n.d.-b). *Wage and hour division*. Retrieved from http://www.dol.gov/whd/fmla/chapter3.htm#.UJP-z1H5L-s.

U.S. Department of Labor, Bureau of Labor Statistics. (2007). *Women in the labor force: A databook* (2007 ed.). Washington, DC: U.S. Department of Labor.

———.(2009). *Highlights of women's earnings in 2008.* Retrieved from http://www.bls. gov/cps/cpswom2008.pdf.

———.(2011). *Women in the labor force: A databook* (2011 ed.). Retrieved from http:// www.bls.gov/cps/wlf-databook2011.htm.

———.(2013). *Union member summary.* Retrieved from http://www.bls.gov/news. release/union2.nro.htm.

U.S. Senate Committee on Appropriations. (2013). *Summary: Fiscal year 2014 labor, health and human services, and education, and related services bill.* [Press release]. Retrieved from http://blog.ruralhealthweb.org/wp-content/uploads/Sen-Chair_- DHHS-Mark-FY-2014.pdf.

Vandell, D. L., Belsky, J., Burchinal, M., Steinberg, L., Vandergrift, N., & NICHD Early Child Care Research Network. (2010). Do effects of early child care extend to age 15 years? Results from the NICHD study of early child care and youth development. *Child Development, 81*(3), 737–756.

Vandell, D., Henderson, V. K., & Wilson, K. S. (1988). A longitudinal study of children with varying quality day care experiences. *Child Development, 59,* 1286–1292.

Vericker, T., Isaacs, J., Hahn, H., Toran, K., & Rennane, S. (2012). *How targeted are federal expenditures on children? A kids' share analysis of expenditures by income in 2009.* Washington, DC: Urban Institute and Brookings Institute. Retrieved from http://www.brookings.edu/research/reports/2012/03/kids-share.

Vesely, C. K., & Anderson, E. A. (2009). Child Care and Development Fund: A policy analysis. *Journal of Sociology & Social Welfare, 36*(1), 39–59.

Vinovskis, M. (2005). *The birth of Head Start.* Chicago: University of Chicago Press.

Voices for Georgia's Children. (2011). *States that exempt faith-based providers from child care licensing.* Retrieved from http://georgiavoices.org/wp-content/uploads/2011/11/ AG_faith_based_exemptions_063011_FINAL.pdf.

Vucic, N. (2013, June 11). *It's time to fix child care—Reauthorization bill introduced in Senate.* Retrieved from http://policyblog.usa.childcareaware.org/2013/06/11/ reauthorization-bill-introduced-in-senate/.

Waldfogel, J. (1998). Understanding the "family gap" in pay for women with children. *Journal of Economic Perspectives, 12*(1), 137–156.

———.(1999). The impact of the Family and Medical Leave Act. *Journal of Policy Analysis and Management, 18*(2), 281–302.

———.(2010). *Britain's war on poverty.* New York: Russell Sage Foundation.

Walker Wilson, M. J. (2010). Behavioral decision theory and implications for the Supreme Court's campaign finance jurisprudence. *Cardozo Law Review, 31*(3), 679–747.

Wang, W., Parker, K., & Taylor, P. (2013). *Breadwinner moms: Mothers are the sole or primary provider in four-in-ten households with children; public conflicted about the growing trend.* Washington, DC: Pew Research Center. Retrieved from http://www. pewsocialtrends.org/2013/05/29/breadwinner-moms/.

Watkins, M. (2013, April 4). *Washington State Senate drop budget ax, leaves family leave and paid sick days untouched.* Washington Policy Watch. Retrieved from http://

washingtonpolicywatch.org/2013/04/04/washington-senate-drop-budget-ax-leaves-family-leave-and-paid-sick-days-untouched/.

Watson, S. (2010). *The right policy at the right time: The Pew pre-kindergarten campaign.* Washington, DC: Pew Center on the States. Retrieved from http://www.Pewstates.org/uploadedFiles/PCS_Assets/2010/PEW_PkN_2010_RightPolicy.pdf.

Weible, C. M., Sabatier, P. A., Jenkins-Smith, H. C., Nohrstedt, D., Henry, A. D., & deLeon, P. (2011). A quarter century of the advocacy coalition framework: An introduction to the special issue. *Policy Studies Journal, 39*(3), 349–360.

Weldon, S. L. (2006). Inclusion, solidarity, and social movements: The global movement against gender violence. *Perspectives on Politics, 4*(1), 55–74.

Wheelock College. (n.d.). *States operating or developing QRIS or other quality improvement initiative.* Retrieved from http://wheelock.educommons.net/courses/qris-training-haitian-creole/qris-training/module-1-1/map.png/view.

White, L. A. (2009). Explaining differences in child care policy development in France and the USA: Norms, frames, programmatic ideas. *International Political Science Review, 30*(4), 385–405.

Whitebook, M. (2002). *Working for worthy wages: The child care compensation movement, 1970–2001.* Berkeley, CA: University of California, Berkeley, Center for the Study of Childcare Employment. Retrieved from http://escholarship.org/uc/item/2050r9pv.

Whitebook, M., Howes, C., & Phillips, D. (1990). *The national child care staffing study: Who cares? Child care teachers and the quality of care in America.* Washington, DC: Center for the Child Care Workforce.

Wildavsky, A. (1979). *Speaking truth to power.* Boston: Little, Brown.

Williams, J. C. (2010). *Reshaping the work-family debate: Why men and class matter.* Cambridge, MA: Harvard University Press.

Williams, J. C., & Boushey, H. (2010). *The three faces of work-family conflict: The poor, the professionals, and the missing middle.* Retrieved from the Center for American Progress and WorkLife Law, University of California, Hastings College of the Law: http://www.americanprogress.org/issues/2010/01/pdf/threefaces.pdf.

Williams, J. C., Manvell, J., & Bornstein, S. (2007). *"Opt out" or pushed out? How the press covers work/family conflict.* Retrieved from the Center for American Progress and WorkLife Law, University of California, Hastings College of the Law: http://www.worklifelaw.org/pubs/OptOutPushedOut.pdf.

Wilson, M. W. (2010). Behavioral decision theory and implications for the Supreme Court's campaign finance jurisprudence. *Cardoza Law Review, 31*, 679–745.

Wilson, S. (2011, November 8). *Obama to change Head Start funding, slams GOP on spending cuts to education.* Retrieved from http://www.washingtonpost.com/blogs/44/post/obama-to-change-head-start-funding-slams-gop-on-spending-cuts-to-education/2011/11/08/gIQA8SaL1M_blog.html.

Wisendale, S. (2003). Two steps forward, one step back: The Family and Medical Leave Act as retrenchment policy. *Review of Policy Research, 20*(1), 135–151.

Wolf-Wendel, L. (2012). *Academic motherhood: How faculty manage work and family.* Rutgers, NJ: Rutgers University Press.

WPRO Newsroom and the Associated Press. (2013, July 23). *NEWS: RI gov. highlights new paid family leave law.* Retrieved from http://www.630wpro.com/common/page.php?pt=NEWS%3A+RI+gov.+highlights+new+paid+family+leave+law&id=18583&is_corp=0.

Yoshikawa, H. (1995). Long-term effects of early childhood programs on social outcomes and delinquency. *Future of Children, 5*(3), 51–75.

Young, D. S., & Holley, L. C. (2005). Combining caregiving and career: Experiences of social work faculty. *Affilia, 20*(2), 136–152.

Zellman, G. L., Gates, S. M., Moini, J. S., & Suttorp, M. (2009). Meeting family and military needs through military child care. *Armed Forces & Society, 35*(3), 437–459.

Zernike, K. (2010). *Boiling mad: Inside Tea Party America.* New York: Times Books.

Zero to Three. (2000). *What grown-ups understand about child development: A national benchmark survey.* Retrieved from http://www.zerotothree.org/site/DocServer/surveyexecutivesummary.pdf?docID=821&AddInterest=1153.

———.(2008). *Early childhood guidelines for infants and toddlers: Recommendations for states.* Retrieved from http://www.zerotothree.org/site/DocServer/Early_Learning_Guidelines_for_Infants_and_Toddlers.pdf?docID=4961.

Zigler, E., & Hall, N. W. (2000). *Child development and social policy: Theory and applications.* New York: McGraw-Hill.

Zigler, E., Marsland, K., & Lord, H. (2009). *The tragedy of childcare in America.* New Haven, CT: Yale University Press.

Zigler, E., & Muenchow, S. (1992). *The inside story of America's most successful educational experiment.* New York: Basic Books.

Zippay, A., & Rangarajan, A. (2007). Child care "packaging" among TANF recipients: Implications for social work. *Child and Adolescent Social Work Journal, 24*(2), 153–172.

Zylan, Y. (2000). Maternalism redefined: Gender, the state and the politics of day care, 1945–1962. *Gender and Society, 14*(5), 608–629.

INDEX

ABOUT THE AUTHORS

Elizabeth Palley is an Associate Professor of Social Welfare Work and Social Welfare Policy at the Adelphi University School of Social Work. She is also the mother of two young girls whom she hopes will not have trouble figuring out child care and early education arrangements if and when they have children.

Corey S. Shdaimah is an Associate Professor at the University of Maryland, School of Social Work. She studies the mismatch of policies and needs on the ground in a variety of contexts, including housing, prostitution, and child welfare. She is also the mother of three school-age children.